D0483797

Living from the Mountaintop

Be the Mystic You Were Born to Be

By
Christian Sørensen

Living from the Mountaintop:
Be the Mystic You Were Born to Be

By
Christian Sørensen

Copyright © 2016 by Christian Sørensen
All rights reserved. No part of this book may be reproduced in any form or by any electronic or mechanical means, including information storage and retrieval systems, without written permission from the author, except in the case of a reviewer, who may quote brief passages embodied in critical articles or in a review.

celestial winds
publishing

First Edition, 2016
ISBN 978-1-365-42237-9
Printed in the United States of America
christiansorenseninspires.com

Dedicated to my wife Kalli who dances with me on the mountaintop.

Linda,

It's been a joy to be on this journey with you through Practitioner training, as you move forward, may your path be filled with richest blessings.

Love,
Linda
&
Christine
June
2019

Table of Contents

"What lies behind us and what lies before us are tiny matters compared to what lies within us."

~ Ralph Waldo Emerson

Introduction

"When we learn to think of things as separate from other things, we give them names."
~ Lao-Tzu's Tao

Mysticism is the Passionate Conscious Union with the Pure Essence of Life Itself.

When exploring mysticism through wonderful texts like the Tao and Kabbalah it can often be confusing and complicated. Plainly put, it's hard to wrap your head around because you can't. Mysticism is a soul experience. It, like many spiritual experiences, can't be described in words. Neither your brain nor the human experience has any frame of reference for its description.

A mystical experience can bring a joyous surge, thrills, electrifying waves of light pulsing, tingling elation, and jubilation through your body. Trembling with intensity, the mystical can lift you by the rapture of a fire in your spine so hot you can't even tell if it's cold outside your skin. It's as if you're Alice in Wonderland growing large or shrinking small. There's a heightening of your senses; smells become acute and your ability to hear becomes extraordinary, one might say even otherworldly. The music of the cosmos, the celestial choir, the hum of the Divine, and the wisdom of the ages fills your soul all in the time it takes to blink a mystical eye.

You can feel the full spectrum of shapes and the history of everything you touch. Your emotions can terrify you in moments of elation like this, beyond description of anguish, delight, and sorrow to enchantment. Past patterns of remorse and guilt can be blown out of proportion and then instantly dissolve like a sugar cube in a glass of water. You might experience uncontrolled movements like shaking and trembling as the energy centers of your body begin vibrating and pulsating at an amazingly new and higher frequency. Your body may experience an opening of the flow of life through your spine removing any and all blockages and bringing up all sorts of images and emotions. Perhaps colors fill your awareness. Moving from the lower vibration of the earth tones to a brightness beyond known colors you have words for, you are absorbed into the luminosity of the light itself. Everything your eyes perceive to be reality glistens as you observe patterns unfolding, directions fulfilled, revelations revealed, past lives understood, and images of sacred sites never visited becoming familiar. In a blink, the great universal collective subconscious is revealed and understood more clearly than you could have ever imagined. The mystical transcendence of self-awareness will move you beyond your emotions into a state of calm equilibrium with a sense of Life itself where all is ever available.

If you aren't prepared for this, it can freak you out. If you fear the potential that your body is dissolving or burning up while your mind demands to grasp an explanation you aren't alone. Add to that the potential for over-powering sounds and images that feel more real than anything you've ever known filling your field of awareness, and the whole experience could definitely be an invitation for a panic attack. Your questioning mind doesn't like getting pushed to the back of the line of importance. Yet, to taste a world beyond the physical is delicious, intoxicating and possibly even addictive. Maybe you've heard stories of others who've never returned from their mystical explorations? That warning notwithstanding, and no matter how beautiful or frightening the sensations, can you see yourself moving beyond the pull of the physical to get to the mystical?

Exploring the mystical isn't about aiming for the beyond-the-body sensations. It's about merging with Life Itself. This kind of voltage can, in an instant, re-pattern and refresh you to the cellular and genetic level of your being and beyond. The veil, through which you perceive and receive, will open a little. This opening will begin lifting you beyond your previous boundaries of reality and perception. You'll be forever changed. Things you thought in your world were permanent will be different and you'll experience an aura of a new liberating calm and joyous freedom. I assure you, you'll never look through your eyes the same way again. But you might ask yourself, "What do I do with this experience after I've had it? How am I to reenter into the world of road rage, lines at the bank, and high gas prices?" Those are excellent questions to *observe* yourself asking. How *are* you going to weave your universal experience and knowing into the three dimensional world of the living?

After your mountaintop experience, you'll find yourself more at home in your body. You'll stop looking elsewhere for your true Self and perceive as much life force 'within' as 'out there'. You'll come to know where you are is where *It* all is. The Guru or the Saint doesn't have anything you don't have. It's not in some afterlife; it's going on in this life. When the Buddha was asked if he was a god his reply was, I am awake.

The mountaintop experience frees you from the constricting trances of guilt, doubt and fear. You'll feel your best when you're the delivery point of the Infinite into form. You'll challenge yourself to look within and call upon resources you didn't know you had. The mystical expression of seeing the good in all things will last forever and your days will be fulfilling and rewarding.

I'm excited to share, unlike what you've probably been told previously, that it's no longer necessary to withdraw from the world and run off to some secluded island, spend 40 days in the desert or become a recluse in a forest monastery to have a mystical life. You don't have to fast, practice abstinence or any other forms of mortification. This book isn't going to require extricating yourself from family or friends to become a greater expression of life. It's a book to support you by re-mapping and guiding you to remain in this world while being a vortex of Life expressing. The context of this literary journey will be to use your world as a mirror and training ground for the insights and understanding of your soul's travels. Being present in your world, which this book will help guide you to be, will lead you to finding blessings and rewards beyond calculation.

Living from the Mountaintop will give you an opportunity to experience joy and happiness beyond words and logic, while folding beautifully into your soul's expansion, evolution and spiritual maturation. All of your interactions within this world will come to be recognized as purely spiritual experiences. This can't be squeezed into words; rather you'll come to an intuitive knowing not reached by reason. The heart knows things the mind knows nothing of. I've filled these pages with soulful adventures so you may come to sense, feel and remember beyond words and earthly description more of who you are. It's in that realization that the actual merging and revealing of the Infinite unfolds. Your soul's intuitive and conscious realization of the Absolute will be unveiled through the mystical connection.

Why no mention of God in this book?

This is the only time in the book I mention the word God because it conjures up so much of what it isn't. Mystics know, as soon as you say It's this, It isn't. I, Christian, love my ever-evolving, emerging sense of the Life of All. To me, It's the Divine, the Eternal and the One and Only First Cause. It's imperative that *you* come to know the *Infinite* beyond what I describe or what was fed to you in your religious upbringing. Whatever spiritual path you were raised on or have been on since, is perfect! There's no reason ever to think any spiritual path is wrong. There are many paths up the mountain. Whatever yours has or hasn't been is perfect because it has led you to this moment of being open to seeing more of the Unlimited Abundant Universal and multi-dimensional order in which you live. It's only as you open to this possibility of an Unlimited Universe that the mystical can help jolt you to a new level of seeing and knowing. This whole journey is about a Divine communion and a Mystical union with Life Itself. The mystic lives from the mountaintop and brings the greater awareness of that expanded view to all situations. You are being invited to live by the dictates of the rhythm and flow of the creative expression of Life. This will allow you to be intuitively aware while expressing the highest and best in all situations. From that viewpoint, you'll be able to speak confidently from an intuitive place rather than a purely logical one.

What kind of terminology will be used to describe things I can't wrap my head around?

You'll find a legend of interchangeable terms in the glossary at the end of the book. What's more important to me than the word itself, is your experience of where the word is pointing you. Feel empowered to replace words that make more sense to your personal mystical experience.

Why should I read this book?

We hunger for the Divine but fear what the revelations might do to our lives which is why the journey through these pages will change you forever. How were you called to this mystical journey? And why are you answering that call now? You hunger for Spirit in your life but don't want to give up the control. Once you truly experience the Divine beyond what you know, you'll have no choice because there's no turning back. There's no unknowing the known. That intoxicating experience will have touched your soul and it will soon be desiring more. Seeing beyond the veil is an invitation from the sacred you receive only because you are ready. It doesn't just appear when you want it. Surrender to the enticing call of the Divine Summon. Your awakening is a remembering of your direct contact with and desire for a more consistent, deeper experience of Life Itself.

This Book is not Formulaic but Soulfully Explorational

The world definitely does *not* need another religion or seven-step process to success. What it needs are people living and expressing their life connections. My personal philosophy has always been living life as your message. It's my view on the key to success. You've come with a gift to give, a lesson to learn and you'll hopefully have some fun in the process of doing both. When you have a higher vision than the chaos of this world, the clarity you develop is transforming. You will heal knowing wholeness while some proclaim sickness. No matter what the situation may be when you speak it courageously others will hear and believe what you say because you're the revealer of an expanding truth in the midst of confusion.

You must be more than just the knower of the truth, however. As a bringer of new thought, you are shining light on a consciousness that changes the world. Living from the mountaintop will show you your entry point into action. Yin and yang, rest and movement, creation and transcendence are all essential.

The Life Force is always prevalent and available throughout your daily life if you have the eyes to see and ears to hear. I recognize that's a big 'if'. The key to always looking through seeing eyes is knowing that, behind everything, the only issue the world ever suffers from is a sense of separation from the Infinite. We need more individuals serving as transparencies for the light and life of Spirit to shine through them. We need more eyes opening to the mystical connection, the abundant universe and a greater acceptance that we are all part of the Ultimate Consciousness. Then and only then will we hear and know the truth of the Life Force.

Imagine a window with light streaming in and lighting up the room. The window is not the light but merely the vehicle which the light travels through. If the window is dirty the light is obscured. The light, itself, doesn't change or become weaker or stronger. Its full potential is just as available as it was from the beginning. It's just not being realized because the window is inefficient. The dullness is created through the filter of a dirty window. There is a co-creative process going on between the window and the light. The light doesn't care and make a big stink insisting the window be cleaned. On the contrary, it just shows up and expresses through the available avenue. The observer of this interaction may see the dull manifestation and decide to clean what's impeding the flow of light, and voila - things will look brighter. You are the perceiver in your world, not the window. Get the glass cleaner out.

Notice the light didn't change but the vehicle it was using became a purer transparency for it to move through. The value of living from the mountaintop and moving in the mystical direction is you are lifted to a place of being an observer, without an attachment to whatever opinion is filtering the light. You notice yourself making choices and are consciously aware of what's prompting those choices and where they'll lead. You're given the option of the cosmic window washing towel for cleaning. Once having the light shine in your world a bit brighter, you'll find other options once obscured from sight become available, though they, too, have been available all the time. When things are brighter, it's hard to return to the gothic ways of the limited life you lived before. It's one thing to believe you can witness clearly, it's another to set down your earthly lenses and truly see the vibrancy of life. For sure, you can talk about walking through the fire; but it's another thing altogether actually walk through the fire. I bet you know a lot of talkers. But, how many of them walk their talk? Do you believe you can levitate above the density of this world, or shape-shift into another expression? These lessons are here to help move you from believer to one who transcends the world of form by merging with the ever available cosmic, Omnipresent, Omnipotent Life.

You can't make the mystical happen, but you can move into a deeper experience of Life Itself by inviting a more conscious relationship to what is beyond your subjective field. What lies within you is unlimited. Your perception is what quantifies and particularizes it into your personality or your character expression. The later chapters will help you ascend to the peaks of the Infinite, or as you'll come to recognize them as an undifferentiated realm of your inexhaustible possibilities.

So the sayings go: after the ecstasy; the laundry, after the vacation -back to work, after the mystical - back to this world. This journey will assist you in integrating into this dimension the revelations that come from knowing your freedom in other dimensions. As in that classic Jim Morrison song, "step on through to the other side." When you do, you might be knocked out-of-sync with your previous earthly hypnotic trance. Your intuitive perception receptors will be attuned to a new frequency which will be influenced from a larger picture. For a while, the clarity of your observing self can continue to influence your choices but, you'll have to decide to live according to a higher authority than the dictates of this world at some point or you'll get sucked back into an existence rampant with fear and scarcity.

Step Back to See the Rapturous Reality of Revelations

Your consciousness, which is just another name for your awareness, has the ability to disengage from whatever is grabbing your attention and refocus on anything it wants. Imagine if it were to focus on a higher aspect of who you are rather than the one currently struggling? Your true self is the one observing your interactions in this world. Indeed, it is the true you who is noticing you feeling the emotions. Your true self is the YOU that is watching your own experience in this world with curiosity. Whenever you watch your mind you withdraw your awareness from the reality of images and stories you are telling yourself.

Inner listening helps open your awareness. The mystical

side of many great spiritual philosophies will guide you beyond the chatter in your mind. When you engage your inner awareness your mental discussion will fall away to the rapturous reality of revelations that aren't bound by the constraints of earthly perceptions. The whole thing conjures up a visual of boosters as they fall away from a space ship as it thrusts into outer space. I'm so thrilled to be able to guide you in finding your inner mountaintop where you'll be able to invite a higher way of understanding to reveal its intuitive impress upon your field of awareness.

"The Secret Place of the Most High is at the center of our own being, where in the silence we wait on the Spirit . . . There is no confusion in this Secret Place; none can enter It for us; none can prohibit Its entrance to us. The door is always open, the gate ever ajar. The Secret Place of the Most High is a place of light, of illumination, of poise and assurance."

~ Ernest Holmes
1887 – 1960

*Theologians may quarrel, but the mystics of the
world speak the same language."*
~ Meister Eckhart

Prologue: Before Birth and After Death

What did your face look like before your parents were born –
Old Zen Koan

One Stopping Point

In this world, we welcome life in birth and we send it off in death. Birth is sacred and natural, as is death. They are both huge life changers. *So why do we as humans have more trouble with departure than arrival?* I believe it's because most have lost the mystical connection and in the process of surviving have forgotten about the continuity of life. In recalling two of the most powerful moments of my life, I'm reminded of that continuity. The first as my son's head crowned and in the time it took me to take my next breath, I was cutting an umbilical cord in support of his arrival to this world. The second on an overcast summer morning as family, friends and a curious dolphin joined me and my brother paddling surfboards through the waves to create a sacred circle and spread our father's ashes. Both expressions of life, arrival and departure in and out of our physical forms, are two ends of a monumental spectrum of sacredness.

Before digital cameras were invented there was film. Film consisted of celluloid strips with individual frames of progressing pictures that held moments of time in perpetuity. One frame would lead into the next, followed by the next frame until the whole story with its intrigue, drama and humor played itself out. The whole story sat upon the reel, one frame at a time. You could tune into any one frame, but there was a story supporting and leading into that picture and an unfolding story on the other side. There was a beginning, middle and end and the continuity moved through each frame whether or not you looked at the frames as a group or as one of a group.

You are part of a current of life that has entered into this time frame. This frame between your birth date and your departure date is merely one stopping point in the continuity of your soul's journey. You've had self-awareness in your evolving progress before entering into this frame and (hopefully) some growth while you've been here. The great news is you get to take those lessons and soul qualities with you beyond this frame which is the picture of your life in this moment. Looking into a newborn's eyes you'll know along with the innocence and trust you sense that there's an "old soul" inside looking out at you. It's as if you know there were frames before the one you see now, as you look in that baby's eyes.

You are needed by Life

On the other side from birth and the arrival into this dimension of awareness, is the act of leaving this realm. It's a yin/yang; black and white sort of thing. It's life and it's death. This flow of death makes it as natural as birth no doubt, as nature provides for it in the same manner. Where your essence comes from is where you return. An amusing aspect about death is that in an instant we are all equal. It doesn't matter how much we've amassed, how damaged we've become, or where and how we lived on the planet. In a blink of an eye you'll get it; we are all of the same Essence of Life that will awaken in another frame minus the accumulated stuff of this dimension. Why wait to the inevitable moment of transitioning from one frequency of expression to the next to realize death isn't an ending? Your existence isn't a series of beginnings and endings; rather, you are a current of awareness moving in continuity from each moment to the next.

If you were told, you'd be making your transition in the next few months, how would you change your priorities and behavior? What aspect of you would take charge? What would come alive in you in order to direct your actions? What part of your awareness would move you to greater joy, love, grace and gratitude? I doubt you'd be wasting any precious time. This is how valuable the time you've been given here is. You lined up to get one of these bodies to incarnate into this dimension. This incarnation is a gift for you to play and grow in, give and enjoy. An often unconsidered gift of this world of form is that it's slower than the speed of thought so you can be fully present to enjoy the expression of each moment. Too many have forgotten the manifestations of this world are just projections thrown in front of them to step into. You, the observer, are what's real; it's you directing your choices.

Without you, Infinite Potential remains just that, potential. It stays unformed possibility. It is you who are needed by Life for its potential to take form. Your journey through this dimension of time isn't about length, it's about width. What's most important is what's gone on in that space of time. Yes, it's the dash between your arrival and departure dates, not how many days or years you've spent on this planet that matters most. It's about quality not quantity.

People often seem surprised when death comes, thinking for some reason it wouldn't ever happen to them or at least not unless they chose it. You are just one breath away from leaving your body behind. It's interesting how the thought of impending death has one wanting to live at the highest level. Apologies are made, forgiveness is rendered, love conveyed, and a bucket list lived out. *Why are you waiting for the unpredictable but inevitable moment of death to start living?* At the time of death, people often want a few more days because suddenly, like a thunderbolt, they understand what's most important to their spirit. Peace feels better than hurt, because it is. Surrender is more graceful than attachment and sharing love is more magical than withholding it. Suddenly you realize that expressing who you are without a need for reciprocation fills you up and you beg for more time. Meanwhile your higher self stands by knowing you lived a lifetime to get to this moment and wonders why it took impending death to act as a catalyst to really, finally live . . .

and, who is this You noticing all of this? *Living from the Mountaintop* will help you to practically integrate higher awareness into your daily activities and remember you are the observer of your life.

Death is a good educator, and expander of what's most important. On their death bed, people aren't saying, "I wish I would have gathered more stuff", rather, they are wishing they would have expressed more love and caring. You didn't arrive with anything and you aren't taking anything with you. Imagine if you looked death in the face and it didn't matter whether you transitioned today or next century. Everything has more significance and is brighter prior to death. Every word and action has deeper relevance knowing it may be the last time to connect with who or what is before you. Imagine living every moment of your life with this kind of presence. *So, the obvious question is, why wait? Do you like who you are being? Is there anything else you'd rather be doing?*

Death is your consciousness, the driver of your body, withdrawing from its vehicle. No longer tied to seeing through the limited filters of the body bound by its five senses and seeing only an infinitesimal amount of the multidimensional realms, you enter into an expanded state of reality. No longer tied to only one frame of the continuity, you see the whole reel at once with its past, present, and future in the now moment. Have you ever had your life pass before your eyes in an instant? How is that possible you ask yourself? Perhaps it could be because everything happens in the present moment. You've chosen to incarnate into this physical expression in order to feel and know love and joy. *Isn't it the greatest irony that we get closest to living when pushed to the brink by our fear of dying?* Our fear around death is because we've created ideas around what comes after here. So often societal myths are believed with no relevance as to what the truth is. Why would what you encounter after death be any different than where you came from prior to birth? Are you not birthing back from whence you came?

Who is looking?

Do you remember looking at yourself in the mirror as a child, later as a teenager and now as an adult? Who is looking? Is the image you see reflecting back at you aging while you, the observer, still feel like a 20-year-old? It's because the body ages but consciousness doesn't. Is it not the same you who was looking at the child that is looking through your eyes now? You are not your body but you are aware of your body. Who is using your mind and feeling the emotions? Do you think and feel by societal appropriateness? Can you answer that honestly by looking at the choices you've made? You'll realize you are not your thoughts though you are aware of your thoughts. But let's return back to who is observing those thoughts. Who's calling the shots and deciding to go with either the joyous or tormenting thoughts? Who's gazing out from behind your eyes? Who is the aware one who senses more than what's known? Who is the one witnessing you looking at yourself looking back at you from the mirror?

The one who witnesses your activities and feelings is noticing your decision making process as well as your emotional experiences but isn't attached to your body or the world of form. The witness isn't tied to the dictates of what you think you know. It's as if there's a third person within. There's the one who is thinking, the body that's acting and a third aspect of your being, the one who is aware of thinking/feeling and taking the action. What part of you notices those interactions? The fact you can notice your thoughts indicates you are not those thoughts.

Are you able to witness yourself making choices? Staying calm and not reacting is one way you can witness yourself. Do you observe yourself being emotional or anxious? A resolve to trust at the moment of an internal struggle is something to watch. The noticer, the observer and the witness are all the same You. Where have You been all these years?

As soon as you became aware that you came into being you rose as a mountain rises from the earth. You'll continue in self-expression as long as you reach out. In the rising, does the mountain forget it originates from the earth even though it has a whole planet to support it? The mountain is of the earth as the soul is of the whole. Who You are is the one who looks out of your eyes and uses your body vehicle to operate in this vibrational reality. You're the driver, builder and choice-maker. You may have created a magnificent structure, but it's not You. It just houses You. If you pay attention and allow awareness to rise above the happenings of your mind, you'll notice you have greater choices about all aspects of your experience.

If my body isn't who I am, what is it?

Have you ever flown from the mountains to the tropics only to get off the plane and be shocked by how different the humid air feels to your senses? How about being flown from one culture to another and stepping off the plane to notice things aren't at all what you've always known as common.

Who animates all those diverse expressions? It's necessary to put on a wetsuit and air tank to dive the sea or don a space suit in order to compensate for the differences in another environment. Your consciousness needs the appropriate suit to function in this physical dimension of awareness. The irony is while you need something to match the vibration of this world to walk in it, the mystical dissolves the boundaries of the form you inhabit.

You've been given a body, primarily made up of atoms. Those atoms are mostly space filled with energy which take on the patterns impressed by your thought-energy. Your parents started the process of coding from their generation to yours the moment you were conceived. Prior to that, their coding came from their parent's parents all the way back from their ancestors. Along with the genetic patterning, you have the normal acceptable behavior patterning which has become the status quo. *If each generation attempts to keep within the edges of the norm, whose world is in your head?* So, whose body are you operating in? Your parents? Your grandparents or great-grandparents? Is it their information that defines your edges and controls your belief of what is possible? When you're too close to something it's impossible to see the larger picture. The defense system of your myopic vision will keep you from going outside the norm and acceptable peer projection.

Is your vision of the world like living behind a crew cut when what you really want to do is let your hair down? Whether it's your job, your sexuality, your socioeconomic status or some other boxed-in view of the way you should be, is it you or your ancestors doing the judging? I hear echoes of, "Hey, Sorensen, you're getting a little too far out there," ringing in my ears as I consider when I've tried to push the edges of social norm. I know I'm not my programming so I'm able to separate from my body and mind's dictates and find an unparalleled integrity to who I am.

Whether you're watching a spectacular sunset or replaying a confrontational dialogue, you know you are not those things. If you are watching some children playfully wrestling in the park or a sexy individual stroll by, obviously you are not those expressions of life either. You are just observing or listening to what's going on in front of you. When you have a conversation transpiring in your head, good, bad or indifferent, you still get to be the one observing the dialogue before you. The difference seems to be when it's inside your head it seems easier to think it's you. But, you are not the inner chatter either; you're the one who hears and observes it. When you attempt to decipher which of the voices is you, you will lose the higher perspective. By entering into the smaller picture you will give up your position as the observer. You are neither the good or the evil twin, the lover or the runner; you are the one watching the conversation and activities while noticing the choices being made.

Your processing controls your experience of the Infinite

You've built your character with every thought, choice, and piece of evidence you've accrued throughout the years. Whatever perceptions you've attached to yourself are the parts of the Infinite You pulled through the screens of your awareness. These have become your creative filters whether this window is dirty or clean. This kind of identification is the energetic imprint on the 100 trillion cells that create your body. Form follows consciousness; awareness will always house and support its perspective, whatever frequency it's playing on. The mystical experience will take you outside your preprogrammed frame tuning into a new frequency, so in an instant beyond time, you'll learn to change your world thus creating new results in your life.

Sometimes the tenacious attachment to your ego can trap you into a false impression that you are merely human rather than immortal passing through on your return to wholeness. You don't need to be narrating what's going on; just experiencing it. Why do you need to be telling yourself in words what is happening to you? With all due respect, shut your mouth. Narrative words will likely confine your understanding to a constricted definition. Imagine that you are strolling through the majestic mountains at sunset looking up at the clouds. On the horizon is a blazed spectrum of fuchsia, purple and orange painted across the bottom of the clouds while the bright Azul-colored sky is reflecting off a still lake. In the water's reflection, you see deer grazing and hear birds singing as the pine trees reach for the heavens all the while swaying in the late afternoon breeze. As soon as this image is described, much of the experience beyond the words is lost.

Processing controls your experience of the Infinite so it can fit into your mind. There are so many dimensions to the picture of your sunset stroll, but your focus picks out just a few pieces for your so-called reality to digest. There are millions of synapses firing in your brain, but you can only process a few at a time. This allows you to live within your mind rather than the cosmos. Scientists speak of frame rates when they talk about this phenomenon. Research has proven the brain sees millions of bits of data, but it can only process 2,000 bits at a time. So, what or who chooses what 2,000 bits of information you focus on per second? Take a minute, be still and notice the one who is observing the picture nature is painting.

What actually gives life meaning is the willingness to be present and experience it beyond words. Stop attempting to get the world to fit into your known vocabulary. Getting the world to give you what you want, which fits your definition can rob you of the gifts it has beyond your own imagination. Notice the willfulness of your character reaching to get what it wants. Who is noticing?

It's not what you do that determines who you are. You are the observer traveling through this time frame, forgetting who you are and falsely identifying with the forms of this world. Your false identity becomes the biggest trap for the controlling influences. You get trapped in the defined spaces. It's within these spaces you have abdicated the realm of infinite possibilities that are forever seeking to express themselves through you.

Your spirit longs to return home

Your spirit longs to return home to Source. After the novelty of this realm wears off your soul's nostalgia cries out for the true peace of the familiar. It longs for its return home and a re-emergence with the Eternal, Infinite, Absolute. The mystical experience will have you transcending creation, mortality and reason, right here in this dimension now! The omnipresent Life Force dissolves the fear of death. Death is redefined as a merging and absorbing back into the whole. Rather than seen as an end, it is the ultimate reunion with the Absolute. It returns to being the Whole, Itself now. It's the mountain eventually returning to the dust from which it originated.

You made a choice to incarnate into your physical expression in order to feel love and joy. Life here is the main attraction because you don't die to become immortal, you are immortal now. You have chosen to experience Heaven on earth now, not at some future date. Why wait for some other point in time? The fear around death arises because stories have created ideas around what happens after here but the truth of many of those images is highly debatable. It's a shame people keep exploring outside themselves for something that can only be discovered within. This dimension offers up high qualities for your spirit to embrace and carry on. These qualities of love and blessing come when you remember not what this world owes you, but what gifts and talents you bring to this existence. The love and joy are yours when you're pouring out, not when you're grasping outside for everything you can get.

When you first have a conscious realization of transcended presence, there's no going back into the safety of the protective womb. Your small story only applies to your small self. When you've been beyond the final frame of the smaller story, it's impossible to go back without a new knowingness. You come back from a place that is beyond the beyond. It's far past personal religion, or the understanding of subjective language. This knowingness is the stream that has carried you into this incarnation.

Maintaining a ritual that reminds you of who you are outside your form is a powerful way to invoke grace and invite the remembrance of the mystical connection. Yet, often the approach to ritual is with expectation. It's a trust walk to approach the presence while staying present without a past or hope for future outcome. Can you enter the now experience of the stream of life rather than the memory of what the stream was? This next ritual is your invitation to living from the elevated perspective of the mountaintop and mystical connection to all Life.

Soul Work

Your Welcoming to the World

The world sang the day you were born! You arrived upon a star which glimmered brightly hovering in the sky after your arrival. Upon your birth, you were marked for significance, for the gifts you bring is what this world hungers for. You were born with a flutter of joy in your heart and a twinkle in your eyes. You bound into your existence with a skip in your step. Your connection with the Infinite was unwavering as you were born into greatness. You have been anointed with an important mission to fulfill and you are so worthy!

You've been given earthly guides to assist you in this world; some may be easily recognizable like your parents or the maternal matriarch of your clan. Some may be from the animal kingdom like a pet who will teach you unconditional love. Others will be friends and some may even be total strangers who appear for a brief encounter but whose presence recalibrates the frequency you operate on. These encounters may be friends or foes who call forth what is slumbering within you.

Close your eyes (you close your eyes in order to see) and take a few minutes to allow the memories of these teachers to come to your heart. . . Never forget, you are not alone on this earth-bound journey. Your support may be undercover, but when you open your heart and eyes you'll find empowerment is there for you. You have signed up for these soul lessons and you have all that will ever be necessary for this classroom of life.

You are welcomed in love and given the freedom to express. Grace is always yours for the remembering. Live in gratitude for the diverse expression and you will ride on great waves of abundance. You are enough for whatever comes your way. Don't take yourself too seriously and remember to live in joy and laugh a lot. You have incarnated so you may feel love and joy. Allow yourself to feel without judgment, as even the warrior needs to be able to cry.

Welcome to this new world. This christening is a mystical welcoming and celebration of your awakening and arrival to this new way of your soul's expression. The ritual of being immersed in Spirit is a realization of the Infinite Power of Life that is within you. You already carry the seed of perfection; it simply awaits your recognition for it to blossom into its fullness as you. Your connection is already true because you live and move and have your being immersed in the wholeness of life. As you walk this world, may you live from the knowingness of the mountaintop view.

Continue on and with your eyes closed touch your heart

and take a few minutes to ask these ancient veil-parting questions. . . Who am I? What is my soul's purpose? What are my gifts to give? Or, if you are comfortable opening your eyes, look into a mirror for ten minutes and ask who you see reflecting back at you and who is observing both the body and the mirror. . . What is my soul's purpose? What are my gifts to give? Who am I?

Have faith in your new adventure; allow your inquisitive spirit to search beyond the edges of what you know. May you come to sense your unity with all things. May your life be conducted as an example of a courageous creator passionately living in harmony with the life-sustaining principle of Oneness. Continue to connect with your soul's assignment and remember to enjoy each precious moment as you listen to all the mystical secrets your heart has to reveal. Don't lose sight of how important it is to take care of you. Speak your name and the soul qualities you have brought! May this time and space know that you have awakened. It is proclaimed you are worthy and welcome to walk in this world of abundant love sharing your gifts.

Soul Adventures

Find some old family photos and spend some time looking at the faces of your parents and grandparents. Enter into their life stories and let them speak to you. Can you notice some traits that have been passed along to you? Do they serve or restrain you?

Find some photographs of you as a baby, young child, preteen, teen, and into your 20's and spend some time with these images. Allow yourself to look out from those times in space. Does it feel like the same you you observed then and now? This isn't so much about what's happened to you on this journey through your life but rather *who* is watching you journey through this life? What streams of consciousness have you followed from then until now? What decisions did you make that continue to impact your life today? What happened to the dreams the younger you had?

- If you were told you'd be dying from your present life

in a few months what would you like to do with the rest of your time as yourself? What would you like to "clean up"? How would your priorities shift? What would be the tone and qualities of your conversations? What would you do now that you may have otherwise put off? What qualities of being would you like to carry with you? Death says now is the time, so why wait to follow your soul's urgings? Claim your birth into this new life now.

- Look at a snapshot of a moment in time that comes to your recall. What about it do you remember? Now, energetically place yourself back into the dynamic of that moment. What else can you now see and remember that you didn't before? Next, go deeper and ask yourself what else you can recall and where does this energetic memory take me? Develop this technique as it will be used later in the book to take you deeper into energetic dimensions.
- What defined spaces are you caught in that it's now time to break free of?

I will be ending each chapter with a Mystical writing. This contemplative quote is meant to open the door of your consciousness so you can sit in the silence and listen. You'll hear, not in words necessarily, but with an inner understanding beyond those words.

Mystical Writing

You Are Me

You are me and I am you.
It's obvious that we are "inter-are".
You cultivate the flower in
yourself so that I will be beautiful.
I transform the garbage in myself so
that you do not have to suffer.
I support you;
You support me.
I am in this world to bring you peace
You are in this world to bring me joy.
~ Thich Nhat Hanh
        1926 -

Chapter 1: You are Infinite

There is a thing, formless yet complete. Before heaven and earth it existed.
Without sound, without substance, it stands alone and unchanging. It is all-pervading and unfailing.
~Lao Tzu

Have you ever experienced lying on a mountaintop facing the star-painted nighttime sky, while allowing your imagination to soar to the furthest galactic reaches, beyond where your rational mind has ever traveled before? Where did your imaginative ideas come from? Are you dreaming those imaginative journeys? Can you recall watching yourself participating in a dream, directing where you wanted to go and engaging in a desired interaction? How could you be lucid while you were sleeping?

Once upon a time, I, Zhuangzi, dreamt I was a butterfly, fluttering hither and thither, to all intents and purposes a butterfly. I was conscious only of my happiness as a butterfly, unaware that I was Zhuangzi. Soon I awakened, and there I was, veritably myself again. Now I do not know whether I was then a man dreaming I was a butterfly, or whether I am now a butterfly, dreaming I am a man. ~ a well-known parable of Zhuangzi (Chuang-Tzu)

You are Infinite Consciousness becoming aware where you are. Nowhere does it say awareness has to fit all neat and tidy into your physical body. As you contemplate the cosmos, you'll find yourself expanding beyond your body. When you think about your survival, you'll constrict into the body's fears. It's impossible to comprehend the Infinite from a finite perspective, but you might just catch a quick glimpse and feel the pull of so much more than you've ever known.

Place a pebble in the palm of your hand and observe as it opens you to the vibration of the lakeside bank on which you found it. If you drop your logical mind and trained answers you just might be able to intuit wisdom about the whole mountain from which that tiny pebble came. You wouldn't be alone if you began asking why would you do such a thing and why would it even matter?

It seems a whole mountain from this small pebble is a disproportionate request to ask of your rational mind as it attempts to understand the majesty of the towering expression of the earth. Though small, the pebble is of the mountain. That is not to say it's the entire mountain, the planet from which the mountain rose, or the universe in which the planet revolves in its spiral galaxy. But all that it is, is of that. The pebble in your hand can be a doorway into the connection beyond its form. What this says is just as you are part of the whole, you are not all of it, but all that you are is of it. What lessons of relevance it will reveal to you can only be found by entering through the doorway of the Infinite stream.

Could the Absence of Light be Good?

In the Infinite and Undifferentiated, you move beyond polarities. There, you are not capable of comparing what your brain knows to what it doesn't know. Revelations are complete and without comparison to anything you might think you know about anything. There's an unsaid deep knowingness of this kind of understanding. Paradoxes and polarities are needed to generate energy, movement, magnetism, description and relational understanding. There's the good (the positive) and the not-so-good (the negative). There's also light and the absence of light. In many circles the accepted knowledge of light is considered superior to the dark.

There are those known as the bringers of light called light workers, and those who move toward the light are considered positive beings. It's only with light you can see; but the greatest potential is in the unformed rather than in the light. The dark force is considered negative conjuring up fears, when in truth the void itself is the place of unformed infinite possibilities. Reflection comes of light, and with that information our thoughtful-self decodes what's perceived. This makes the brain happy. But talk to a friend who has no physical sight and find out if it's light in there? Or, consider when you enter the gap, or silence. Is there not an all-knowing void of light through which unlimited expansion and potential is waiting to be known? *Why is the dark considered bad?*

Do you believe for something to exist it has to have form or can you consider an existence without shape? In the thunder of silence all sounds are possible until you start making sound and pull out of the infinite a phonic form. All possibilities exist in the formless. There is no paradox within the unformed Infinite; only potential. Polarity doesn't exist in the realm of unlimited possibilities. When you shift your attention from your body back to your consciousness you can experience freedom. The mystical journey will help you shift your dependence from the rational need-to-know with explanations and guarantees upfront, to the security of trusting your inner states of awareness. This is where surrendering to trust and perfect timing in the emerging directive is imperative. The mystical journey is a relinquishment to the interior kingdom beyond language's description. It's an absence of negativity, ridicule, and anxiety. It's a field of grace where calmness resides, and it has nothing to do with the brain or the mind.

To experience a true mystical journey, it's crucial to move beyond the boundaries of needing to know the linear explanation and open to your soul's impress. To understand the images of telepathy and clairvoyance, which is the language of awareness, you have to move beyond insisting it to come through your brain. The brain deciphers the world of senses, but it's in the energetic realm that we're all connected. In that realm, the direct impress, which is the One communing through you, is rerouted as the lower energies of the subjective take up the available space. Your inner skeptic comes from a fixed position and filters out all evidence contrary to what it knows. You receive a direct impress minus the interpretation of your belief filters. Some might call it intuition which is a whole being experience. But, in order to receive messages of the mystical your brain needs to be unlocked.

I once helped lead a retreat in Russia. It was a magical time with an interpreter conveying back and forth through language, my words and the attendee's words. As the week progressed the deeper experiences didn't need to be verbalized because a collective feeling that was beyond words emerged amidst the group. On one of the scorching hot days I was there, a participant at the retreat who had brought her new baby, asked if I would baptize her. I said yes to welcome her spirit to the world and asked her to bring the child down to the pool. Soon, a crowd followed to watch me announce this child's name. Symbolic of her purity, I dabbed a little bit of water on her forehead and proclaimed her child as a positive force of love on this planet. Before I knew it, someone else jumped in the pool and asked me to do the same for them, so I did the same for them. That person was followed by another and another and before I knew it, there was a mass welcoming of many into their new phase of life, proclaiming their names with a new vibration of being. The amazing part was none of us knew what the words being spoken were, yet there was a profound understanding beyond the sounds of those words that resonated deeply within all our souls. I came out of that water a changed person.

The old barracks where this retreat on love and compassion was held, and which surprisingly were still being used by the local military, were remote. I had to leave early in the morning to catch my flight, but I failed in my attempts to slip out before anyone should have been awake. A couple of people who came to my room to wish me a pleasant trip helped me to the car and as I drove along the perimeter of the campus, I saw balconies lined with people waving good-bye and shouting their blessings. I couldn't understand their words but could absolutely feel their gratitude. When our car arrived at the exit there was a delay because the guards couldn't find the keys to unlock the locked gates and had to fetch a new set. While I waited, people came down from their balconies to the driveway to hug and wish me a safe journey and to express their love and appreciation. After spending a week in that soulful place the deep emotions were palpable. When a young girl looked deeply into my eyes touching my soul with her unconditional love I couldn't hold back my emotion. She reached towards me and gently wiped the tears from my cheeks and placed them on her heart. There was no need for my brain to interpret anything in that moment. The experience was far fuller than language could ever describe. It doesn't matter what you call it, there's an energetic connection to all things, *if* you want to pay attention. That's a big *if.* If it's your intention to pay attention you'll dial right into the Infinite.

Whose History is it?

You can enter a spot in consciousness where past, present and future all meet, are one and available. It's in this space of the now moment where the pull of past and future lose their grip to the newness of the creative potential of now. When you enter this state of unity you are able to commune through anything because everything is of the same energetic wave length. The challenge comes if you get stuck in the manipulated societal perceptions of 'it's not possible'. As a society, we're taught how to think through our education, culture and religion rather than through our awareness. History was written from only one side. Years later it was again rewritten to fit the agenda of those who weren't there to begin with, and over and over this occurred until what you have been taught as history is accepted as truth.

When the educated, who are only locked into the physical universe, hear about converging with the subtler realms - many will laugh. However, just as healing was once only considered possible through means of chemical and cutting, now energetic fields are once again being understood and involved in thought and form. Science continues to verify what mystics have always known. Case in point, sometime around 400 BC, Democritus, an ancient Greek philosopher, claimed that everything was made of atoms.

Since the energetic and vibrational fields are now accepted, equipment measuring these fields were made possible. But until there was a belief system in place to support the energy fields' existence, equipment to measure and adjust them couldn't be created.

Those who continue to laugh have their time and energy vested in their position at all costs carving out little pieces of the unlimited that they'll defend. It often looks like they are belittling, threatening, and ostracizing the unpatriotic of their acceptable norm. So those who aren't willing to accept there is so much more to the Infinite, choose to intimidate those who embrace a less constrained perception. In order to rise and expand above all that noise, you must be ready for the mystical ride because it alone will take you beyond the language of words and thinking to the language of awareness and image. Are you open at the top?

The Idiomatic Battle in your Head

There's no foundation or framework to support an idea you aren't sure you believe. As long as you're locked into your linear brain's parameters you'll remain earth-bound. The physical earth-bound world keeps you in servitude to its design by continuously feeding you limiting thoughts. Freedom from those limitations offers more options, but first you must allow yourself to be inspired from beyond what's known in the physical dimension. Your brain will continue to edit allowing you to see only the reality of your fundamental beliefs. Remember, the brain can only process a finite amount of seemingly infinite messages. The ones it chooses not to release are those it has a relationship to through its beliefs.

To look at what it takes to embrace belief, let's take a look at suspending disbelief. It's been said the suspension of disbelief is critical to the success of any storyteller. The last time you went to the movies, did it haunt you to stare at a one-dimensional screen projecting a two dimensional picture? Was your brain confused by the fact that it wasn't really happening to you, but instead in front of you? You had to suspend your disbelief to accept the film as reality in order to follow it as the story unfolded. If you're able to open yourself to suspending disbelief you can open yourself to the Infinite.

The question to ask yourself is whose reality did your beliefs come from? As the manipulated material realm closes the doors to your greater awareness, which is beyond the edge of your field of view, it locks out understanding that falls beyond the five senses. It doesn't really matter what solid beliefs you have. They could be religious, political, or otherwise. But, as long as you have one, you'll be trapped in a dense realm of belief and the fight of one ideology against another will keep you locked down in that battle. It's those who are able to see and know a greater reality beyond idiomatic beliefs that witness the lunacy of the battle. Your knowing a greater reality than the battle of ideology becomes dangerous to the power of the controlling element. You must unlock your brain so you can see beyond the separation of beliefs. Stepping back from the myopic view of reality to your mountaintop perch enables you to gain a broader perspective of possibilities. You need to quiet down and listen to the part of you observing the battle of the idiomatic world going on in your head.

Medicine and science have done amazing things with the body and provided unforeseen insights into the physical universe. There's a lot of good to be said for these practices and discoveries. For some, science has become a new form of 'religion' in our time. But imagine if just as some of the historical facts around world religions have been proven untrue, the factual science we assume is proven may also be debatable. There was a time the pantheon of mythical Gods was believed to be the absolute truth. What if some of premises around the physical sciences we hold to be true just aren't? Some have already been proven untrue. It wasn't so long ago that physicians who believed that leeches were a better alternative to surgery were in practice. What if the science of Epigenetics is true? Let's just say it is and your DNA can be influenced by making changes in its environment. Could you accept it's just that simple to modify genes in the human body? Change your diet, change your life. What if you're made up of more energy than mass and you're not living in a solid universe? There was a time not too long ago when the physical sciences would have had a challenge with that premise.

What if the things you're seeing are really made up of more space than solids? This is the philosophy of a great many quantum physicists who have much support in the field of science. It's already been proven if you really are made up of atoms, then at the atomic level you're more space than matter. It's now common belief that atoms are mostly space with electrons whizzing around a nucleus which is mostly space itself. This space is a vibration of energy holding the pieces together at a frequency that works for this dimension. So goes the entire premise that matter is mass when in reality it's space. It's an entire paradigm shift from prior scientific thinking and is rich with energetic ramifications that traditional sciences haven't yet begun to understand or explore. Is it too far-fetched for you to believe you can direct energetic vibration?

It's Your Body

Children learn through school projects of growing two similar plants with the same variables at the same time that if they love one of the plants by speaking to it or playing lovely music for it, it thrives. Alternatively, when the child treats the other plant with harsh music and yelling or "bad vibes" it shrivels up. All else being equal, e.g.; sunlight, soil, water - there's hardly a doubt that the physically intangible variables made the difference. There's a responsiveness from all living beings, plant and animal, at an energetic level. There exist numerous experiments showing how water crystals take on dissonant patterns from energetic input of angry thoughts, emotions and music, while beautiful patterns emerge from loving, positive thoughts and calming music.

As you open up to the Infinite realm of possibilities, it seems logical the observer, who is You, can give the operator of your body direction in choosing what energetic patterning is desirable to impress on your vibrational space within the atoms of your body. You'll be imprinting the water molecules which make up the majority of your physical form.

Rather than having news, cell phones, bad relationships, the toxicity of the environment and food dictate the impression of the energy waves in your body, you can choose your vibrational imprint. All of these outside toxicities impede your redirecting as the observer. Our societal norm supports allowing an assault to your system that re-patterns the water crystals of your body. This re-patterning takes the control of your physical form away from your conscious direction. Maybe your new direction for the return to wholeness and balance in life and the body could lie within energetic and vibrational healing?

Keeping your body healthy is integral to staying on track vibrationally so your spirit can operate. Staying healthy through the choice of unmodified live foods, daily exercise and meditation enables your body to be the best conduit for your mindful thoughts to take form.

It's imperative we step away from thinking we live in a solid universe dominated by manipulation. We can change all that by choosing to cooperate with the flow of the energy of Life that gives direction to form. If you resist that flow, you'll be trapped in your body which is trapped in a world of form.

Pretty ugly stuff. To expand in the Infinite you must free yourself from the slavery of fixed positions, including science and religion. This isn't done by having another fanatical point-of-view which just becomes another position to defend, but instead by honoring people where they're at and knowing there are other choices. Just because everyone thought the world was flat didn't make it flat. What's true is true whether a lot of people recognize it or not.

The challenge arises when you look with the belief to confirm what you want to prove rather than recognizing what's new and emerging. To move beyond the collective norm or external deceit you must look beyond mass media outlets, politicians and established institutions. There's just way too much at stake for those voices to come around to an emerging thought that's contrary to their long-held positions. It's your choice to move forward through the door to a greater freedom; one that's beyond all the mind control of thoughts and beliefs others are planting in your head. You have direct access to the Infinite because you've been coded with a gift to bring to humanity, but you must step beyond the belief that your physical reality is all there is. What's your gift? The Infinite is not denying you. You are denying you. The one who is your issue in this moment is sitting in your underwear. It's you! Step back and observe yourself making choices or acquiescing to the physical information you accept as fact. Remember what appears as solid fact is just being held together at a common connecting vibrational agreement, and generally it's a pretty low one at that.

Your brain is a biological computer capable of being programmed by any knowledgeable persuader, unless you deny access to the intruder. Neuromarketing and neuroeconomics are being practiced by companies of the controlling influence of our times. What's different about our era is the technique is not shrouded in mystery schools for the privileged few like it once was, but instead is widely available to any curious inquirer. The mystery schools of our day are some of the great universities who are pushing the edges of the envelope and sharing new discoveries with the masses.

Indigenous people have always known that living from the frequency of the heart vibration is the key to real living. It allows one to see much of the lunacy of participating in the acceptable societal norms and their conversations of importance as opposed to being in-sync with the rhythms of the earth. A realization of a transcendental Presence and Power is the activity of the heart space and soul, not the mind. This kind of sight sees the connectedness of all life and doesn't allow for constricting another's behavior, but rather the safe encouragement of all vortexes of life.

When living from the mountaintop, you'll move into a realm of expansive knowingness rather than the limited view you receive when you're immersed in the picture. When you trust your inner knowing without question, your intuition will serve as a delivery system of the 'you' that can dance with abandon in the Infinite Awareness. You'll find yourself being lifted from the manipulated pull of 'the world' and becoming comfortable not having to define what you see and sense. Thought transference is the language of awareness so you'll no longer need to explain yourself and what you know to be true to the demands of the defining minds.

Are You Caged?

I once stayed in a hotel in Costa Rica that had caged wild animals from the surrounding rain forest on display on its lower property. I walked down to see the display out of curiosity and remember looking into the eyes of a jaguar. What a powerful life force! In his glance, I could feel its memory of moving freely through the mountains leaping across the rocks and stealthily jumping from tree to tree. Have you ever seen a bear, the king of the forest with its awesome power and size, who once roamed free now chained and used as a show piece in a circus? When you connect with the essence of these animals you know in your soul they are expressions of life not meant to be condemned to such small, confined and humiliating existences. It's not what they are coded for. My heart space was uncomfortable with what I saw in that jaguar's eyes. I felt his pain and exploitation. He was a jaguar now dominated in a way that was never intended. How horrific to have to spend the rest of his life trapped and confined to a cage.

It's not the most comforting of perspectives but this is exactly what you are doing to yourself through limiting thoughts. Your persona has taken the freedom of your soaring soul with its infinite ability to explore the multidimensional cosmos and locked it up in your body. Your controlling mind, and once again who knows who programmed it, only allows your consciousness so much exploration before it cuts off its communication link. If your known world is breached, it yanks your chain and pulls you back to the circus, demanding words which must use the definition of your known reality, rather than the intuitive impress of a greater realm. You have been caged and chained to such small quarters you've forgotten how to roam free through the expansiveness of life. You are an Infinite expression who has submitted to a confined living space; a body and world only your mind knows. Though the guards at the gate never sleep, all they have to do to keep you imprisoned is press the buttons of your limiting beliefs. Ironically, the door to your cell has always been unlocked and the guard is helpless in keeping you put.

The diagnostic mind can't and won't deal with the Infinite. It will take the indescribable and put it into your words so it can control the Infinite or at least the perception of what the Infinite is by its definitions. This mental model has been passed from generation to generation and from the time of your gestation it's been imprinted into your belief system and genetic pattern. Forgetting everything is all energy, it's easy to believe you're stuck with an unchangeable genetic code. Thus, it becomes your truth and worse, your new religion.

But, science is now proving you are not bound by heredity. You'll spend a good deal of your lifetime identifying what's good and what's bad based on these coded mental models despite new proof that it's all hogwash. But alas, something will come along giving you a shake down, rattling you to the core of your being. A heartbreak, a disappointment, a revelation. Something will come from a higher place attempting to help your tethered soul escape back into the Infinite realm. It might be something devastating or painful, like the death of a loved one or near death for yourself, loss of a soulmate or something extremely important, betrayal, divorce, financial collapse, chronic illness, environmental disaster, etc. When it comes, know there is something prophetic calling you into a greater freedom through the pain. So far, planetary evolution has always come out on the other side of every cataclysmic upheaval. Taking lessons from nature, it seems possible and even plausible your personal world could and would emerge better after being hit with chaos.

When your life is seemingly in balance, you aren't caged by thinking about aches, pains and what's not working. You don't think about it because a naturally healthy body doesn't call for your attention. Your spirit is free to use your life and body as it sees fit. When you're in balance you aren't thinking about it. You aren't dealing with fears, insecurities or how to love right. If your neurotic personality wasn't constantly calling for your attention, like an addict for drugs, how much more present could you be for the joy of life's expression?

Once the parasitical thoughts are in your operating system, however, it gets difficult to cleanse. Plucking them out one at a time is a tedious, painful and laborious process. You can do all the analysis you want including spending countless hours and dollars on a process which may or may not have some value, and in the end, only makes your counselor a little more affluent. Or, if you're open to it, the mystical alignment with the Infinite can blow through and purge it all. You pop into a new frequency through the mystical connection and the vibrational patterns that don't match just fall away. It's a little like how barnacles fall off the ships entering the lakes of the Panama Canal because they can't live in the fresh water. Before they enter the canal though, they're hard pressed to be removed. It can be that easy, or you can defend why it can't be that easy. Either way, the choice is yours and you'll be right. Just allow your mountaintop-self to witness the conversation.

Freed From the Cage

As with a faucet whose slow leak is accepted and adjusted to, its gradual increase is no longer noticed until a visiting friend asks, "Why is water pouring out of your faucet?" Gas prices slowly creep up little by little when all of a sudden you realize you're paying a buck more a gallon than you were six months ago. Little by little you put on a few extra pounds and when you stop to pay attention you notice, there's an unfamiliar number on your scale and your jeans really aren't shrinking. Life slowly gets tighter but the loss of freedom and comfort isn't too noticeable because it's usually a gradual process. People can be blind and often don't realize how much of the infinite aspect of their being they've already abdicated. The parasites of this world; fear, jealousy, envy, arrogance and anxiety have taken up residence and made you their oblivious host. They have no life other than what they can suck from their carrier. People don't realize how much pain and discomfort they're in because it crept in so gradually that the constriction of the cage seems normal having forgotten what it was like not to suffer.

When you catch a glimpse of something not working in your life and attempt to change it, the mind takes charge and points out items on the outside which seem to be the culprits. Suddenly everything outside of you is worthy of blame and change. These external issues block the passage to your internal cause. Maybe it might give up a little of the thinking inside, but those deep rooted causative beliefs aren't giving up their stronghold so easy. The mind may give up some interesting game pieces but the inner kingdom will be kept out of reach and locked up tight. The mystical revelation is like a cleansing from the Infinite, providing a new thought and vision from beyond the painful place, reopening the blocked passage for a while.

As your newest growth spurt kicks in, your notions and thoughts in combination with your theories of what a higher power is, become more flexible. The conceptual traps which previously held you back and denied the emerging flow of life, release their grip. The expansion from the inside bursts through the holds of the outside like Marvel's classic character The Hulk. As you awaken from the societal trance, you'll leave behind the manipulative influence of the norm and enter into the cosmic realm. Feeling a connection to the entire universe, the cosmos comes alive in your thoughts and actions in an extraordinarily positive way. You are the activity the Infinite is having.

Your expansion doesn't guarantee the mystical encounter; it only readies and extends the invitation to you. It takes a lot of tenacity and resolve to get to know your spirit. You awaken into a fuller realization of the magnitude of your true being and the fullness of who you are beyond the personality and your point of attention. The mountaintop helps you live from a higher, broader perspective of the observer of your life. It takes some bravery to climb to heights you've never been. You need faith because it's unknown territory. If you knew what was there, you wouldn't need trust. When it's outside your comfort zone, by definition, it's not comfortable - at least for your mind which is acting like a dominating parent begging for an explanation as to what's going on. Analogies and metaphors can give you a hint of the greater engagement with a long forgotten aspect of your fuller self. What they can't give you is the soul strength that will come only through the direct experience of the journey itself.

Spiritual experiences are temporary. It is living from the

revelation of the mountaintop that returns you to your freedom that is everlasting.

This journey is of the heart and not the head, so you must stop following the unreasonable voice of reason echoing in your mind. The universe doesn't have to follow your understanding of how it should work. Words can't give you the experience of being in South Africa, the ecstasy of love or an understanding of the Infinite. Your brain isn't going to be able to heal your spirit's wounds through logic or analysis. Healing cancer, genetic diseases and incurable prognoses is your spirit's work because your head just can't grasp how it's even possible. Your earthbound mind will give you reason after reason why it can't be done while your heart will tell you all things are possible. As long as you need to know why things happen to you, you lock yourself into that particular frequency fueling the pain and closing the door to the Infinite. People will defend their fears like a mama bear does her cub. Looking for answers will keep you in the past while the transformative process of life is in the now.

It's Not a Head Trip

What gives value and significance to your life is your willingness to live it - so say yes to your spirit's urgings and answer the call stirring you to follow your heart into the unknown.

Your spiritual leap comes when you move beyond the part that is not OK with living outside your interpretation of the world. Who would you be if you weren't so tied down by being so busy? What's keeping you from living those qualities now? The modern day mystic brings those qualities to bear wherever they are, knowing all of life is part of the Infinite. The spiritual leader who sees from an elevated perspective will bring clarity to confusion, love to hurt, trust to fear, generosity to scarcity and healing to pain.

The Universe is a safe place and you are Its outlet. If you are dealing with an Infinite Life Force, then there can't be two

Infinites, can there? There's only one Life Force animating all things. Its nature is creative and it seeks to express Its nature. Because you are of the Infinite, you never know when you'll see beyond the veil of your personal character, but your soul will always become aroused when it catches a glimpse of the spiritual vision of truth. Your observer, the higher aspect of your spirit that's never been hurt or violated, is your soul's connection to the Infinite and always has been. It's what brings the Infinite into form or what some might say heaven on earth and its memory is always there. Much to the dismay of your mind, this unimaginable phenomenon can only be experienced through your spirit. It's not a head trip.

Imagine if your growth was in leaps and you popped from one classroom to another. Let's say you don't hop a linear line of point A to point B but instead, you just simply appear from point A into point G. Infinite consciousness is having infinite experiences through infinite points of attention and you can choose where in the Infinite you want to become aware. This would make living out lifetimes sequentially in linear time obsolete and yet not impossible, if that was your belief. But, with its cause and effect inescapable until handled, this explanation would render the whole idea of being stuck on the karmic wheel an irrelevant theory. The soul doesn't need to be continuously reincarnating into this vibrational dimension for its soul lessons. It's not the only classroom in the school of the multi-dimensional Infinite.

Truth isn't made truth because a lot of people believe in it religiously, truth is what it is, whether people believe it or not. Being aware of your Infinite nature would never be good for mass control, whether it's getting you back here into this world through your belief or imprisoning you with your own thoughts. When your limiting beliefs and constricted thinking have more authority over your behavior than you do, you're possessed. The good news if you fall into that percentage of the population is that your Infinite nature can free you at any given moment of your choosing! Choose to live from the mountaintop now and watch all the pieces of your life connect and playout.

Preparing for Meditation

It's important to create space in the busyness of your day to tune into an aspect of yourself revealing images and insights from beyond the filters of form. It's valuable not to tell your awareness what to think but instead to be receptive to the impress coming from something larger than the sum total of your subjective thoughts. A guided meditation is filled with visual images of what you're supposed to see, thus directing it in particular ways. This often puts one into a hypnotic trance defeating the purpose of connecting with something greater than what's in the mind. What this book will attempt to do through these visual invitations to your mountaintop is help you create a fun spot in your field of awareness. Some specific exploratory questions will give you the opportunity to do some self-directed inner work to assist in dissolving separation from your connection with the Life Force. Bigger than the mind that is operating in the minutia of your world, the awareness these exercises are meant to reveal will give way to valuable perceptions and understandings for observing unattached discernment.

There's a Perfect Order and Wisdom guiding the universe and it's this Intelligence that is operating through you. Quieting your consciousness filled with chattering gatekeepers keeping you captive in the tried-and-true, will enable you to slip past the surly bonds of your defining mind. There is no mysticism without meditation. Meditation parts the veil to greater understanding and an awareness not seen during your normal operating hours. It will widen your vision to new ways of seeing. It's imperative for you to be consistent with your conscious connection to Source in order to develop a clear quick path to a peaceful place of understanding above the chaotic world of appearance. You'll be amazed with a dedicated practice how it gets easier and easier to tap into this familiar place. You aren't taking this inner adventure to muzzle the mind, but rather to realign with the higher part of you that's watching the one making the choices. At the end of each chapter you'll find a mystical writing. Consider it a contemplative piece. Read it first, then set it aside and allow it to launch you on an inter-dimensional journey without written guidance. Taking the time to soar and merge with the Infinite on a daily basis, with no soul assignment, dissolves time and space with a rich relevant knowingness.

In preparation for your conscious connection with awareness above the gravitational pull of the world of affect, find a location where you can still your mind. When first developing or realigning with your practice the noises and demands of the outside world may distract you. Peacefully, take care of the distractions you must deal with and allow the other distractions to float through your awareness without any resistance from your aggravated self. It's likened to the experience of clouds passing through a sky. A quiet environment where you can sit your body down and close your eyes works nicely to establish a connection. Almost like a dial tone, you need to be grounded to tap into the unconscious network. This is a helpful approach particularly when getting accustomed to this regular conscious connection, but not necessary once familiar with it. You can align with this deeper knowingness anywhere, anytime, and in any environment. It just takes some consistent practice to familiarize yourself with this mountaintop view so you can get there with ease.

For now, ready yourself to receive a gift as you go on an exploration of inner space. Let go of all expectations. There is nothing you are supposed to 'get' or receive. Be gentle on yourself, as you are most worthy of a few minutes of peace, quiet and possible insights every day. However you 'perceive' your inner guidance is your perfect way. Some may see clear images in color or black and white, others may see full stories unfold, while some others may yet perceive through words, thoughts, imagination, hunches, and inklings. The only way to hone your skill and be sure to know your own unique style and inner voice is to listen to your inner guidance and watch your elevated awareness consistently. Your regular meditation practice will teach you and is the only way you'll learn what works for you individually. The gifts received from meditation can't be conveyed through books or teachers. You must experience your higher self's communication style and sound to know it.

Through your consistent attempts to quiet the mind and body you'll learn the ways to still all the demands vying for your attention. Occasionally you'll have a 20/20 hindsight where you'll say to yourself, "Oh yea, I should have listened to my intuition". You'll soon learn what 'I don't know' feels like, in advance, but in the meanwhile why wait for haphazard occasions when daily tuning-in will serve you greater? Going to a place of stillness within, you'll familiarize yourself with the sound from the one watching as you notice your mind and actions. You'll become conversant in a new language, discerning the differences between the imagined and the truth. From this height of awareness you'll be able to see paths of fear and trust play out before your eyes, leaving you with a complete knowing you are at choice. You can either choose the path with anxiety around your life lessons or the one with peaceful trust.

Bring a journal and something to write with to your meditation time. It's also great to sit in the stillness without worrying about writing down your revelations. But, it's great to have the tools there if you have some contemplative questions and revelations. You might want to capture them, but remember there's no need to stay fixated on them for the next 20 minutes. Instead, gently open your eyes and jot them down. Then softly close your eyes and return to where you were.

Near the end of each chapter of this book you'll find meditations which look at different aspects of your world from your mountaintop. You may want to read through these scenes and soulful inquiries a number of times until you can recall them. There are several soul-reflective inquiries within each mountaintop experience. You might want to choose only a couple to reflect on in any particular journey. Close your eyes and allow the remembrances to guide you. Alternatively, you might want to find a quiet place to read a few sentences, and then close your eyes to reflect on the meditative suggestions. Follow that by opening your eyes and writing your thoughts down before reading the next sentence. Contemplatively, close your eyes and slowly move through the entire meditation repeating this pattern. Another approach might be to record your voice speaking these soulful directives. Yet another powerful approach is to meet with a group of like-minded spiritual explorers on a regular basis. Within this coven of friends, you can identify someone to be the designated voice for the journey.

Establishing Your Mountaintop

Before meditation, take a moment to state:

I know all is well and wherever I go in my expanding awareness, all is good and I am safe. I'm surrounded by and live in an Omni Dimensional Life Force that can never be violated, because there is nothing opposed to it. I move on the very currents of Life Itself and I'm free to notice all things without attachment to anything. Free to move beyond any image at any time and courageous enough to remain in it. I open to graceful guidance on my soul's adventure, surrender my demands to logical understandings, and I welcome new and unknown states of consciousness for my soul's evolution.

Take a few breaths to bring your attention back to the center of your body. Find a natural rhythm for your breath to fall into. See if you can follow your in-breath into your body . . . Allow your exhale to take with it any tension, worries, or concerns while creating more internal room. Find a natural rhythm to your breathing . . . Now, follow your next breath, letting it take you deeper into the space beyond your body temple, where past and future dissolve into the present. Your inner awareness becomes the threshold you move across, where now your exhale propels you further into the openness of the void. Allow yourself to become available and receptive to a deep hearing and heightened awareness to move you to greater good.

Notice you are in a vast expanse with infinite points of light as if you are one in a galaxy of stars . . . Allow your awareness to be drawn to a beautiful blue orb that is calling you home . . . feel an attraction and relational remembrance to the vibrancy of this world. You move in closer and when you do, you can see the pristine snowcapped mountains, the wooded forests, the lush green jungles, the expansive deserts, deep canyons, still lakes, running rivers, and the all-embracing blue ocean . . . Your soul is deeply moved by the physical beauty. As your awareness of the magnificent of this place is heightened, you feel the call of this earth for the gift you have to bring.

From this elevated perspective you feel drawn to a particular mountaintop to rest. You know this is your special connecting place between the celestial realm and the earthly world of form. It's your personal vortex where you can always return to remember that you are more than this world. You have come here for a time such as this because you have something to give to this time and place. You have come with joy to share who you are and what you have and it's perfect. You are enough for all this journey will ever ask of you. If you ever forget who you are, all you have to do is close your eyes and bring your awareness back to this spot for it is always with you on this adventure and no one or no thing can ever take it away from you. Find your perfect mountaintop . . . Find yourself lying on your back looking up at the star-painted sky from where you just came . . . Take notice of the trees reaching to the heavens. Open your senses to hear the sounds of nature and the birds singing . . . smell the fresh crisp air tasting its fragrances traveling on the breezes and brushing your skin.

Look out from your mountaintop and become familiar with your expansive view, with its rivers, lakes, canyon, caves, and valleys. Take note of any animals noticing you moving in and what birds are soaring through the sky. Make this space yours . . . Feel free to move some boulders around with your mind or build a rock ring for a sacred circle; draw any icons or totems your spirit feels like adding to your sacred space . . . Become aware of the many paths leading up the mountain converging upon your sacred center . . . Ask your observing-self where it sits in the midst of all this noticing . . . What does holding a higher view mean or look like? Take as much time as you desire here in the silence enjoying your new location . . . Allow yourself to be filled with wonder and amazement, astonished in these images and insights that have not previously been part of your consciousness. Being that they are new and enticing, know they will linger in your cognizant awareness and be available for easy recall when you come down from the mountaintop. Welcome the revelations from on-high that will have you rethinking much of the known facts of your world. Take some time now to review some of the earthly facts that you'd like to have reevaluated from a higher place . . .

Seeing uncomfortable dynamics in your world from this higher place doesn't necessarily make them go away, but it allows you to see them with a different kind of representation and meaning for your life. From this elevated perspective you can see healthier options for resolution. Where you struggled previously, you'll see ways through that you never knew were there. As you awaken to your mystical connection, you'll understand other's perspectives and stories and find new answers you were unaware existed. You come to a spiritual understanding and its relevance for your soul's growth. In your journey through this book, what dynamics would you like to see resolved in your life? Know that you'll have opportunities throughout its pages to transform these dynamics of your world, but for now, it's time to come back to the conscious interaction of the world in which you are walking . . .

You return to your world of activity refreshed and

renewed. Know once you've been somewhere you can easily return to that somewhere by simply calling it back to your awareness. There is always more work to be done, but for now, pull yourself back into your body permitting gratitude for your discoveries to fill your field of awareness . . . Feel a joy knowing you'll be consistently returning to your sacred space, but for now, choose a path down the mountain . . . Familiarize yourself with this trail back into the world of form. Know there is always this corridor, this passage back to the elevated perspective of your world. Touch some of the trees as you pass by them and feel the earth move beneath your feet.

As what you saw in a distance comes more into focus, return your attention to your breath. Breathe . . . When you are ready, slowly move your fingers and toes, stretch, gently open your eyes and sit for a moment to reacclimatize to your physical world. Take your pen and take some time to write out your experience. It doesn't matter if it was memorable and you are certain you'll never forget it, you should still capture it on paper – later, you'll be glad you did.

Soulful Adventures

- Sketch your Mountaintop.
- Take a walk in nature, find a rock or some object, sit on the ground and contemplate it. See if it has any history to share. Observe what images might come into your field of awareness.
- Where do you feel caged in your world? Where do you sense you are tied down to some circus act which feels like it has nothing to do with your spirit's intention? What's really keeping you there? If you knew the cage door was unlocked, would you leave? If you stepped freely into your fantasy what would you do? Take those fantastic energies and use them to transform your life.
- Remember a time you held a position to be true, like

you were right and 'they' were wrong, rendering you unable to hear a new possibility. Then identify when something in your awareness shifted in you and you were able to hear new information. In this new openness you were able to discover so much more. This could have occurred in a relationship, political or religious opinion, or at work to name a few places. What gift did you receive? Where, in your life now, could you be a bit more open to a new perspective?

- Take a step back and look at some of the headlines in magazines and newspapers sitting around your house or those that pop up on your computer screens. Ask yourself, how do I see the media directing my thoughts to their position? If you listen to news or gossip shows, allow yourself to wonder if there could be more to the story you're hearing or another side not being shared?
- If your body is truly energy at the atomic level, what new energetic direction would you like to take on?
- Look at your health, eating and drinking habits, exercise, sleep, etc. How can you be kinder to your body? Where can you improve the partnership between your spirit and body by taking better care of the body you were gifted with so it's a healthy vehicle to move around in?
- Where is your spirit's energy being diverted from its intention? What's valuable for you to learn from this wrestling match? Your observer of this interaction has some insights. What are they?

Mystical Writing

I am Wisdom. Mine is the blast of the resounding Word through which all creation came to be, and I quickened all things with my breath so that not one of them is mortal in its kind; for I am Life. Indeed I am Life, whole and undivided -- not hewn from any stone, or budded from branches, or rooted in virile strength; but all that lives has its root in me. For Wisdom is the root whose blossom is the resounding Word . .

.

~ Hildegard von Bingen
1098 -1179

Chapter 2: Prison without Bars

I freed a thousand slaves I could have freed a thousand more if only they knew they were slaves.
~ Harriet Tubman

In my country we go to prison first and then we become President.
~ Nelson Mandela

The 2:00 A.M. Alarm in Your Head

Waking at 2:00 AM with a heavy feeling in the pit of your stomach, heart racing and mind contemplating the horrible scenarios that might befall you if the situation doesn't improve, is a trip through hell. Losing sleep as a result of that anxiety taking you captive by hijacking your creative imagination is sadly commonplace. This intruder of consciousness has you believing you've lost your ability to direct your internal faculties. As you fall into a hypnotic trance by staring at the object of your concern for too long the anxiety is compounded.

Often, I'm struck by the sheer number of very wise people who come to me seeking spiritual support as they find themselves facing financial demands they are unprepared to handle. If I were to create a composite picture of them in one person - let's name him Caleb - several common behaviors would become apparent.

Caleb's initial response to his financial woe is like a blow to the gut that brings him to his knees. The anxiety runs rampant filling his mind with scenarios he doesn't want to experience. Next, his sense of hopelessness shuts down his ability to see a way out of his hamster wheel of panic. As Caleb relentlessly reviews and dramatizes horrific scenarios over and over as if they are his truth, he directs his creative power to create the very thing he doesn't want to happen. The next thing Caleb does is pray. Even those that are the farthest from faith fall to their knees, begging for iconic intervention they don't even believe in. I've seen it hundreds of times. Caleb soon begins looking outside of himself for the ultimate bailout - buying lottery tickets and trying too-good-to-be-true business schemes. In the end, out of exhaustion and depression, Caleb finds himself enveloped in despondent energy disabling him from making any other attempts to generate a positive outcome. That's usually when I get the phone call.

Do you know a Caleb? Have you been a Caleb? Living from the mountaintop will help unlock your psyches grip on your brain so it can process freely again. Fear shuts down the total operating system on a physical level and slams the door to your higher vibrations. The density of fear in your field of awareness is so heavy; it can weigh you down to the degree that you feel like you can't lift above its paralyzing view. Fear locks you behind the prison bars of a logical horror sequence projecting itself through fear-based beliefs onto the screen of your mind. Your subconscious doesn't know the difference between something vividly visualized and actually seen. So all of your fear-based programming is activating your biological system and leaving it totally out of whack. No wonder your adrenalin is pumping at 2:00 A.M.

These logical horror patterns have been spoon-fed to you by media images, tales of woe and the what-if-something-bad-happens mentality residing at the control panel of your operating system. These controlling fears keep you searching for the safety of the herd. There is no doubt that fear complicates everything. Imagine you have nothing to concern yourself with except bringing forth your spirit's vision and whatever real particulars are at hand. You'd certainly have a lot more energy to bring to whatever you take on without imagined what-if scenarios attached to that task. Your desire for safety is what holds you back and keeps you stuck in the concern vibration. Without fear and what-if's, you'd know innately that you're safe and able to trust the Universal Intelligence. Guidance would be there when you needed it supporting a much more comfortable approach to living.

No Longer Bound by Sequential Unfoldment

Intuitive knowing comes in an instant and isn't relegated to physical or linear time boundaries. The Infinite moment can deliver in all of Its fullness everything you need to return to a place of peace and calm, even at 2:00A.M. It's the law of cause and effect that operates in the linear construct of the vibrational world of form. Infinite isn't bound to sequential unfoldment because It's already where the unfoldment is going. It's Omnipresent, not here and there constricting It within duality. It's One and Everywhere Present already, so there's no place for It to go. Within the Changeless, all change takes place. The Infinite has the same potential today, yesterday and forever more.

Before the issues you are currently grappling with, there were others. When these current issues are handled, there will probably be more. When you duke it out with a problem, you've already slipped into believing there's something outside of you needing to be fixed or changed. When there's a disturbance in your field, it's time to go within for clarity rather than searching ceaselessly outside of yourself. Your internal dialogue created the projection you are walking in. Step back to see what's directing your attention. Remember to ask yourself, who's looking at this scenario? If you notice who is looking at the mess, you'll realize you are outside of the mess itself and need not be upset and lose who it is you are to it. To free yourself from the prison of reactionary fear you must be able to watch yourself in all situations.

If anxiety takes over, its density pulls you back into your body. At times, it can feel impossible to escape the gravitational pull of its physical reality. Your awareness must separate from it effectively creating distance between you and the issue so you can observe it objectively. The understanding of the need for this separation comes from realizing you are always at choice, no matter what. At any instant you can decide to be free and return to your mountaintop. So, how does right this instant sound? Yes, now.

If not now, then you remain shackled to the issues which continue to activate your unresolved weak spots. Whether they be anger, shame, guilt, sorrow, pain, or regret, your triggered energetic experiences will lock you into a mirrored prison. Within that prison, you'll be taunted with hurtful events of the past and vulnerable potentials for the future. Don't betray yourself by giving into your troubled emotions. Even mystics of the heart embrace their full range of emotions, they just don't allow themselves to be controlled by them. The Indian poet, Kabir, wrote, "Wherever you are is the entry point." What he meant was whatever is going on for you, is the perfect opportunity to enter into the stream of Life with its infinite potential for resolve.

You must remember you *are* awareness. The objects you're aware of aren't you. You are boundless. When you forget, you bind the totality of your infinite potential-self to a limited in-form experience. Most people will remain trapped in a belief that what they see and hear is the truth, particularly if it comes from the authorities. These individuals have no chance of breaking out of their prisons until they escape through their portal of death of the physical body. Sometimes people don't embrace their freedom even then, because they're still bound to a belief in repeatable lifetimes to get it right. Some individuals leave their awareness in the womb and acquiesce to the programming of their body and upbringing as rationale for their lifetime's sickness and responses. After 'proper education' in repeated well-meaning misinformation you're ready to go out and do life. At the end of the day, those duties leave little energy to continue an exploration of what you are beyond your physical form. You're just too tired and imprisoned to experience the finer vibrations of true unconditional joy and love of your true nature.

But what if you weren't too tired to experiment with the imaginal body outside your physical manifestation? Jean Houston popularized the term imaginal body, which is commonly accepted as the separate externalized image of the self that carries awareness through different dimensions. Have you considered using yours to create new experiences for yourself? It's a powerful way to extend your awareness beyond society's encroachment squeezing you into an experience you don't want. Through its use you can step beyond the boundaries of the body's confinement and past the prison bars you're feeling locked behind. Form follows consciousness and you can visit your heart's dreams before your physical world manifests them. You can be a co-creating conduit of the Infinite by being the center of your world and not its prisoner.

Develop your skill at being the conscious link between your envisioned world and your physical reality and see the differences in your perceptions every single day. The ability to inhabit the imaginal dimension, which was natural to your ancestors, is a vast difference from today's value lying in the quantifiable realm dismissing whatever it can't touch. It's time to re-familiarize yourself with your subtler body so you can be released from the casting of other's desires. Step free from your cellular memory and enter the imaginal realm of the immeasurable.

The Few Control the Many

Many people unknowingly, but freely, surrender most of their inalienable rights of freedom so they might feel a sense of 'safety'. The more you forget about the Infinite aspect of your being and True Power, the more you'll become bound to a physical, fear-based reality. Beyond endemic surveillance of cell phones, internet, smart meters and the eye in the sky, there's still an untraceable quantum consciousness that presents itself to those who stay in touch with their observing selves.

As the next generation is brought up unfazed by being watched by cameras in school and traced through their electronics, there will be a natural acceptance of this infringement to privacy as 'just how life is'. Where today you might say I have nothing to hide, no big deal, what if tomorrow the controller decides to abuse their observational position? Unquestioning submission is what keeps the herd penned in. The last thing a rancher wants is the herd stampeding through the fence, which it can do at any time it unites. The crowd mentality teaches those who listen that it's more comfortable to go with the flow and live life on autopilot than it is to push against the accepted norm. When you go against acceptable behavior, the peers you previously aligned with turn against you. In other words, your community begins to police itself and report fringe-dwellers as detractors to the authority.

Real force for change comes from the ground up. It's a grassroots philosophy. To be expressed, Life needs you to break free from the imposed limitations of your imprisoned self. The few control the many through fear and separation. Those who direct the collective awareness do not want individuals uniting for any purpose other than their own. And, as long as you continue to identify with your personality rather than uniting with the Life Force of your being, you'll remain susceptible to the vibrational battle for supremacy. It's your thinking that thinks 'this is me' putting your ego in charge. But the ego is a little like a bull in a china shop, not that that's such a bad thing. Its muscular nature has its value. Your ego gives you confidence, chutzpah, a healthy competitive edge, and watches out for your wellbeing in the world. But when you relate to your experiences, titles and belongings as who it is you are, because that's what you've been falsely taught - you've got a problem. Usually, later in life, even if you never took a journey to the mountaintop, you'll submit your ego to the greater concerns of the soul, but why wait that long? You need a journey to the mountaintop for a more expanded view of the truth of who you really are. If you want to evolve spiritually you don't need to get rid of or even overcome your ego. You simply need to learn to access the part of you that's already beyond it.

You're so much more than your experiences, but as you become more imprisoned in your entrained fears of failure and loss, you forget that who you are now truly can't fail. Giving up your freedom to protect your freedom is oddly illogical, don't you agree? There's an unleashed strength when many individuals break out of the herd mentality. When enough people refuse something, it becomes unenforceable. This stirs the greatest concerns of those with the biggest sticks. But when the enforcers, themselves, refuse to execute an edict that's been imposed and instead choose to sit down with the protesters, it generates fear in the controlling elite.

Attempting to create a calculated and controlled world in which to feel safe, is entrapment, and honestly, it's the most ideal environment for anxiety to breed. When you're trying to keep things from happening, entitlement to fear and worry grows. Being on the fear-filled lookout for prospective problems will work against you big time by keeping you imprisoned by them. Remember, it's in times of flux when life is increasingly difficult and issues seem impassable that the greatest opportunities for change and newness emerge. It's at the point where hope becomes hopelessness that you can choose to engage faith instead.

My personal experience with this entitlement of fear came as a complete surprise to me and everyone who knows me. It didn't hit me immediately but gradually a foreign feeling whittled away at my abandon to the call of the moment after I became a parent. That foreign feeling? It was the subjective concern filter of fear. Something I'd never experienced before having never been afraid of death. I spent decades chasing physical adventures, jumping out of airplanes, skiing glaciers, diving the depths of the ocean and trekking the heights of

Himalayas. Now, as this father-person who isn't afraid of my own mortality, I find myself with a bit of anxiety at the thought my death will leave my son fatherless. The potential, which is just too painful for me to process, has tempered my adventurous undertakings.

So, where did you get the idea life's unfoldment is not going to be alright? What has been your experience of a subjective concern filter of fear? Was it an unfortunate trip to the dentist? Or, a near-miss with another car during rush hour? Perhaps it was when you had children and realized how many tables with pointed corners the world was filled with? Only your choice to give fear a presence in your world keeps it fed. Trust your inspiration more than your fear.

At any moment you can either, take notice of your choices and go within to have a look at your options from a higher place, or stay imprisoned in your anxiety. There are many more possibilities on the mountaintop than exist in the physical moment of form. Getting past your fixation on the limited human perspective from a fear-filled mind will invite a grander picture into view.

There's always a way through the subjective filter of fear. When you pause to return to your mountaintop, you'll discover all the trails through the difficulty. Your observing self knows the way and will never forsake you, no matter how insurmountable the situation may appear. Your confidence grows as you feel your soul's power and authority influencing your decision. The mystical connection will strengthen your whole life. Allow this power from within you to grow into its greatest promise.

The Boot of the Bouncer

You can look for miracles or be the miracle. Stop fighting creation and be the creator. If you really look at it, fear causes you to fight while Life causes you to create. The experiences and the people in your life will change; that's just the nature of things. The form in your life will be in a constant state of change. It's always been that way and always will be. Feeling stuck in attachments will suck you into battle mode and equip you with an armor that's so heavy it becomes almost impossible to move. The densities of these parasitic emotions don't belong in a light heart. If you were fearless you'd be happy and living in Joy. This graceful field awaits your choice. Decades ago I left a position with a substantial amount of responsibility for a life unknown to follow my dream of starting a new thought community in Hawaii. I followed a vision rendering any fears that tried to creep in impotent. That didn't mean they weren't there. I heard the questions, "how are you going to pay for this" and "who's going to show up when you start talking" but I didn't give them any power. The end result was the Aloha life that birthed a new spiritual community on the windward side of Oahu. You may hear that story and think I was lucky, but I believe it demonstrated being in alignment with the mystical union of my soul's purpose.

Sure, you can hold onto the anchors that keep you miserable and shackled to what doesn't serve you. Or, you could create space for your imprisoned perspective to know all of your current challenges are serving your tomorrows just perfectly. Which sounds like the better choice? It takes some trust to hold this position. If it was so obvious or just a matter of luck, it wouldn't require trust.

Choosing faith will transmute your fears into blessings. Your greatest pains are here to help you escape your prison without walls. Your inner bouncers will tell the torment where to go, showing it to the door of your consciousness after its mission to make you miserable is complete. When you let go of your earthly expectations of how everything should be, you become lighter, and gain a higher perspective from an ever greater elevation. From this sight line, you'll see more of the landscape and what's possible in your life. What's going on in the density of form will no longer matter when you're above that level and your vision is turned upwards.

Where you look is where you go.

Dark Night of the Soul

While it may sound quite frightening and initially feel it too, the dark night of the soul is an exquisite journey during which you'll find your false self being destroyed and your true nature emerging. The path can be excruciatingly painful though you'll be strangely grateful for it in the end. The realization of never being the same afterwards is mind blowing. The greatest challenge of making it to the beautiful end where you'll find yourself forever changed, is the feeling that the pain will never end. This is what makes the dark night of the soul so frightening. The journey through the dark night brings up a lifetime of fears and past mistakes and rubs them in your face over a prolonged period of time. The period of painful introspection seems endless. I've rarely heard it to be a quick passage.

The good news is most survive it and those who don't will have bought themselves another life. The dark night is an invitation to open the mystical connection by bringing you to your knees, both literally and figuratively. Saint John of the Cross', now famous poem, "The Dark Night" was partially prompted by the wrongful imprisonment by his Carmelite Brothers who felt he was pushing the edges of the order a bit too much. He was held captive in a small space under the stairs and taken out midday for public beatings and humiliation. He finally escaped to the safety of Teresa of Avila's convent.

Having the experience, like Saint John, as a powerless victim wrongfully and forcefully humiliated is a classic catalyst that will throw you into a dark downward spiral. It's not unusual for seekers of truth to pass through a dark night on their way to higher consciousness. Many consider it to be an integral part of the journey to unite with the deep joy of one's true nature. It's a very private, personal matter during which you'll feel a profound sense of aloneness as you're initiated into elevated states of awareness.

No doubt at some point in your life you've experienced some sense of union with something greater than your earth-bound self. These deep connections shine a light on the inappropriate control your ego has in keeping your true nature at bay. You're searching and faith is developing as you either dig deeper on your own or are pushed. Your controlling mind will attempt to hold onto the tried and true despite your hunger to merge with the Infinite and gain mountaintop perspective. It can feel like being pushed into a hole. Simultaneously, you are pulled by the vision of new ways, yet still imprisoned by old ways, and find yourself wedged in-between. This unclear, vague realm of possibilities torments your stuck-self when you don't seem to fit in either place.

You might find yourself struggling to function in your world of form attempting to be positive or by going about your daily routine, all the while the truth is that you're just barely showing up. Life appears bleak, the passion is missing and it seems as if you are wandering in the wilderness. You feel lost in the dark barren desert with no hope of seeing the light again. The abyss you are looking into seems bottomless. They don't call it the dark night for nothing.

The struggle continues despite knowing the truth of the mystical realm is a path of joy, ease and grace. It seems you're hanging on for dear life as you persevere because there's nowhere to turn back to anyhow. Your prayers aren't working, your meditations feel empty and even in those brief moments when you do catch a glimpse of a lighter life it's only fodder for your tormented trapped-self. Friends see your pain, they invite you out and you put on a good show, but your heart isn't really into it. You feel like you're with them, but it's almost as if you aren't in your body and the conversations are just muffled sounds. The irony is you can function fairly well in spite of the inner anguish and most of your friends won't even know the depths of what you're experiencing.

The funny thing is how commonplace this is. Many others have plunged into this same kind of soulful darkness and have come out on the other side. These are the guides who, through this experience, have developed profound passion for fellow travelers and will encourage you to trudge ahead rather than giving in to your old ways. Transformation of your total being is awaiting you on the other side of this cataclysmic soulful event. And yes, there is something greater calling you. Check in with your higher self who is observing your journey through pain and your mind's torment. Commit yourself to remembering this is a rite of passage and a spiritual detox which will bring you to a higher understanding of everything once you've passed through it. The dark night isn't everyone's path, but if you're in it, it's yours. The truth is, the more relentless your sense of incompetence becomes the longer you are held down by your mind's attempt to figure a way out of it. As you find your friends' can no longer reach you, the more alone you feel. The pursuits of the physical world aren't making sense to your way of seeing and you'll find yourself awake at 2 A.M. tormented, despondent and anxious, wondering if you should even bother to keep on living. Past mistakes play through your mind like a strange movie and you're left wondering what you've done to create this horrific dissonance in your life. Suppressed emotions keep bubbling up at bewitching hours paired with haunting adrenalin rushes of shame, victimhood, anger, regret, guilt, and woe-is-me. The pain lies in the stories you're telling yourself.

You've lost your connection with Life, seemingly annexed from your Higher Power and the sense of aloneness is debilitating. Even your dearest friends seem unable to love you back. All your spiritual work can't even lift you out. All the earthly belongings you worked so hard to collect don't seem relevant. Even the thoughts from your brain can't seem to lift you out of this underworld of unrelenting funk.

The Light at the End of the Tunnel

Sometimes it takes being weak enough to be willing to return to the stream of Life. With a total sense of destitution, you're unable to do anything but accept your fate and surrender. Giving up all of the struggle and desire to control your way out, your heart breaks open and the light returns. You're immersed in a peace that fills the room and a warming calm easily fills your mind, body and soul. You are coming to life again, unfrozen by the warmth from the fire within. There's a purification that breaks open thus allowing the heart to expand with blissful peace and love, leaving you both empty and full. What you thought you knew to be true was diminished by the greater view from the mountaintop awareness.

This blissful expansion of understanding obliterates the logical mind. You can hardly take it any longer. You're pushed to the very edges of the experiences you believed were possible. There's such an overwhelming expansion in your emotional field that it annihilates what you knew about anger, fear, arrogance, despair, joy, ecstasy, and love. It's like birth. You must get pushed through this canal. Your ego mind no longer knows what to do but jump into the fire where, after it has finished spitting, hissing and smoldering, you're consumed and become the flame Itself. Total union is now known. You stand as the light, transformed.

Your insufficient sense of self is gone. It could no longer support your new Spirit's expression. The prerecorded limiting mind that only knew a small part of your magnificence and dictated your life, had to die for your true expression to come forth. The collision between the controlling mind and your true nature was inevitable and, once on the other side of the dark night, is seen as a blessing only you could go through. No one else could have dealt with your demons other than you as you've uprooted and cleansed them from your being. Your ego had gained too much control over your heart and operating system dictating all your thoughts and emotions.

Don't be fooled into thinking your ego has been subdued forever. You must continue to reaffirm your true nature's authority. Over the long haul, your controlling mind will always have an opinion in all matters. It wants to be part of your transformation as it reaches for its reestablished dominance. But now you know your ego stands between you and trusting Life fulfilling its promise of a higher consciousness. As you, it can't direct matters of the heart which is what healing is really all about. You want to trust this all-embracing love, but like most, you suffer from fear of the very thing you desire. This internal battle is what keeps the false identity of the ego alive. In the mystical there's nothing to fight because there is no otherness. Fear keeps you stuck in its tightening grip but an acceptance of the ever-available unconditional Love will free you. If it's complicated, it's all ego. Spirit is simple!

When the night is over, the dawn will come, and you'll get to walk in your life seeing with new awareness and experiencing your existence in a new world. Your life is redefined as it becomes aligned with the vision from the mountaintop. You've become an expression of brilliance because the mystical has prevailed in transmuting any sense of separation from the Infinite Source. You might not be able to articulate what you experienced, but you know things are very different. There's an ease and grace in your world. A joyous appreciation for all of life, and an acceptance and self-love for who you truly are after the dark night has passed will keep you from going through another. You'll find yourself home wherever you are as you realize the light you've been looking for has been within you the whole time.

Stepping Free From the Prison

With its sense of violation and hopelessness, the dark night of the soul is not only experienced by individuals but also by whole nations. What chances do people have in war torn countries when major media sources are spinning their stories to satiate the transnational corporations, thus supporting hidden agendas? Only those on the ground have a sense of the true pain and maybe the reason for it, while images seen by the world are carefully choreographed for a particular response.

What's awakening is the global heart as a stronger vibration in the collective unconscious. It's becoming available to those who want to tune into this rising spirit of love and understanding. Change is difficult no matter which way you come at it. If you're in pain, it's tough to tap your higher abilities to push through it. Yet, if you feel like everything is ok, there's no motivation to change anything. People are so used to getting their information through words, which are limiting. Compared to stepping into the image of thought pictures, words are so one-dimensional. Before the proliferation of words, there was still communication. Many children born today have difficulty putting words into sentences and invite you to communicate in a more telepathic way. Forgo your perceived way to enter into communication another way. If you continue insisting your way is the only way rather than listening to your spirit's guidance, you'll be looking back with a sense of self-betrayal saying, "I should have listened." Your intuitive guidance is available all the time, not only in times of need. Tap it for creativity, communication, and higher insight to tie into your awakened global consciousness.

Humanity's advancement has brought people to the point of no longer needing their root chakra protective energies to forage for food and fight off saber tooth tigers. Instead, we've modified our protective desires to our physiological personas. Our angst is as real as any other force we have to deal with. Now, we're playing in the energy fields that are out-picturing. To quiet those inner rumblings, people shut their life force down and in doing so they build walls of defenses, which only serve to imprison the builder. Life becomes dark and dank when you live in the protection of your treasured thoughts of reality. You just can't live a liberated life if you're distracted and running scared. You must realign with the observing self if you don't want to live out the rest of your days in solitary confinement.

The new fight isn't in your physical world; it's in your psyche where you fight those saber-tooth tigers of consciousness. This dimension's images and energy is as real as the world of form our ancestors fought in. This is the realm where you must find peace, otherwise the internal struggle will keep you imprisoned. Can you recall a story of humiliation or embarrassment enough to make you blush today? Humiliation has a lot of juice and you might find yourself impacted by that experience in ways you've never acknowledged. It's hard to feel your oneness with the love of all things in life when you want to crawl under a rock.

How does that experience of humiliation from so long ago still affect your decision making process today? What and who do you avoid? *Have your decisions about going out with certain people, going to specific places, dressing, or careers been a result of ancient wounds still imprisoning you?* In retrospect, how have you humiliated others? What were you afraid of that prompted that? What choices do you think that person makes now based on that experience? These are the kind of soul experiences that have implanted their remembrance into your cellular level. Looking back now from this distance on the mountaintop and knowing the pain you inflicted, how would you change your interaction?

Do you have a secret you wouldn't want anybody to know? Whether you did something or just had thoughts about doing something, would you fess up to it? Have you done something that would embarrass you or others if it was made public? When your self-doubt takes hold, you've got a lot more to deal with than what this world is throwing at you. The self-questioning aspect of you is always sitting in the background waiting to raise a hand to be acknowledged and take over the situation. How is it possible to feel so good one day and filled with despair the next? One negative piece of information and the footing can be knocked out from underneath you. You'll be shrouded with such indecisiveness that you are truly in a prison without bars. Don't let doubts incapacitate you while the mountaintop view is available to emancipate you.

Do you have doubts about your mystical exploration? There is an aspect of you watching your journey and the choices you make from an elevated level. Are you ready to trust this guidance again and step free from your self-imposed prison? Or, are your doubts around being humiliated and unsupported keeping you from listening and trusting? *Is your desire to control the universe stronger than your willingness to surrender to it?*

If the downdraft of fear comes up, let it go. If resentment tugs at you, let it go. If worry grasps for you, let it go. If judgment pulls at your attention, let it go. Fear, resentment, worry, and judgment are not what will open your heart to the gifts of the Infinite; instead, they'll all close in and pull you down. The sooner you let go, the more liberated you'll become and the more beautiful your Life will grow to be. You must trust where the divine current carries you. The moment you come out from the prison cell, you'll notice the light has been shining the whole time. It's been ever available to you, it's just now you've said yes by joining those who've been enjoying the light the whole time you were in hiding.

Try those ruby slippers on for size, remember all you have to do is click them to get out, and step through the unlocked prison doors of your limited thinking. To be a mystic you must make a conscious decision to stop being motivated by fear. Too many fear intimacy with the Absolute and Infinite Source of all things unless it's on their own terms. It's natural to be challenged by the wants and the how's. Wanting to know how everything is going to turn out, how long it will take to happen, and seeing solid proof before submitting to the process of surrender is common.

The shadows and parasites of the darkness, like the fears

of not being able to make it in this world, or being unable to provide food, clothing, or a roof over your head, feed on your concerns about survival. It's tough to continue believing in your higher self when this kind of dark, reptilian survival energy fills your mind. The mind of earthly beliefs will try to take control and blackmail you with images of humiliation, failure, disapproval, poverty and if you aren't proactive, it will be successful. These beliefs will keep you from expressing your true nature. It takes courage to move from fear of crisis to living in integrity with your inner vision of what's possible. People start believing the most rational choice is the easiest one. While this makes the most logical sense, it really turns your power over to your small mind because it entails the least amount of risk to the ego's comfort zone.

Alternatively, if you're willing to risk and stretch beyond where you're comfortable, you'll align your true self with the mystical pulling you through to higher ground. Yes, it will be uncomfortable, but oh, the ecstasy on the other side is so worth it. You'll be liberated from the fear only when you listen to your soul's calling and courageously follow the guidance from your higher coding.

No Space

People talk about mind over matter, but what we must learn to have is awareness over mind and higher perspective over the genetic make-up. If you've always believed that you're a slave to your genes and DNA, cell biologist Bruce Lipton argues otherwise, advocating the idea that a cell's life is not controlled by its genes, but instead, by thought and the physical environment.

Have you ever used a DVD? It's a perfect example of how you can access a particular part of a whole at one time. Throughout the whole movie, it's ALL available and present at once. Just like viewing that DVD, you can bring your attention to your past or future; it's all available at this moment. You can put your attention on health and wholeness or you can direct your attention to dis-ease and sickness. It's your choice. So, while your mind is playing out the sequential unfoldment, your world is fully available at this present moment. In human form we live by linear timeline whereas in consciousness, where life can pass before you in the blink of an eye, there's no such thing as time as we know it. You can dance with time if you know it's not real. If you're locked into time's reality, then that's your reality. Rushing, moving, running, anxious, and late are all words used to describe the negative dance with time. Perfect timing, synchronicity, and déjà vu's, are all words that describe a joyful positive dance with time.

Those who control the perceptions of this space in time have your mind in their prison. But more and more people are breaking free from the grip which keeps them separated from the Infinite Source. Those who control the present, also control the perception of the past and what's to come. You might forget you're watching a movie titled with your name and have the option of walking out and into another show at any time. Most are so emotionally engrossed in what appears to be their total truth on the screen they are rendered incapacitated. Don't let the images you see before you fool you into submission. Walk out of the theatre and choose a different ending.

How things resonate through the morphogenetic field has physicists exploring subatomic particles which make quantum leaps from one place to another or communicate across vast distances of the universe without any linear connection. This has scientists thinking and talking about no space as we know of it. Mystics have always known about the fields of no space connecting us all.

The Infinite Potential needs you to break free from the imposed limitations of your imprisoned mind thinking everything must be logically connected. There's hardly any room in that theory for there to be a space that is no space at all. The few control the many with fear and separation. The last thing those who direct the collective awareness want is a uniting of the many in the morphogenetic field. As I shared, the real force for change comes from the grassroots. Everything you ever wanted is on the other side of your sense of separation from the Infinite Source.

What you can't change on the outside you can transform on the inside, however. Allow the challenges in your life to support your growth. Your strength and inner resolve to know the Power within you is greater than anything outside of you. The events of your life are your spiritual gym in which you can gain strength and stamina to break free of your present levels of fear and constriction. Keep identifying with your personality thinking 'this is me' rather than uniting with the life force of your true nature, and you'll remain in a battle for supremacy at the vibrational level believing you are your experiences.

Meditation

When leaving the body behind, it's always a good idea to know how blessed you are in this field of grace in which you play. Before meditation, take a moment to state:

I know all is well and wherever I go in my expanding awareness, all is good and I am safe. I'm surrounded by and live in an Omni-Dimensional Life Force that can never be violated, because there is nothing opposed to it. I move on the very currents of Life Itself and I'm free to notice all things without attachment to anything. Free to move beyond any image at any time and courageous enough to remain in it. I open to a graceful guidance on my soul's adventure, surrender my demands to logical understandings, and welcome new and unknown states of consciousness for my soul's evolution.

Take a few breaths to bring your attention back to the center of your body. Find a natural rhythm for your breath to fall into. See if you can follow your in-breath into your body. Take with it any tension, worries, or concerns while creating more internal room. Find a natural rhythm to your breathing and following your next breath, let it take you deeper into the space beyond your body temple, where past and future dissolve into the present. Your inner awareness becomes the threshold you move across, where now your exhale propels you further into the openness of the void. Allow yourself to become available and receptive to a deep hearing and heightened awareness to move you to greater good.

Notice you are in a vast expanse with infinite points of light as if you are in a galaxy of stars . . . Allow your awareness to be drawn to a beautiful blue orb that is calling you home . . . feel an attraction and relational remembrance to the vibrancy of this world. You move in closer and when you do, you see the pristine snowcapped mountains, the wooded forests, the lush green jungles, the expansive deserts, deep canyons, still lakes, running rivers, and the all-embracing blue ocean . . . Your soul is deeply moved by the physical beauty. As your awareness of the magnificence of this place is heightened, you feel the call of this earth for the gift you have to bring. You return to your perfect mountaintop . . .

Scanning the surrounding beauty, hearing the enchanting songs, you find yourself resting upon and feeling the support of mother earth. Connecting your roots deep into the heart of the planet, you are grateful for the support and nurturing of the bountiful good . . . sensing the breeze, you feel a pull to a canyon in the distance. You lucidly head down one of your many forested paths to a greater connection with the mother earth . . . all the while noticing a nurturing, supporting and embracing feeling as you bond with Gaia . . . What else do you notice on your way to the canyon? . . . As you come out of the trees onto the valley floor you see the rim of the canyon in the distance and you feel a pull to its edge . . . What agenda does your loud-mouth mind have for calling you to peer over the edge? . . . Do you feel a temptation to jump? . . . What temptations in your life are calling you to compromise your spirit in spite of inner guidance to the contrary? . . . Could your journey be about overcoming duality with inner conflicts and doubts? What are your doubts and conflicts? . . . Where are your internal power struggles? NOW LEAP FROM THE EDGE.

You are on the dark canyon floor with towering walls blocking any of the sunlight where reptiles and insects are scurrying in the shadows just outside your periphery.

Where are you being less than honest with who you are to others? What hidden life have you been living? . . . What don't you want people to know about you? . . . Be honest, do you have defensive traits that can be difficult for people to be around? What are they? . . . Could it be, rather than being rejected if you were truly seen, you drive caring individuals away with these behaviors? What makes you difficult to be around? What is it that won't let you be seen that must control the perception of others? . . . What tormenting grief and pain reside within you? Can you see beyond your ego's agonies to the pure tranquil unviolated true self that is observing this whole journey into darkness? . . . How can it get any worse, you ask?

In the darkness, you're barely able to make out the opening of a cave, but you are drawn to venture into the dark silence of the womb. It's mysterious, but in the absence of light there is infinite potential, your senses are heightened as you are overwhelmed by a feeling of being all alone. What does it feel like to wander in the darkness alone with fear creeping in? . . . Where else in your life does it seem like your fears are creeping in? . . . What does despair and doubt feel like? . . . Remember, this dark night can be the forerunner to your transformation. What do you fear most happening in your life? . . . Where do you fear being a failure? . . . Could failure be a profound insight to realign your path? Listen to your doubts and fears and the painful chatter of the whimpering ego and learn what lessons this moment has to reveal . . . Freed to see beyond the ego's agony of grief, you see a hint of a light further in the cave, you debate whether you should explore or turn back . . . but your temptation overwhelms you and you move closer to discover it's a ring of fire shining bright from within the depths of darkness. You are drawn to this light, you feel its warmth, you dance with this discovery as you partner with the remembrance of joy, and you recognize an urge similar to the one that told you to jump over the edge into the darkness. But this time it says to... NOW LEAP INTO THE FLAME.

Become consumed in the glory of oneness with the fire of Life, and recognize there is an absorption that purifies and unifies. As you burn away the personal torment and torture and learn to love again, you are illumination Itself lucidly opening to the light in every moment . . . You embrace the gifts that make you magnificent, wonderful, powerful, omnipresent . . . These realizations cannot be contained because they are forever expanding through your bursting heart. Ecstasy is known . . .

From this total immersion in this womb-like nucleus your awareness awakens as you gaze out again upon your sacred circle on your mountaintop with a renewed conviction to live your purpose. You take a few moments to allow this exploration into your psyche and soul to settle into your conscious mind . . . Comfortable in your skin, being who you are, doing what you love and moving in unity with your spirit's mission creates a formula for joyous success. Dazzled by a new found lightness and freeing commitment to be used by the flow of Life and having had the walls around your heart shattered, you're now ready to experience a truer expression of yourself.

You return to your world of activity refreshed and renewed. Know once you've been somewhere you can easily return to that somewhere by simply calling it back to your awareness. There is always more work to be done, but for now, pull yourself back into your body permitting gratitude for your discoveries to fill your field of awareness.

Feel a joy knowing you'll be consistently returning to your sacred space, but for now, choose a path down the mountain. Familiarize yourself with this trail back into the world of form. Know there is always this corridor, this passage back to the elevated perspective of your world. Touch some of the trees as you pass by them and feel the earth move beneath your feet. As what you saw in a distance comes more into focus, return your attention to your breath. Breathe . . . When you are ready, slowly move your fingers and toes, stretch, gently open your eyes and sit for a moment to re-acclimate to your physical world. Grab your pen and take some time to write about your experience. It doesn't matter if it was memorable and you are certain you'll never forget it, you should still capture it on paper – later, you'll be glad you did.

Soulful Adventures

- What kind of thoughts race through your mind when you are abruptly awakened with concern at 2:00 A.M.? Is there a similar pattern over the years?
- What do you really need to address but are trying to fool yourself into believing you don't have to? What excuses are you telling yourself that keep you locked in those behaviors?
- What is keeping you from expressing yourself in a greater and more liberated way? What's got you imprisoned?
- What do your walls of defense look like? What stories do you tell others that keep you from being truly known? What is it you're ashamed of that you don't want exposed?
- Where is there a fence you'd like to see humanity stampede through? Where would you like to see social change take place?
- Stop and become aware of what electronics are tracking you?

- What are your beliefs about the sequential unfolding of time and circumstances? Is there space in your thinking to expand on those ideas of time? What are your thoughts about being able to take a quantum leap without a direct progression from point A to point G?
- What scene is your internal dialogue creating for you to walk in? How would you like to change what's playing on the screen in front of you?
- What are your fears, where did they come from, and how do they control you?
- Wherever you are is your entry point into the Stream of Life. Observing your life from your mountaintop, how would you describe where you are? Can you see how it's an entry point into the Stream of Life?
- Consciously take a hot shower to symbolically wash away any of the psychic crud you might have lingering after you've journeyed through this chapter.

Body and Soul Practice for Connecting

Body connection for Opening Your Root Center

To open the root energy at the base of your spine, try stomping your feet, do some squats, walk barefoot on the earth, march in place, or pound a drum.

Soul connection for Opening Your Root Center

Walking Meditation

Walking meditation can be just as profound as a sitting meditation and can bring the insightful awareness into your activity. Walking becomes the focus, bringing a mindful awareness to the activity of walking which keeps the awareness involved with the experience of walking.

Walking meditation is a simple way to practice mindfulness and can be used anywhere but the traditional walking meditation finds a pathway and simply walks back and forth. Keep your eyes cast down without looking at anything in particular. The purpose of not wandering about is so that part of your mind that usually negotiates your walk can rest. The art of the walking meditation is to develop a natural rhythm and a wakeful presence. Find a place where you can walk comfortably back and forth, indoors or out. Before starting to walk, spend a little time standing still while allowing your awareness to be with your body...Close your eyes and center yourself. Take some deep breaths, inhaling deeply then exhale . . . Put your full attention on the sensation of breathing . . . Then allow the breath to return to normal and notice it finding its own natural rhythm after a little while . . . Now bring your awareness to your body . . . noticing how your body feels as you are standing . . . become aware of all the sensations going on in your body. Notice how the body feels in great detail as you walk as the entire body is involved in the act of walking. You'll want to start with your awareness of your feet connecting to the earth, let your hands rest where they may. As you take your first step feel each muscle engage . . . Notice the points where your feet touch the earth and the natural sensations of movement as your arms swing in their perfect rhythm.

Walk with an ease and grace. As you walk back and forth, find a pace that gives you a sense of ease . . . After you've found a pace of ease, let your attention settle into the body . . . Let your body take your awareness for a walk. If the mind starts getting caught up in thoughts, easily bring your attention back to the experience of walking . . .

Once you feel connected to the body, let your attention settle into your legs and feet and the sensations of the tensions and release of each step . . . Instead of alternating breath, try bringing your focus to alternating stepping. Whenever you notice that the mind has wandered, bring it back to the sensations of the feet walking. Getting a sense of the rhythm of the steps may help maintain a continuity of awareness.

Witness the lifting of your foot and leg off of the earth and be aware as it comes down and touches the earth again . . . Be fully present with each step and all that it takes to move your body through time and space comfortably. Notice every muscle's movement . . . Practice moving mindfully slow, then pick up the pace . . . find your perfect pace, but whatever pace you move, remain mindful . . .

As with any meditation your mind will want to wander, bring it back to present moment with your mindful awareness of your walking . . . When caught wandering, honor the distraction by gently saying to yourself, "noticing or be here or come back" so you're present for your next step.

Noticing is a Vipassana (insight) approach to meditation. As you slow down and note the rising and passing of each moment in its fullness. Every moment brings new awareness. A little bit of time brings a flood of moments. This walking meditation will help you become calmer in your body, so you don't lose your connection in stores, crowds, standing in line or walking through life in general. You'll learn to walk for the pleasure of walking instead of solely for the purpose of getting somewhere.

Mystical writing

'The Voice Celestial'

It is expedient I do not stay
Lest you should turn from your own self away
And think causation rises from without
And not within. Such concept put to rout!
When *first* the soul becomes of *self* aware
He thinks *another* self, *another* mind is there -
He has no scale, no laws, no abacus
By which to measure out the rapturous;
But when a voice is heard, believes some Power
Above himself, beyond the present hour,
has come to visit him, some *being* from afar,
Some astral form, some spirit from a star;
So thou, whose vision glimpsed eternal; Me,
Ascribed the inner voice to outer deity.
If now that voice seems faint and far and dim,
It is because *thy self* embodies him.
Henceforth his voice encased within thy tone
Shall speak with force, but it shall be thine own.
Forevermore thy wide-eyed soul shall be
Awake, aware that thou thyself art Me.
                  Ernest Holmes/Fenwick Holmes
                           1887-1960/1883-1973

Chapter 3: Beyond the Senses

Man has no Body distinct from his Soul; for that
called Body is a portion of Soul discerned by the five
Senses, the chief inlets of Soul in this age.
~ William Blake

Making Sense of the Senses

The body is an amazing organism. It's a gift to be able to taste the sweetness of life, touch and feel physical pleasure, see the light of the world, hear the music that abounds, and smell fragrances that fill the air. Computers may be able to record these sensations but never will they have the soul to feel them. The nervous system has a specific sensory system or organ, dedicated to each sense. This system provides you with pleasure, pain and an inordinate amount of data to help you perceive the world around you. You lined up to get one of these bodies with all of these amazing abilities. Remember, it's your receiving system for this dimension - so taking care of it is of utmost importance.

Just beyond the physical sensory system is a subjective field called the psychic realm. This is the space that carries the impress of previous thoughts and remembrances of your actions. There are those who have clairaudience (clear hearing), clairvoyance (clear vision), clairsentience (clear feeling), clairalience (clear smelling), clairtangency (clear touching), clairgustance (clear tasting), and clairempathy (clear emotion). For these, this psychic realm is extra sensitive and serves as a conduit for these gifts.

There are also those who have telepathic gifts. Telepathy which is also referred to as thought transference is the natural communication link between the psychic and physical realms. If you have this gift, you're able to see the possible unfoldment of uninterrupted scenes and know true motives for people's actions. You can even connect with those in other realms. Exciting abilities for sure, and because they *are* so exciting this is often where people get stuck.

The psychic realm isn't the mystical realm at all and there's a chasm between the two. People dabble in this subjective field and get stuck going parallel while becoming addicted to their newfound abilities. The mystical realm is a vertical trip transcending through this realm accessing the All Knowing; merging with Life Itself. And while it sounds like, in words, it's a place to travel to, there's nowhere to go and nothing 'out there'. You are present in the All Present here and now.

Your Heart Knows Things Your Mind Can Not See

Poet Rainer Maria Rilke once wrote, "Go into yourself and see how deep the place is from which your life flows." If you hunt for awareness inside your head it's akin to watching a movie and looking inside the screen for the characters. To get beyond the five senses, you must move from thinking through the brain to perceiving through the heart. The authority of your soul doesn't require evidence. Your gift is an intuitive knowing. To that end, a Divine download is not necessarily a divine message rather, it's a message from the Divine. There is only One Mind that you are now intuiting. The Egyptians believed the heart was far more aware than the brain, and I tend to agree with them. The brain has to think and work things out while the heart knows intuitively. Intuitive awareness comes from levels beyond rational information. Put your hand on your heart when you need to make a decision or say something important and see how it feels. The head will defend its position since that's its job. But the heart, the extraordinary one and only beating heart, lets you know what's right and wins out with a higher, different perspective every time. That is, when the observer chooses to back it. When you decide through your heart, you don't see reality as it is, but as you are. What's real is not outside of you, it's inside of you.

Too many people are moving through their lives unaware they have the option to be aware. It's like dreaming and not being aware you are dreaming. When you're aware you're dreaming, you become the director of your dreams. Being lucid in your dreams allows you to be present in the environments as well as noticing yourself as a character in the movie you're observing. You're able to tap into the awareness of what the character is hearing and seeing but you're also observing what they're hearing and seeing. In a lucid dream, you aren't controlled by the events you're observing. You can even change the scene's location and those with whom you are interacting with. You are detached enough from the events that you're beyond their controlling of your senses. When you're able to move the awareness from the dominant energy demanding your attention in a dream, or life for that matter, you are able to lift yourself to see the whole picture from the beginning, to the middle and end. It's as if the whole story is already in the can. Your clarity allows you to perceive without fixating. It's brilliant!

People are so comfortable living within their thought patterns and beliefs they'd sooner spend their energy keeping that space familiar rather than expanding it. Go visit an unfamiliar neighborhood, a different country or take a walk in a dark forest and you'll notice a heightened awareness and the ability to take in so much more. This hyper vigilance will have you stretching and searching within what's beyond the edge of your basic five physical senses. Start a new job and notice how much more explorative your searching self becomes. Why get cornered in defending the beliefs that keep you in the comfort of your home of thoughts when the alternative is so much more rewarding? The more you defend your environment the more you'll have to defend. It takes faith to walk among the possibilities and vibrations of new dimensions because of the unfamiliarity of what's there. If you knew what was there, it wouldn't take faith. There could be perils and danger in the new realm, so believing in something greater than what you already know is necessary.

Your senses know in advance what they'll have to deal with and your greater self knows you've got everything you need to deal with whatever comes your way. The mystical expression isn't only for calm meditative times but also for times of peril and upheaval. As a spiritual leader you are called to be a revealer of a higher truth and greater reality than what's happening in the world with its neatly labeled descriptions. From the mountaintop, a level of reality beyond the human experience awaits you.

Your mystical connection mediates into actuality what's beyond your senses.

But those senses aren't pushovers and will be quick to jump in and present the first interpretation. Physical reality likes to recollect through the filters of shame, failure and disappointment, and in doing so will pull you off the mountaintop. Your reptilian brain will be quick to add more negative thoughts, pouring gasoline onto the fire, too. There's so much more to who you are than your five or six senses.

You'll manifest people who match your energetic expression and they'll be attracted into your experience. Watch the growth as your energetic seed plants itself in the sensual world. Fear moves you down the death spiral, while your senses accelerate your descent into its darkness. Alternatively, the seeds of vision from beyond the physical senses offer the expanded view from the mountaintop revealing more paths of opportunity and infinite perspectives.

Lift Your Gaze

Relax and let go of what you're defending or holding onto to free yourself from the downward suction and rise above it. Stop looking down and getting dragged into and emotionally involved with the gloomy forecast of the senses. If you hadn't noticed, this kind of vision doesn't dispel the gloomy predictions. This sensory-supported vision only augments and exacerbates the worldly challenged. Lift your gaze to the invitation of what's possible rather than adding your energy to what you no longer want in your life. If you feel guilt, release it. If you feel fear, release it. If you feel discouraged, disgraced, or angry, release it. You can defend it and keep it, or let it all go and rise above it all.

Let me give you a simple example that will illustrate the basic mechanics of how to do this. Imagine, for a moment, that an animal you love has been injured in an accident. As you look at your beloved animal lying on the grass, what do see? How do you feel? Now erase that image from your mind and imagine, for a moment, the same animal bounding across the grass towards your outstretched arms. What do you see? How do you feel? Notice a difference? How did you do that? You just switched the picture in your mind. You, as the observer, chose a different reality to embrace.

Evolution can stir the senses with pain as a way of helping you to let go of the familiar. People will do what they can to avoid pain in their physical world. Authentic evolution occurs when you're willing to push past the threshold of your pain. This pain can be physical or it can live in your emotional body. Either way, it's calling for your attention and you must be the one who notices and separates the awareness from the call of pain. Do you go to the dentist regularly despite your discomfort in the chair? There's something in you that is greater than your concern about pain. I know it operates inside of you, as it does in all of us. Have you ever stayed away from a relationship because you were afraid of getting hurt? Perhaps you haven't taken up a sport because of concern of injury? Have you not followed a dream for fear of loss of your reputation and everything you hold dear? You are the observer of the call. *Are you doing something to avoid pain rather than moving through it? Are you allowing the pain to run your life? Are you ready to give up the director's seat that easily?* This physical world evolves on the other side of chaotic upheaval; it would make sense that on the other side of your pain is the birth of something greater. The mountaintop view will give you an ethereal peek at the other side before you return to your existence in the human world of your five senses.

Just Passing Through

Are you getting locked inside the womb of your five senses refusing to enter the new world? When you guard yourself, what you're really doing is defending your edges. A paradigm shift would allow your awareness to lift you above the field of engagement. The engagement is with your five senses as they attempt to define everything through known descriptive vocabulary and a categorization of whether what you experience is good or bad. Stop defining and start knowing. This knowing I speak of doesn't come through the brain, it's a whole being experience. You are Infinite Awareness. It's a felt sense coming through your intuitive system and it's a definite vibration beyond the knowing of your biological computer system can pick up. A knowing doesn't need to explain itself. It isn't an either or scenario; it just observes from the mountaintop how all the pieces are part of the picture. It's akin to a quantum leap where something comes of nothing. A knowing may not arrive on the natural algorithm but is a momentary glimpse of an unseen picture that wasn't visible before. There's a bigger pattern for your life wanting to make itself known.

Have you ever just kicked back and watched the clouds move through the sky? Have you seen storms pass through, maybe even tornadoes, waterspouts or rainbows? Did you find yourself noticing how the sky in which all the change took place remains unchanged? Disturbance and beauty all move through the unchanging atmosphere. When you can remove yourself from the storms of your senses and observe the passing of experience, you don't need to cling to any of it.

You can allow the experience to be what *it* is in the moment and then leave that moment where it *is*. Your awareness is always there and it's unchanging and unaffected as you observe the experiences of this realm. Go back to your observation of what was passing through the sky; like your awareness, it's the sky that remains the unchanged constant. You are the observer who is beyond the five senses. More importantly, you are the observer of the thoughts that support what you're noticing. You can obsess and become fixated with one aspect of pain moving through your life (like thunder clouds passing through the sky) or you can accept that same experience as part of a larger transitory journey. Where you place the focus is entirely up to you, the observer. Don't let your five senses determine your experience.

How Culture is attempting to Control Your Extra Sense

Race consciousness and societal norms and their images as options are constantly passing through your individual subjective or sky of your awareness. Any of those you choose to focus on, rather than those you allow to drift by, slow down for you to make more real. The more attention and energy you give them the denser and more real they'll appear to your five senses. The mind's job is to help you feel secure in your skin. It'll talk up a storm to keep you clinging to that limited viewpoint as your true reality. With so much more undefined real estate to experience you can shift from your deeply encoded earth-bound consciousness into an awakening of the realm of Infinite Possibilities as You.

Within the mystical experience, time collapses and dissipates so you can sit down with an older version of yourself and have a conversation that you'll remember clearly when you arrive there. As you shift your shape into the next great version of yourself now, and look back upon this moment in time, can you sense your older-self telling you everything is going to be ok? You can visit that version of yourself any time and look back upon now with the knowing from then. What's fun is when you actually arrive at that point in time in this life you'll have a recall from then of now of that visit.

Rigid belief systems are everywhere, they're even held by those who feel they have been liberated by the truth. Science is the new religion of our times. People are enslaved to the scientific truth, just as they once were to the old religions or mythologies which were believed as absolute. What science proves today can morph into something else tomorrow. What was measured by the five senses was considered fact and provable, until now, when a lot of the focus is being put on energetic healing. Medicine is realizing, observing and measuring other influences with equipment recently created like frequency gauges and generators. Until those vibrational fields were believed to exist there wasn't any equipment invented to measure energy. When people don't believe or understand a different perspective, it will often be ridiculed. Yet often the only thing that will move life beyond boundaries is something that can only be seen from beyond the boundaries. It doesn't matter how many times the controlling influences repeat a lie, it doesn't make it true no matter how many people believe it. When the controlling influences of the traditional media outlets or political-speak don't welcome or invite our freedom of thought, we must step up our own initiative. Set yourself apart from the herd. Know that you are blessed to live in a time when there's an open and free exchange of conversation beyond the norm in the global brain of the internet.

As the fight for your mind heats up, watch out for instances of circuitous activity usurping your freedom. One example might be the microchip, Radio-frequency identification (RFID), now being placed just under the skin of animals so they can be found when they're lost. Imagine a similar microchip now being placed in your driver's license. Did you know that was in there? Did you know it can help locate you if the 'authorities' think you are lost? We just might start to see media encouraging the value of putting them in our children so they can never be lost; or in the bodies of criminals so they can be tracked. Or, we might begin hearing stories about lost hikers or Alzheimer patients being located through their valuable use. Be wary of giving away more of your independence and freedom despite hearing stories about how the technology has saved lives. You'll be seeing more individuals who are willing to give up their freedom because of the fear imposed on them if they don't. The delivery of microchip technology might seem circuitous in commonly embraced products such as cell phones, computers in our automobiles, or even vaccines. Who knows, maybe chips will be implanted at birth in our futures just like a social security number is assigned now. Maybe credit cards and cash will disappear because recognition of your chip could easily replace currency. Perhaps, someday we'll not only see information transferring from chip to computer, but also from computer to chip. With this kind of transference evolving, you must be cautious of who turns the power switch on and off.

Most people repeat what they call their opinion when it's really nothing more than what someone else has implanted. Control of the mind enables somebody else to think what you want them to think and believe it's their thought. Can you wrap your mind around that? If you can't get the brains of the many to see the world as you wish, you've got no chance to direct the masses into a singularity of consciousness. The greatest fear of the manipulators and the controlling elite arises as the mass collective unites from the grassroots. Teaching children a common concept to think, rather than how to think, eliminates their ability to think outside the box. As the bridge between the two hemispheres of the brain closes down, the left side of the brain gets stuck in the analytical five senses, forgetting how to transfer creative expression into form. It's imperative to go beyond the five senses to create something fresh and resilient. Where there once was nothing, something will rise through your alignment with the mystical. As you go to the mountaintop and rise above the earthly senses you'll find yourself crossing through the fog bank at the base of the mountain. As you rise above this haze left behind is your mind's inner dialogue espousing that your self-expression has no value, you're unworthy and no one is interested in what you have to create. Your imagination is liberated as you climb further and the channel through which it flows supports its abundance. This is what it feels like to open the creative energy center.

With all the monies that are appropriated to the area of public education, why are music and the arts going radically unfunded? Aren't our children's abilities to be free and creative thinkers at least as important as their ability to memorize and parrot back the curriculum creators' core concepts? Isn't learning how to stay receptive to what's beyond the five senses the most important tool for the advancement of the individual and humankind? Beyond the border is the Infinite. Do we no longer want to know what our ancestors knew about accessing their multidimensional selves?

You're bombarded everywhere by programming attempting to shift you from the creative thinker you were created to be to a shepherd of the herd mentality. Prearranged sound bites are slipped to the masses like pills for control of consciousness. Words can direct and redirect the body's pre-programmed system and prefabricated collective opinions are repeated until they're spoken from the mass consciousness as a forgone truth. Any questioner is framed as unpatriotic and then publicly ostracized compromising all of their credibility. The human psyche is the ultimate prize. Whether it's repeating a history that isn't true, believing a current story that's been spun into a truth that isn't, or ingesting chemicals that are doing more harm than good to your body, if the persuader's perspectives are coming out of your mouth, they've won that round. This is why you must continue to bring your awareness as the observer to all things. *Are you noticing what's happening in the world around you?*

You are a perceiver; a receiver of the Infinite. You are necessary for the unformed to take form. Your five sense programming started in the womb. Indeed, you heard me right. Your natural coding began with the biological makeup of your body and nutrient input during the time of your gestation. Along with the programming, you couldn't help but hear and feel what happened around you as you were forming during gestation. The knowledge that seeps into your subjective realm is seldom consciously questioned or even known to most. As a child you're told who to listen to, shown what to watch, who to talk to and what is or isn't acceptable behavior. Your education is sculpted by societal standards so everyone will claim the same generic story. Other cultures' beliefs are wrong and our cultures' beliefs are right.

If you are curious what this predetermined programming does to you, consider TV as an analogy. Television is all about programming. Whether it be blatant advertising or subtle messaging in mass produced storylines, your subjective soaks it up, while the conscious mind recognizes and acknowledges only infinitesimal amounts. You've been desensitized to violence, shown one-sided stories, and exposed to parts of the world with someone else's goal of stereotyping your understanding of them.

It's been said perception is reality. Those who control the perceptual output tend to be the ones who direct the collective consciousness and its behavior toward fear or peace, whether it be in a world without borders or one where patriotism rules. *Were you taught if you aren't for us, you're against us?* But who is "us"? Is it not our brothers and sisters around the one planet we all share? When you didn't agree with authorities' actions, were you labeled unpatriotic? What's more beautiful than the mystical connection with all of life? Is being part of a collective more rewarding than being connected? If you've traveled the world and visited other cultures you'll know, we all love, we all care for our children's future and we all have dreams we'd like to see come true.

One of the big challenges to realizing ones dreams is the weakness to the body's cravings. If you're imprisoned by a body that's demanding its fix, you're possessed and have lost control of the vehicle. Your awareness goes to placating the craving and your mind is no longer free to explore what your heart pines for. Addiction is addiction no matter what you tell yourself it is. Whether it's an adult beverage every night to wind down and relax, or a medical expert's daily prescription you can't go a day without, you have cause to check in. Do your hand over your heart practice and as witness, observe the discussion between your reasoning and your heart's desire. From this higher perspective what you hear from your heart will be vastly different than anything your brain conjures.

Your body is actually made up of the elements of this world, and its root desires are just fine in moderation. It's when those root desires become your boss and you pay the price with your life that you'll find a higher intervention is necessary. The mystical is able to touch all of Life and those with addictions get trapped into one aspect rather than seeing the greater picture. It's a lot easier to control the numbed, lethargic fog-brained person whose body isn't quite treating them right than those dialed into a higher vision with new possibilities. The latter aren't available to listen to the nonsensical programming of this world because they're busy speaking out against it. They're in love with Life, on purpose. They're on fire and merging with what turns them on in a healthy way. Your channeled sexual energy is one of the most powerful, creative forces; and even though it's expressed through form, it's one that can take you beyond your five senses. When this Life Force moves through you, all things are possible.

When Love Moves Through Your Body

When you open your mind and heart to the Infinite that is

you, the Divine programming drifts through your field of awareness just like clouds drift through the sky. The divine operates not in a static mode but in an ever-evolving and innately personal knowing beyond language. Language is inadequate for describing something beyond the five senses. For example, there's a big difference between experiencing love and describing love. A closed mind doesn't know what it's missing and will defend its thoughts and fears to keep control. Language is limited by the cultural definitions that are inherent in the stories it weaves. But if present form yields to the formless allowing the boundless expression of Spirit to take on a fresh appearance, language dissolves leaving only the experience of love.

Making love is one of those magical experiences when your soul manifests through your body. Time disappears and the boundaries of separateness dissolve. Infusing spirituality into your sexuality makes for an out-of-this-world interlude. Connecting with your beloved is the best aphrodisiac, dissolving all concern around performance. The mutual vulnerability of opening your heart and soul for another to see into the depths of your being is transformative. Making love doesn't require you to be young, beautiful or athletic; it's an opportunity for souls to merge into one body. Taking time to connect, listen, and share feelings before touching allows spirit to come into your body. Your body's ability to feel pleasure is one of the greatest gifts of having a body.

Be mindfully present for each moment and watch as your spirit opens to deeper love. With beautiful emotions flowing, you'll become more receptive, more forgiving, and find understanding on a new level. Allow your partner into the small, hidden places inside of your soul and body with each powerful and tender touch. In a unified surrender of passionate love you'll courageously soar beyond the bounds of the body, reaching peaks beyond your five senses that are so real and so wonderful you'll never want to return. But despite the ecstasy of being lifted through this love into Life Itself, come back you must, in celebration and exhaustion.

Your experience is beyond compare and words, much like the universal truths of the mystical. Do you always need to be so spiritual around making love? No, but the days of unfulfilling lovemaking will long be forgotten when you do.

Meditation

When leaving the body behind, it's always a good idea to know how blessed you are in this field of grace in which you play. Before meditation, take a moment to state:

I know all is well and wherever I go in my expanding awareness, all is good and I am safe. I'm surrounded by and live in an Omni Dimensional Life Force that can never be violated, because there is nothing opposed to it. I move on the very currents of Life Itself and I'm free to notice all things without attachment to anything. Free to move beyond any image at any time and courageous enough to remain in it. I open to a graceful guidance on my soul's adventure, surrender my demands to logical understandings, and I welcome new and unknown states of consciousness for my soul's evolution.

Take a few breaths to bring your attention back to the center of your body. Find a natural rhythm for your breath to fall into. See if you can follow your in-breath into your body . . . Exhale. Take with it any tension, worries, or concerns while creating more internal room. Find a natural rhythm to your breathing and following your next breath, let it take you deeper into the space beyond your body temple, where past and future dissolve into the present. Your inner awareness becomes the threshold you move across, where now your exhale *propels* you further into the openness of the void. Allow yourself to become available and receptive to a deep hearing and heightened awareness to move you to greater good.

Notice you are in a vast expanse with infinite points of light as if you are in a galaxy of stars . . . Allow your awareness to be drawn to a beautiful blue orb that is calling you home . . .

feel an attraction and relational remembrance to the vibrancy of this world. You move in closer and when you do, you see the pristine snowcapped mountains, the wooded forests, the lush green jungles, the expansive deserts, deep canyons, still lakes, running rivers, and the all-embracing blue ocean. . . Your soul is deeply moved by the physical beauty. As your awareness of the magnificence of this place is heightened, you feel the call of this earth for the gift you have to bring. You return to your perfect mountaintop . . .

As you look out to the south, the sun warms your face and from your elevated mountaintop view your awareness is drawn to the beauty of the expansive valley floor with its rippling golden grains, ribbons of green where the river runs through, lakes reflecting the sky, clusters of trees and various animals roaming through your view . . .

Find yourself lucidly wandering along an earthen path on the valley floor reflecting on when you first awakened to the possibility of a realm beyond the physical senses, an awareness beyond what the world of form is telling you exists . . . The first duty of love is to listen, listen to what your body has been telling you, what it has been feeling, notice yourself noticing and realize you are not the body – you are the listener . . . You witness your body's experiences floating through the mind. Allow those sensations to move on out from your screen . . .

Remember some of your early soul lessons . . . What physically keeps calling for your attention? Consider the earthly teachers who inspired you to awaken to the options of the heart. How have these shifts in your consciousness played out over the years? What life lessons have your trials, tribulations and unexpected circumstances brought you? . . . How have these lessons served you and how will they serve you as your life journeys forward? . . . Where have you noticed societal programming being presented to you for your consideration? . . . Observe where you feel your thoughts are under the influence of outside directives . . . What does being connected to the Flow of Life really mean to you and how do you see it playing out for you? . . .

Are there any battles you are fighting in your world, in your body, or in relationships that you'd prefer to avoid or deny? Bring them into your field of awareness with kindness and compassion without judgment or combative energy and just allow them to sit with a gentle benevolence eventually passing like clouds in the sky . . . Feel the warmth of love fill you, be filled with appreciation for where you are in your life and the path you've taken to get here. There is no need to make anyone or anything wrong for any part of your journey to this moment. Be with a sense of honoring of your choices and all those who have crossed your path . . . See your future-self looking back on this moment in time and sense what the older, wiser self is telling you . . . What lies before you is, the natural unfoldment from your calling of the new dimension of awareness and your present practices.

You return to your world of activity refreshed and renewed. Know once you've been somewhere you can easily return to that somewhere by simply calling it back to your awareness. There is always more work to be done, but for now, pull yourself back into your body permitting gratitude for your discoveries to fill your field of awareness. Feel a joy knowing you'll be consistently returning to your sacred space, but for now, choose a path down the mountain . . . Familiarize yourself with this trail back into the world of form. Know there is always this corridor, this passage back to the elevated perspective of your world. Touch some of the trees as you pass by them and feel the earth move beneath your feet. As what you saw in a distance comes more into focus, return your attention to your breath. Breathe . . . When you are ready, slowly move your fingers and toes, stretch, gently open your eyes and sit for a moment to re-acclimate to your physical world. Grab your pen and take some time to write about your experience. It doesn't matter if it was memorable and you are certain you'll never forget it, you should still capture it on paper – later, you'll be glad you did.

Soulful Adventures

- If you knew the beginning, middle and end were already in the can and it all turned out well, how would you relax more?
- What scenes in your life would you like to detach from so you could easily move to another location?
- What are some of the addictions that take over your thinking? What are some of the conversations coming from the healthier part of your mind saying before you muzzle them with logic in support of your ongoing addictive behavior?
- When has the root essence of your being united with a force from beyond your five senses propelling you into action? What did this new found strength feel like? What did you do with it? What did you accomplish and where did it take you?
- What are you passionate about now? How have you seen powers you didn't know you had just show up, seemingly out of nowhere? What's getting in the way of following your passion and unleashing these powers now?
- Where could you use a bit more faith? Go take a walk alone, contemplate a sacred or inspiring image, read a soul-stirring piece of poetry, listen to some music and just be with it. Watch your faith rise.
- Do you remember when lovemaking was so incredible, there were no words to describe it? Close your eyes, sit there and be with that memory as you transcend time and space. Remember it in this moment and savor the feeling that arises in you.

Body and Soul Practice for Connecting

Body Connection to Open Your Sacral Center

Here's a great practice for opening up your Sacral Center.

Pull out your old Hula Hoop and start moving those hips. This energy center is located right below the belly button. It's the location of personal power, creativity, vitality, sexuality and is known as the seat of emotions. When you're in balance, you're more comfortable expressing rather than suppressing.

Soul Connection to Open Your Sacral Center

Mindful eating meditation for the soul

Before eating, mindfully sit down and practice a few slow deep breaths to get more centered in your body and to be entirely comfortable with yourself. If others are at your table, look them in the eyes, smile and allow your spirits to connect. It's good to appreciate the others you share your world with. Take a few moments to be grateful for the food you're about to partake and allow your awareness to catch a sense of what it took to create this opportunity - from the seed, earth, rain, sun, farmers, harvesters and all the people involved in your food's travel to get it from the field to the grocer. This food is a gift of the earth, the sky. Yes, some people can see the whole cosmos in the food sitting on their plate. Establish yourself in the present moment, so as to consciously eat in joy, love and appreciation. Take your time as you eat, giving your full attention to the awakening senses from taste, texture while chewing each mouthful completely. When you chew be aware of what's in your mouth. Don't chew and digest your troubles, worries or fears. Just pay attention to your food. When you eat in silence, the food becomes even more real with your mindfulness and you can become fully aware of its nourishment. Upon finishing your meal, take a few moments to notice you've finished. Embrace the feeling that your hunger is satisfied and your plate is now empty. Be filled with thanksgiving in realizing how blessed you are for this nourishing gift.

Mystical writing:

While I stood there I saw more than I can tell
and understood more than I saw,
for I was seeing in a sacred manner
the shapes of all things in the spirit
and the shape of all shapes
as they must all live together as one being.

Black Elk
1863-1950

Chapter 4: Changing Frequencies

The intuitive mind is a sacred gift, and the rational mind is a faithful servant. We have created a world that honors the servant, but has forgotten the gift.
~ Albert Einstein

Energy beyond your body

The journey into the world of form is merely a series of instantaneous shifts in perspective. Have you ever been embarrassed? Spooked? Startled? Enraged? Turned on? Have you ever listened to an inspiring speaker that moved you into a new dimensional awareness, heard bad news that brought you to your knees, or had an out of body or mystical experience that changed your life as you knew it, forever? Perhaps you lived through the death of a loved one, the loss of a relationship or a child and realized in an instant your entire life was different. The adrenaline rush of that instantaneous shift into a new channel has the power of Niagara Falls. Adrenaline can be addictive to the degree that base jumping becomes the norm. Dare I suggest you base jump from your mystical mountaintop?

Adrenaline, albeit a big one, is just one channel in the physical world. Don't be naive enough to believe that like the adrenaline channel, the rest of the channels in the physical world are the only ones that matter. Multitudes of unseen frequencies in the astral world exist right alongside it. You might delude yourself into believing you're alone and untouched by these frequencies where you're sitting quietly reading this book. But, there are Electromagnetic Frequencies (EMF's) impacting you and me right now. They are everywhere at all times. Among them, multiple radio and television stations, cell towers and the like are broadcasting through the airwaves. Despite, of course not being able to see them, there are so many frequency vibrations at this very point in time around you, it's actually sort of crowded where you sit. If you're keenly aware of your greater and higher senses, it's highly credible that you'll be able to tune into these various unseen frequencies. Just as some can read the subjective field, or what some call the Akashic records, there's much beyond the typically entrained human view. The fact of the matter is, what gets played on the frequency of your awareness tends to dominate the conversation and direction of your activities, rather than changing the dial to tune into the Infinite Awareness.

Nikola Tesla wrote, "If you want to understand the secrets of the universe, think in terms of energy, frequency and vibration." When your awareness is in sync with the human body you become an amazing receiving station and able to pick up subtleties your brain never suspected were even present. Through this sensor, you have the ability to tell whether you've entered into a good or bad situation before it even materializes. Your talent as an emotional weather meteorologist is actually more accurate than your local forecaster. When you pay attention, you'll often know if it's a good deal you're about to enter into or if it will go sour before you even utter a word. You just feel it. *But, the more important question to ask yourself is, do you listen?* Let's say you meet someone serendipitously and find they hold the missing piece to your business plan. Do you still consider it serendipitous? Or was it your internal tracking system that delivered this so-called chance meeting?

Your body is affected by certain frequencies. Have you ever just innocently walked by someone and found the hair on the back of your neck standing at attention because there was something so wrong? Perhaps you've even seen a medical intuitive who, just by being in your presence, could read your energetic aura and see potential or existing illness in your body. Some can smell chemo or feel anxiety when it enters the room. Or, have you ever just known you had to talk to someone you saw from across the room because they exuded a sense of Life you were attracted to? Be it illness, separation, betrayal, loss, pain, death or war, all carry a frequency that effect your perception and action. The same, of course, goes for the lighter, more welcome frequencies of love, joy, fun, and fulfillment. They dial you into different, more positive energetic options. Your vibration is always searching the dial for something to match your mood and validate your environment. You always have the choice to align with an energetic vibration that soothes your soul or sends you into action.

Your intuitive and reasoning selves are at constant odds, working to catch your attention as you're exploring what possibilities to tune into. As an example, think back to a time when you thought you'd met your perfect mate and your mind went a million miles a minute. Oh, that's the person for me. That's my soul mate for sure, your reasoning-self pronounced before you even had the opportunity to flex your intuitive muscles. Then, your dream date opened their mouth proving your gut instinct right again. Your rational mind was lost in the fantasy of a lifetime of memories while your heart screamed, are you nuts? It's a perfect demonstration of how your heart knows so much more than your mind sees.

If you remember to allow your observing self some space to notice your choices, you'll be free to take in more than just the physical facts. Alternatively, if you muzzle your intuitive side you'll have welcomed parasite-like energy suckers to feed on your anxious, low vibrational energy. Sadly energy suckers often look like friends or coworkers, sometimes even soulmates, but after you've been with them for a little while you feel like they've sucked the life out of you. Truth is, it's because they have. If you don't want to slip, don't hang out in slippery places. In other words, when you're trying to shake an addiction, the last thing you want to do is play in the field where your addictive habits are awakened.

If you're constantly attuned to just surviving, paying bills, defending religious myths, arguing for littleness, watching reality shows (other than your life) or the sensationalist gossip of others people's lives, you're missing the greater opportunities of your life. It's important to recognize the low vibration energy of mass consciousness is not reality, or at the very least it doesn't have to be *your* reality. These planted beliefs can be addictive. To move beyond the societal thoughts being spoon-fed to the masses, you have to change the frequency but, breaking the addictive habit of falling back on low vibrational frequencies in order to rise above the lowest common denominator isn't easy. In fact, it's quite difficult because people are trained to embrace a fascination to the lower lurking physical energies that make up the tabloid consciousness.

How can I change my energetic vibration?

So how do you rise above it? Start shifting your energetic vibration by cutting down your brain-numbing screen time. Take your awareness back to Life's Originating Source. With so many of our lives revolving around technology, this might ultimately be the biggest challenge in this book. Remember, your genetic codes are vibrational and the propensity of their energy fields can be changed by transforming your mind. That transformation is accomplished in your shift of awareness. See the domino effect there? If the observing self isn't allowed to have its new perspective, your genetic codes will continue to hold the shape of the container they've been placed in. *What kind of transforming thoughts are you creating in your life?* Shift the container, shift the shape of your life.

Be careful not to get drawn into other people's competitiveness when they throw down their challenge. As hard as it is to shift your awareness, it's easy to get caught in spiritual competition. Pronouncements like, 'my prayers are stronger than yours' or 'my meditation is deeper than yours' have no place in your spiritual and vibrational evolution. There's just no space for pre-school antics that sound like, 'I healed a back', 'I dissolved a tumor' or 'my energy is hotter than yours'. What's with all the competition? What is there to fear from others' success when we're all in this together? Encouragement and praise will lift you up and take you much farther than competition will. Competition will only serve to pull you down.

Observations from the Canyon

Fear, like competition, is a low-density frequency that pulls you into descent. Energy vampires and parasites looking to suck the life out their host, operate in this low level frequency. As you bring your awareness to many different frequency options you'll find others who are also looking for someone to play with on your higher wavelength. They're there because they relate to the vibration. Birds of a feather flock together, or is it, reptiles of the scale scurry together? While you're welcoming a higher frequency from the realm of Infinite possibilities your vibrations change. In fact, there is a huge vibrational shift that starts at the cellular level and works all the way out to the auric level. The part of our animal world that hasn't been 'educated' out of their sensitivities, feels everything from fear to calm. Many children on the autistic spectrum are ultra-sensitive to energy fields outside of themselves because their minds haven't been indoctrinated into the cultural think. They haven't fully aligned with the framework of our manipulative world and are blessed to catch a bit of what's on the other side of the veil.

The higher the frequency you come from, the more support you transmit to others with a sympathetic vibration. You don't eliminate the other stations as you rise in frequency, they're just left behind because they aren't part of your reality anymore. Those who lurk in the denser realms will still have their place to bottom-feed while those who choose to soar in the light will find no ceiling to the Infinite.

There will always be a beyond-the-border-of-the-known to play in.

From the mountaintop, the higher perspective is always present and waiting to be discovered by you. From that vantage point, you'll know which earthly activities will bring you joy and fulfillment while you make a difference in the world. You'll no longer need to use your energies to fight or overpower anyone or anything. Just step right up to a new channel where the perspectives and options are different. It's exciting to know harmonious alternatives are here now.

False Flags

People are often too easily diverted into perceiving the irrelevant so, as a result, they don't recognize their options, or even that they have them. As you look at the meaningless, you miss the meaningful. As the collective observes the broadcasted distractions, like any good magic trick, or illusionist, much is done under the un-watchful eye. Don't allow yourself to digress to accepting the lower frequencies as the truth. While a little bit of distraction can be a good thing, acquiescence to an addiction such as entertainment, sports or pleasure is not a good thing. Alternatively, you can lift your vision above the confusion to see what's really going on.

As corporations become far more powerful than politicians, the research that counters anything supporting the corporate profit is silenced. The funding for that particular research often comes with an intended outcome, which means it has strings. What's best for the whole is not always the way those in a position of influence want you to see things. Major information delivery systems present information through filters and the corporate media outlets are the ones who own those filters. It's not unusual for the influential to distrust the populous and democratic process in their goal to keeping their highest interests intact. Their objective is to keep the masses entertained, not too inconvenienced, tired, in debt and unaware of the truth in reality for the ultimate outcome of keeping the herd from rising up against the position of the few.

We've all heard stories of idealistic youth, not yet set in their ways, who are willing to risk it all for a greater vision of equality. Their uprising is a paradox to the apathy of the masses. They resist any kind of authoritative directive and choose to tune into a higher vibration. That kind of idealistic, youthful energy still believes in the higher possibilities. *Where has your courageous youthful energy gone?*

Dis-ease, Your body and the Electromagnetic Field?

There seem to be a lot more energy-centered diseases these days; labels like stress syndromes, headaches, chronic fatigue, burnout, infertility, difficulty focusing, brain illnesses, you name it – either you or someone you know has been diagnosed with an illness resulting from an internalization of low vibrational energies. Homeopaths will tell you that all disease begins in the energetic realm. In the end, it's pretty simple. The choice lies only with you as to whether you will hold onto stress and be bitter or just let things roll off your back. Throwing medicine at the symptoms telling you there is a problem on a physical level will never address the source.

Some feel the pineal gland functions as a third eye or the access point to other-dimensional abilities. As this gland is physiologically damaged by the bombardment of many unseen energies and as a result of the repeated insult you become stuck in the most common earth frequency present. Microwaves operate on their frequency, cell towers on their radio waves, and power lines exude their crackling escaping energies, all of which scramble and impact the sensitivity of the human energy system and, in particular, the pineal gland. You are a sensitive antennae able to pick up electromagnetic frequencies whose pulses disrupt and alter your personal energetic field. These vibrations can and do mess with your biological function, at the cellular level, among others.

Your bio-electromagnetic frequency is as unique as your fingerprint. As electromagnetic pollution invades your body's field in multiple ways, it de-stabilizes your ability to connect with the Infinite. With foods no longer carrying the natural nutritional energies of the earth, the addictive additives are scrambling your natural frequencies through your digestive system. Everything from noise to light pollution assaults your body daily. The toxic air you breathe carries nanoparticles of pollutants into your cellular makeup. You aren't solid, you're boundless through consciousness. Yet, as one would imagine through the barrage of electromagnetic pollution, you're becoming more body-bound as the truth of who you are is forgotten.

As interference is thrown at the natural brain rhythm, you disconnect from the restorative life flow. Anything that requires itself to be plugged into an electrical outlet to work creates an electrical field of its own. Just as the currents around power lines can be measured, on a lesser scale, your everyday is impacted by the movement of electrical waves all around you. All of this electromagnetic pollution and activity in the atmosphere overwhelms your body's natural currents. It's a perfect storm.

In this time of rationalism, people who live by the process of reason have become reliant on their logical thinking. When you're only operating on lower dimensional frequencies, it's easy to forget there's a higher source of knowledge accessible from the mountaintop view. Even some of the most logical people can find themselves stuck on one station of perspective. It can be difficult to push past generally accepted positions or favorite stations.

The scrambled brain waves of today, make the fight for one's mind control of utmost importance. Blurred and blocked, a higher awareness has been relegated to the back of the line while your mistaken sense of self embraces your rather warped states of thought as who you really are. This confused embrace of the truth of who you are can cause emotional upheaval, as well as, physical challenges when accepting the way of the physical world as the highest reality. The accumulation of subconscious mental impressions along with physical evidence can influence you into believing this is the truth. With paradoxes at hand, not to mention the pull of earthly motion, your intellect is rendered useless in finding the mystical. Experiencing Life Itself is your spirit's assignment not your head's undertaking.

With change often being the outcome of an intuitive directive from a higher frequency, the rational mind (which by the way, deplores change) will tell you to stop listening to that channel! It will prompt you, instead, to turn your attention to a different area of your life. Next comes the clash between your lower self in the frequency from its known world which wants to keep you in familiar territory and your higher connected self who perceives options from the mountaintop. Your higher self is pulling you with guidance toward a greater expression you've not yet realized while your lower-self pushes you towards the lower vibrations you are already intimately familiar with. This conflict is waiting to happen through the controlling domain of your physical form. You're always being called to reclaim your life force. Interestingly, when you languish too long without honoring your higher calling you'll eventually exhaust your earthly strength. The death spiral which follows will leave you in a depleted place, often referred to as the dark night of the soul, which I spoke about in Chapter 2 on Fear.

Most make it out of their dark night, prolonged state of depression or isolation. The dark night of the soul is not meant to be medicated or treated, but journeyed, explored and understood as part of the soul's unfolding path.

Changing the Question Changes the Frequency

Changing the question, changes your frequency, and *will* change your life. You've lived for a long time dominated by questions, how much can I have? How can I be safe? Who loves me? Can you shift your questioning mind to matters of the soul instead? Asking questions of your soul invites the fire and intoxicates you with The Divine. Questions like: Who am I? For what purpose was I born? Or, what's the meaning of my life? Offer deeper soul-searching options so you can ditch the darkness.

Have you ever found yourself so engrossed in a movie you lost the feeling of who was watching it? Perhaps you were so caught up in it visually, aurally, and emotionally that it became a real experience. This is what life does. Life grabs you and synchronizes you with its frequency so your mind believes it's true. When you get drawn in, you lose sense of self. As the witness becomes the object of the experience, you simply disappear. To move up the frequency dial, you must reclaim your independence from the experience you are witnessing. It's your choice. You can focus on anything; why not allow yourself to focus on Infinite Awareness? As you move your awareness to the observer you move away from the grip of form and it's obstruction to the truth.

When you explore consciousness instead of form, you step beyond the boundaries of imposed limited perceptions. The Life Force is infinite. When you open the door to It, It fills all space without ever being depleted like the way the sun fills a morning sky. The mystic knows how to be a conduit for Its flow without exhausting personal self. As you dial down into the lower, denser frequencies you shut down, which blocks that inexhaustible flow. Healing happens when the Life Force flows, purging anything unlike Itself.

One of the big challenges to a natural state of life-flow is many people think they must protect themselves by closing down their heart centers. You might delude yourself into believing you are protecting yourself by building a fortress so you won't be hurt again. But, what you're really doing is cutting yourself off from the fresh arrival of good. In an awakened state, energy flows. Notice how your energy, positive or negative, excited or depleted affects people around you. When energy is flowing life opens like the petals of a flower. The heart serves as the transforming spot between the celestial realm and earth.

When your energy flows, your vibration is raised. The best you've ever felt is a result of this upliftment as the force moves through you with an unparalleled strength. It's a wonderful reminder of how good you can feel. When old negative patterns, jealousies, or unhealthy perspectives return and vie for your attention, let the energetic current of the truthful life force wash it away. Clinging and defending the heaviness anchors you in time. Open the drawbridge around your heart allowing the pain in and trust the Divine frequency to transform the situation at hand. Your world doesn't have to implode to see where you might still have some attachment to lower frequencies. The mystical quest to the mountaintop perspective lifts you out of the shadows.

Past experiences, which is really what you had been and aren't anymore, too often become the defining expression of who you are now. Are you struggling to keep your position rather than trusting the flow will bring you higher up the mountain forever expanding your view? What took place in your life was perfect exactly as it appeared in your lifeline and appropriately belongs in that spot of your evolution. But that moment's now past and you must make yourself available for the next moment's vibrational pull today. What was, doesn't need reinforcement. Let it go, stop rehashing it by telling the story over and over and allow the new to emerge as the unfolding petals of your life reveal your blossoming flower.

Suffering was once thought of as a way to salvation. There was a long-held belief that suffering kept you mindful of the Creator. People held to the understanding that constant pain was a reminder of Spirit. This old-school philosophy has been carried over into today's practices with the belief that suffering and punishment are somehow spiritual. People embody the unique notion they're no better than the worm of the dust rather than being entitled to soar. Don't get me wrong, there's nothing wrong with a worm, unless it makes you think you are low life. As a creator, you'd never want your creative expression to suffer, would you? Of course not! And if your answer is yes, I'd want no part of that creator and highly doubt you would. If you're holding on to old thoughts of unworthiness, you can give those up now because it's an outdated concept which doesn't serve your higher good. A sense of unworthiness will keep you dialed into the lower, denser end of life.

Tension only occurs when there's resistance. When fighting for your life you become exhausted and plunge to the depths of heaviness. If instead, you let yourself be moved with the current, you must commit yourself to not resisting it. If you give up the struggle, you'll be able to see where it's taking you because you'll no longer be blinded by the panic fighting energy. Activities might still be taking place around you, but you can remain centered while on your ride downstream. It's exhilarating to go white water rafting but if you fight the current, you'll end up caught in the eddies, on the rocks, and eventually flipped into the water without a paddle, not to mention, black-and-blue. Rather than clinging to fear you can come from a place of being unattached allowing observation from a harmonious place of balance. During the activity of your life, you can notice your choices unfolding without disturbance. At any time your observing self can switch to another channel's current.

Years of YouTube surfing, channel hopping and dial turning with an attitude of impulsivity has helped to prepare you to switch focus quickly. You're not clingy or stuck. By being open to receiving what comes next all of your yesterdays prepare you for all of your tomorrows. There's always the possibility that a challenge coming your way isn't necessarily your life's natural unfoldment but rather something you've called into your space through your frequency. What happens in your life is a reflection of the attention your subconscious paid to the sum total of your thinking. A scary aspect of the Orwellian philosophy is the idea that thought police are watching you through your TV screen. Little did Orwell realize back then we'd be voluntarily offering up the sum total of our thoughts and our location, not to mention actions through our web searches, emails, social media, cell phones, micro-chipped cars, cards and more that we don't even know yet. Do you realize how much is known about you and your activities within the privacy of your home through the monitoring by your smart meter?

Through the internet, it's getting easier and easier to determine what you think as you put your searching and expressing thoughts on the screen for the accumulators of data. How many people today carry their phones with them for fear of being out of constant communication? If you want an interesting insight into your subjective, go without a cell phone for a month and notice what conversations come up in your field of awareness relating back to why you can't go without a phone.

This exercise can be a gentle frequency changer. Often it takes big frequency changers to catch your attention. If you've ever jumped on a trampoline with a friend, you'd know that you bounce higher and with greater ease when you're in sync. But if your friend jumps at a different rhythm than you, your knees will buckle and you'll instantly and effortlessly collapse. This is what it's like when you're out of sync with life. You simply can't sustain your stance and instantly collapse when you're up against resistance. When you are one with the current, you'll be launched ever higher. The experiences of life will show up unannounced and bring you to your knees. So, Why? *Why must you land on your knees in order to get back into the rhythm of what is truly important?*

The view from your knees might appear like a loss of everything, a career shake up, a death, tragedy, major separation, betrayal, or a disease. Pain will push, but remember you can turn to a vision calling you to the mountaintop for a greater perspective. This is why spiritual practices are essential to the mystical path. Regular daily connection or communion with Source, through silence, contemplation, self-inquiry, observation, and listening will assist in keeping you aligned with the sacred bounce.

The sacred pearls of insight you find in the peaks of the new elevated moments gifted from the higher frequencies are not to be tossed around lightly to unwilling or uninitiated ears. These soul revelations are only esoteric images, inklings, and hunches pointing to something greater and can't be put into words. You'll get shot down by those who can't wrap their brains around there being more than the five senses. Why submit yourself to this kind of mockery? The new conversations coming from your expanded perspective are not for casual conversation at cocktail parties. Constricted fear-based individuals can't possibly comprehend what you've seen. They're moving and grooving to a different frequency and while they might see your lips moving they have no ability whatsoever to hear what you're saying.

Reclaiming certain soul qualities like patience, trust, faith and gratitude will also change frequencies for you. They'll bless and serve you as constant stabilizing forces since you won't always know what to expect next. The choices which demand the most soul will be the greatest conduits for grace to shift the frequency of your being.

And yes, in case you are wondering, it's possible for you to affirm your true spiritual nature before fully understanding it. Turn your dial from the cry of the commotion around you to the call of a higher frequency. Do this by calming the mind, tuning your breath with the rhythm of life, and stilling the impulsive triggers that activate your anxiety and adrenalin centers. Be the Divine Communion or the Mystical Union and await the sensation as your body stills. In this relaxed state, the door is unlocked, the blinds are opened, and the drawbridge is lowered.

Living from a higher vibration allows your entry into a new non-sensual picture of possibilities. This mountaintop view alters the perception of what you see which creates a domino effect changing the shape of the world you live in. There are as many options for the out-pictured experience as there are frequency waves right where you are standing. The vantage point you're watching from can't be described, but you can live and create from there. Don't just pine to be there. Imagine yourself already there. The lower vibrations don't have the capacity to understand the finer, higher ones. Just like lower math doesn't understand higher math and the heaviness of the needy can't comprehend the activity of the affluent, nor can the wealthy understand struggle over a grocery bill. There are many vibrational fields as an option for living and at any time you (the observer) can move from one frequency to the next. Just remember, you're so much more than the vibrational field you're in.

What Dimension Are *You* Coming From?

One dimensional reality is a line. Two dimensional objects are a flat surface, and it's the third dimension that most people operate in, with shape and form presenting itself in time and space. The fourth dimensional realm is where it gets interesting with ideas and imagination infinite in potential. It's in this dimensional field that your imaginal body gets to play. In the fourth dimension you can be at a particular awareness level at a particular time but you don't have to travel to get there. As you raise the quality of your awareness, you change the pattern of your experience. In the realm of the fourth, you can experience change without movement and you don't need to travel to get around because it's without space as we know it. The gauge of your experience changes in direct correlation to your changing intentions. It's as if you are shape-shifting.

Shape-shifting is the ability of a known form to physically

transform into another being or form. It can be an extraordinary experience and with time and practice, you can really perfect the art of shape-shifting. Not too long ago I had the most glorious afternoon attending a celebration of the environment. I had been asked to offer prayer to open up a sacred circle within which a Native American stepped, dressed from head to toe in bands of eagle feathers running the length of his arms.

It is a common belief in Native American folklore that the Eagle is a sacred and symbolic bird because it is able to fly so high in the sky thus it moves gracefully between heaven and earth. In fact, Eagles are often regarded as capable of carrying messages to the gods and so the Eagle Dance is a sacred and powerful ritual. With his authentic costume he proceeded to imitate the movements of the eagle turning, flapping and swaying while portraying its cycle of life from birth to death. While eagle dances like this differ from tribe to tribe, they all bring much of the same experience to the observer; an alignment with a human being who before our very eyes transforms into an eagle. I was captivated, even spellbound, as the dancer flew through the circle until there was no longer a difference between man and bird. I witnessed this human form turn into an eagle as his feathers shimmied with flight, his body pulsated with the eagle's energy, and then dancer and bird merged into one. Floating, catching the wind, gliding around and above the circle, everyone present watched his spirit lift off to become one with the eagle. Here's an exercise to introduce you to the unparalleled insights you can gain from that practice.

Shape-Shifting Exercise

When a transcultural story appears throughout time around the globe, it's worth listening to a little deeper discovering the piece of truth it carries to fuel its continued emergence from the shadows of myth. From the darkest jungles, hottest deserts, and busiest corporate urban civilizations come stories of shape-shifting galore. Since the beginning of recorded history shifting has been depicted as not only possible, but necessary for survival. In Neolithic cave drawings it gave rise to hunting techniques and in works such as the Epic of Gilgamesh and the Iliad, where it is called therianthropy, it was induced by the act of a deity. As we entered the Middle Ages it was said only a sorcerer or witch could take on an animal shape as is often illustrated in many classical modern day books, plays and films. Dynamic tales of indigenous cultures are rich with stories of the shaman's ability to physically transform into another appearance, change shape, slide into another form, or drop their present appearance altogether. If you're only seeing one frequency of a multidimensional reality, then you're missing so much!

Shape-shifters can tune perceivers to their dial of choice without others knowing they have tampered with the dial. Your viewing is limited within a spectrum that's infinite in perceptual choices. With an ability to consciously occupy a multitude of forms through the multidimensional levels of consciousness the shifting experience has the potential to guide you into new areas of awareness and altered realities expanding your understanding. Do you believe dual expressions of reality exist? Is it possible to have awareness in the first reality and simultaneously have your attention in the second? Could this explain how a departed loved one can communicate with you here and be active in another dimension? What if the gifted shape-shifter can teach the person who has only awareness of one frequency to see the second and hold that vibrational reality so that's what is experienced? Yes, metamorphosis can be yours.

So, for fun, use your creative imagination in guiding your imaginal body to take on other shapes and allow yourself to see through the filtering vibration of that particular consciousness. You can be a corporate giant looking out from the towering high-rise or a fearless panther walking the observational tree branches in the jungle. Either way, enter their form and draw on their spirit of courage to face difficulty and complexity. How does that body see, hear, taste, touch, feel, think, and remember? What are you taking in through those eyes? Embrace the positive traits and leave the undesirable ones behind. When you are complete (and don't stay too long), always leave with gratitude as you return to your present earth body.

Extending your awareness into the imaginal body of the mythic realm will deliver a never-before-imagined expanded esoteric experience. Just over the threshold of the subjective lies the ability to release yourself from present form and shift the perspective beyond the continuum that rules your earthly reality. Shape-shifting into different forms, whether they be current or historical, allows for a beyond-science experience as you observe the differences in perception through each shape you take on. In other words, you not only take on their shape but, through this practice you also know their knowingness. The most exciting part is you can take the new knowingness back into your world of present form. Indeed, as you hone this practice, you will begin to observe the world around you with the ability to filter it through the information you received while you shape-shifted.

Since you will be traveling from your own eyes and ears when you leave your body, I recommend recording this meditation before practicing. Read it once, determine where you will put pauses that will make sense for your process, and then proceed to record it in your own voice.

When leaving the body behind, it's always a good idea to know how blessed you are in this field of grace in which you play. Before meditation, take a moment to state:

I know all is well and wherever I go in my expanding awareness, all is good and I am safe. I'm surrounded by and live in an Omni-Dimensional Life Force that can never be violated, because there is nothing opposed to it. I move on the very currents of Life Itself and I'm free to notice all things without attachment to anything. Free to move beyond any image at any time and courageous enough to remain, I open to

a graceful guidance on my Spirit's adventure surrender my demands to logical understandings, and welcome new and unknown states of consciousness for my soul's evolution.

Take a few breaths to bring your attention back to the center of your body. Find a natural rhythm into which your breath will fall. See if you can follow your in-breath into your body. Exhale taking with that breath any tension, worries, or concerns while creating more internal room. Find a natural rhythm to your breathing and follow your next breath, letting it take you deeper into the space beyond your body temple, where past and future dissolve into the present. Your inner awareness becomes the threshold you move across, where now your exhale propels you further into the openness of the void. Allow yourself to become available and receptive to a deep hearing and heightened awareness to move you to greater good.

Notice the edges that separate you from the Infinite blurring. The 'you' that exists in the world of form is almost digitizing into smaller holographic versions of you. As your form becomes a transparency for the energy that vibrates as you, you find yourself recreating that energy in other forms and identities.

Think and choose an archetype or identity you'd like to try on for size. Whose eyes would you like to look through? Whose spirit would you like to blend with as you take on an enhanced creative process of shape-shifting your energetic vibration? In this imaginal realm of identity you choose; feel the body first. Look through the eyes of the new shape as you try on the perception the archetype, animal or person experiences. Look down at your hands or your paws. How are you dressed? Where are you? Do you have a tail? Are you in the water? Are you in the sky? What do you see? How do you feel? Look out at the world through your new eyes and the compassion, senses and knowingness of your chosen shape. Continue seeing for a while . . . and when you feel comfortable, release your first imaginal body. Take a deep breath, clear your slate of consciousness and when you are ready, choose another form to experience life through.

Now, try on a shape that is a complete departure from the last shape you chose. If you were a person last time, try an animal. If you were a ground mammal, try a reptile. If you were in present time, try historical time. The practice to observe the outside through the knowingness of other energetic beings invites much richness into your experience, both in the imaginal and the world of form. Make the sounds of your shape, speak in tongues, bark, swim through the wake of a strong tide, be at one with your new shape and feel into it. Move around a little, or a lot. Soar, crawl, jump, walk or run.

Now you are ready to release this present form with appreciation and slip back into your own energetic vibration. Again, observe the world from inside the form and knowingness of the universe in which you are vibrating. What do you know as this person, animal or thing that you didn't know in the first body likeness you took for a spin? What is new to you but with the essence of being something you've known all along? What comes naturally that surprises you? Take some time, as you did in your first imaginal body, to experience this new perspective. When you have traveled in this new vibratory form for a while, it's time to release it.

As you enter back into the body of your own beautiful human expression, know that you have traveled within the One Mind of all and with that, the knowingness of all are within you. Be at peace knowing all of the energetic beings and their knowledge live in you, and you can tap that perspective and understanding at any time. Breathe, and when you are ready, slowly move your fingers and toes, stretch, gently open your eyes and sit for a moment to re-acclimate to your physical world. Take your pen and take some time to write out your experience. It doesn't matter if it was memorable and you're certain you'll never forget it, you should still capture it on paper – later, you'll be glad you did.

Now that you've had a chance to play in the reality of the fourth dimension, it gives greater perspective to the shapeless fifth dimension. When you choose to listen to your observer who is not bound in the three-dimensional realm, you are instantly lifted to a mountaintop view that is outside of the world view. You can begin to have a soul experience rather than an earth bound one. Your spirit is not something you have, like a talisman you carry in your pocket. You are spirit. You are spirit with a body to function in and direct about in the three-dimensional world. You are not the vehicle, but it's yours to use and it must respond to the driver from the fourth dimensional realm.

The fifth dimension is neither spatial nor chronological but brings space and time into relationship with the changeless thereby creating motion in pure unformed consciousness rather than movement in the realm of form. This ripple enables you to see the inner-connectedness of all things while the third dimension is demonstrative of disassociation between all things. From this mountaintop you'll know you are not separate from your brothers and sisters, but connected in the One.

River Meditation

When leaving the body behind, it's always a good idea to know how blessed you are in this field of grace in which you play. Before meditation, take a moment to state:

I know all is well and wherever I go in my expanding awareness, all is good and I am safe. I'm surrounded by and live in an Omni Dimensional Life Force that can never be violated, because there is nothing opposed to it. I move on the very currents of Life Itself and I'm free to notice all things without attachment to anything. Free to move beyond any image at any time and courageous enough to remain in it. I open to a graceful guidance on my soul's adventure, surrender my demands to logical understandings, and I welcome new and unknown states of consciousness for my soul's evolution.

Take a few breaths to bring your attention back to the

center of your body. Find a natural rhythm for your breath to fall into. See if you can follow your in-breath into your body . . . Exhale. Take with it any tension, worries, or concerns while creating more internal room. Find a natural rhythm to your breathing and following your next breath, let it take you deeper into the space beyond your body temple, where past and future dissolve into the present. Your inner awareness becomes the threshold you move across, where now your exhale *propels* you further into the openness of the void. Allow yourself to become available and receptive to a deep hearing and heightened awareness moving you to greater good.

Notice you are in a vast expanse with infinite points of light as if you are in a galaxy of stars . . . Allow your awareness to be drawn to a beautiful blue orb that is calling you home . . . feel an attraction and relational remembrance to the vibrancy of this world. You move in closer and when you do, you see the pristine snowcapped mountains, the wooded forests, the lush green jungles, the expansive deserts, deep canyons, still lakes, running rivers, and the all-embracing blue ocean . . . Your soul is deeply moved by the physical beauty. As your awareness of the magnificence of this place is heightened, you feel the call of this earth for the gift you have to bring. You return to your perfect mountaintop . . .

As you look out to the east, from your elevated mountaintop view, your awareness is drawn to a flowing river whose banks are lush with trees and plants. Originating in the peaks of the mountains, this meandering ribbon of green and blue crosses the valley floor eventually merging in the vast expansiveness of a placid lake that's calling for your exploration . . . find yourself lucidly wandering under the canopy of the trees along the bank of the river, hear the sound of the water dancing over the rocks, smell the river'd air, feel the moisture in the environment . . . Mysticism is a release from attachment to form and the separation it creates from the One All Animating Life Force. An important aspect of walking this world is detaching from frequencies that have captivated your attention, making it tough for you to move on to what's next. What significant part of your life do you have struggles releasing . . . who's there . . . where is it and what is the thinking that is holding your awareness there? . . . How have you made this frequency your drama . . . If you changed the channel, so your perspective was now the opposite, what would that feel and look like? . . . Take both perspectives, throw them both into the river and let the river wash them away . . . Listen to sounds, notice what you see and allow any feelings you have to rise and pass away as if they are being washed down the river. Continue this practice and let more images come and go despite how bright, loud or dull they are . . . just allow the current to carry them all away. As they appear and disappear without struggle, observe yourself in the allowing state.

If you are an expression of joy you'll see your world as joy. If you are combative, your world will be a combat zone. Your ride in the river of life can be one filled with fear of what's around the bend or one of pure elation as you welcome the next adventure. You dial into your consciousness the lower or higher frequency and life will bring the experiences to match the vibratory choice.

Get into the raft that's tied to a branch along the river, cast off into the current and let yourself go with the flow. . . When the current's speed picks up you begin to see a bend in the river. You recognize it as a metaphor for your life . . . what is awaiting you around the corner – what's downstream for you . . .

Can you recall times when you had the opportunity to trust and enhance your perception by moving to the elevated mountaintop view frequency but ended up reverting to some old familiar frequencies of anguish, discouragement and complaint? Do you remember watching yourself give in to the image of contracting pain rather than elevating your vision and catching a greater glimpse of a possibility? The current you're traveling in has power and only you decide where to direct it. Knowing you did the best you could at any time in your life, familiarize yourself with the feeling from that deceiving crossroad so you can remember in crucial moments you have options. Your liberation is born when you are free to be present enough to handle what's around the bend whether it's rapids or calm.

As you come around the bend you see white water rapids tumultuously boiling and bubbling. Let your raft catch the swift current and head toward them . . . You have the ability to enter all frequencies of complexity - picturesque or barren, challenging or placid, but all with a sense of wellbeing. So nix the negative and run the rapids with a sense of exhilarating joy and fun . . . where do you see your life a bit more tumultuous than you'd expected it to be . . . Listen to your higher perspective which sees the end of the rapids and understands what a small patch on the river of life it actually is. Listen as it prepares and tells you to drop into the white water field with a shift in attitude... you have all it takes to make this an exciting and entertaining thrill ride in your adventure of life – go for it.

You head toward boulders in the middle of your run, you can't deny them or suppress them so rather than fighting them you let the natural currents of the river take you toward them and effortlessly around them . . . What boulders in your life have you been using all your energy to
avoid . . . Resistance doesn't work be it in the river or life. Face the challenge head on, invite it into your path and trust the natural currents to take you around them effortlessly. Flow with your innate frequency and you'll find you are one with all that is necessary . . .

As you go with the flow, hooting and hollering with joy thinking you have a handle on it all, you playfully bounce off a rock pile in the middle of the river and find boiling in front of you a giant pit, the size of a swimming pool, opening up and ready to devour your raft. You drop into this giant bowl, covered by the wave folding on top of you from the other side. What feelings from your life come up when the weight of it is crushing down on you? . . . When things are going well, and oh no, here comes another challenge . . . The most challenging of times require the most self-compassion. Even in the most difficult of times your true identity wants to be remembered, its brilliance and connection with The Absolute is far greater than any challenge this life can cover you with. It doesn't matter how many psychotic breaks, bouts with cancer, or broken bones you've had to endure, if it all moves you closer to your union with the Whole of Life it's a good thing.

Feel the power of the river lift and push you through the wave, launching you with delight and elation to the other side, into the sky and delivering you back to the sacred circle of your mountaintop . . . Wow, what a ride!

Pause to reflect and integrate what you just learned from your mountaintop view.

It's time to return to your world of activity refreshed and renewed. Know once you've been somewhere you can easily return to that somewhere by simply calling it back to your awareness. There is always more work to be done, but for now, pull yourself back into your body permitting gratitude for your discoveries to fill your field of awareness. . . . Feel a joy knowing you'll be consistently returning to your sacred space, but for now, choose a path down the mountain . . . Familiarize yourself with this trail back into the world of form. Know there is always this corridor, this passage back to the elevated perspective of your world. Touch some of the trees as you pass by them and feel the earth move beneath your feet. As what you saw in a distance comes more into focus returning your attention to your breath. Breathe . . . When you are ready, slowly move your fingers and toes, stretch, gently open your eyes and sit for a moment to re-acclimate to your physical world. Take your pen and take some time to write out your experience. It doesn't matter if it was memorable and you are certain you'll never forget it, you should still capture it on paper – later, you'll be glad you did.

Soulful Adventures

- Do you remember a time you had a negative premonition and you listened? How about a time you didn't listen? What does it feel like when your body picks up warning signs, and do you listen to them?

- Your energetic vibration is always searching the dial for something to match your mood. You always have the choice to align with an energetic vibration that soothes your soul or sends you into action. When in the past did you notice your world validating your mood? Where could you use a frequency change to shift a particular experience you seem to be caught in right now?

- Who or what do energy sucking vampires and parasites look like in your present life?

- It's exciting to know harmonious alternatives for your viewing and listening pleasure are readily available. Step up to your channels of consciousness and pick a different option than the one you're bored with. What does this new picture look like?

- While a little bit of distraction can be a good thing, are there areas in your life you imbibe more than a little bit? Is there something that has pulled you out of your sense of Oneness with the Infinite, locking you into a repeating desire?

- What can be unplugged in your home to soften the electromagnetic field? Go unplug.

- Where does your logical mind keep you from exploring more controversial subjects that might actually have some truth to them? This week explore one or more of those subjects.

- Changing the question, changes your frequency, and changes your life. You live for a long time dominated by questions. What questions aren't reaping answers? How can you change how you can look for insights going forward?

- Close your eyes and sense what needs to be released from behind your protective walls for transformation to occur? Clinging and defending the heaviness will anchor you in time. Open the drawbridge around your heart allowing the pain out and trust the Divine frequency to transform the situation at hand.
- Consistent spiritual practices are essential to the mystical path. What are your regular daily spiritual practices? Connecting or communing with Source, through silence, contemplation, self-inquiry, observation, and listening will assist in your momentum as you climb to your mountaintop.

Body and Soul Practice for Connecting

Body Connection to Open Your Solar Plexus

If your willpower is dwindling, you've lost your drive or you are struggling with stress, self-doubt, or guilt, this practice will help to diminish those anxieties. You might want to try opening your solar plexus region more. Give Belly dancing a try or just go out dancing and get your body grooving. Exercise and yoga are always great releases. Dress well, stand taller, speed up your walking pace, speak up, look people in the eye and smile more.

Soul Connection to Open Your Solar Plexus

Find a place to sit in the sun. Close your eyes and feel the sun on your body and notice all the life enhancing gifts it brings your life. Sense the sun soothing and energizing your solar plexus region dissolving any disturbances in the area. Visualize a warm healing yellow ray blessing your solar plexus center and revitalizing your life force. Sit there for ten minutes while the healing energy envelopes your body and soul.

Mystical Writing

Because Thou Art

Because Thou art All-beauty and All-bliss,
My soul blind and enamored yearns for Thee:
It bears Thy mystic touch in all that is
And thrills with the burden of that ecstasy.
Behind all eyes I meet Thy secret gaze
And in each voice I hear Thy magic tune:
Thy sweetness haunts my heart through Nature's ways;
Nowhere it beats now from Thy snare immune.
It loves Thy body in all living things;
Thy joy is there in every leaf and stone:
The moments bring Thee on their fiery wings;
Sight's endless artistry is Thou alone.
Time voyages with Thee upon its prow
And all the future's passionate hope is Thou.
~ Sri Aurobindo
1872-1950

Chapter 5: Love and Diversity

Humankind is being brought to a moment where it will have to decide between suicide and adoration.
~ Teilhard de Chardin

The Heart, the Center of Unconditional Love and Acceptance

Ah. The heart chakra, the energy center of unconditional love. Unconditional love, as I've discussed, is an energetic frequency of the most powerful and creative kind. It can help you through the most challenging of times in your human experience and is available to you whenever you need it. As long as you focus your awareness and observing-self on love, it will free you from fears and limits. The heart center integrates the celestial and terrestrial realms bridging them as one into the earthly experience.

The Upanishads say, within the heart-center, mystics can hear sound without the striking of two things together as form and formless unite without ever touching. Not a bad depiction for something that is best described without words. Mystics, who commonly affirm extraordinary insights beyond all expression, write and speak with a boundless passion about great love pouring out on them through their spiritual seeking. Rumi often spoke of being intoxicated with the Divine. He wrote, "Not only the thirsty seeks the water, but water seeks the thirsty, as well".

The essence of love is one of those boundless feelings; an expression of aspects of living and Life that is almost impossible to communicate. How does one describe the taste of pure joy? How do you find words to paint a perfect sunset? How do you convey the flutter of your heart experiencing first love? It's really difficult to describe what love is, but rather simple to describe what heartbreak feels like. Heartbreak comes of expectations in this world and it follows a more physical, form-based experience. But love, love is otherworldly and there aren't as many words to describe it, though countless poems composed and analogies attempted. What's more likely than an accurate description of that kind of awe-inspiring love is a description of the depth of heartbreak that no doubt, everyone feels at one time or another. Whether as a result of shattered expectations, or the change that comes with the passage of time, so many look at love in the rear-view mirror. No one wants to experience loss, sorrow or the pain of a broken heart but as Buddha taught, we're each given ten thousand joys and ten thousand sorrows. The challenge not to get stuck in the quagmire of the emotional pain is a hurdle. We must keep our hearts open and soft instead of closed and constricted and that's where the journey up to the mountaintop is so vital.

Opening the front door to find our son's Godparents unannounced and looking nervous took me off guard many years ago. Their visits were always welcome but this one felt different in some way. Little did I realize my wife, Kalli, and I would be heartbroken by the observations they would soon share with us.

We didn't know what they wanted to talk about, but we felt an energetic awkwardness by the looks on their faces. As we followed them into the living room nervously, expectation suddenly getting the best of us. I wondered, what could possibly be bringing them here on this fall day?

What followed seemed like endless benign chit chat until they shared with us their deep concern for the well-being of someone our lives revolved around. Our son, our only son, was nearly a year and a half old and wasn't speaking or walking yet. It was the elephant in the room. We were of the mindset that he needed support, but we never saw it as something that would override his ability to speak volumes in time. Heck, historians say Einstein didn't speak until he was nearly five years old. We had plenty of time. As hard as it was for these loving friends to share their unease, their love pushed them through their discomfort as they felt obligated to share their insights that our baby boy was not maturing in a typical way. As they expressed their observations, all my ego-based perceptions of what my parenting journey was to look like were obliterated as my only concern was now for my son's future. In that moment, and in truth, for some time after, we were still in denial - yet soul seeking to figure out if their apprehensions were right. It was only years later I'd realize the crushing blow of losing my joyful expectations around playing a game of catch with my son, never having him share with me how his school day went, and the other typical milestones most parents get to experience. All parents tell me parenting looks different than they'd ever expected, but still, I experienced heartbreak until I aligned with the joys of how different my experience looked and continues to look as I parent my incredibly special son.

So, why do I bring up heartbreak in a chapter on love? I'm not a great believer in getting life lessons through heartbreaks or the ten thousand sorrows the Buddha speaks of, but if they come there's no need to deny them. Instead, I'm all for immersion in the gifts they bring. As I mentioned, my heart split wide open when I thought of not being able to have a conversation with my son, but what he's since taught me about wordless communication transcends our logical world with so much more. I now know full images that need not be described in words. I can feel beyond description. He has taught me that I can love beyond measure.

I've come to know that I'm not bound by the frequencies of the major communications of the five senses. I can travel further into the Infinite searching for broader possibilities in all areas. I've since become comfortable in searching beyond the edges. By introducing me to the peripheral, my son has unlocked the prison door of my physical senses and opened me to the diverse expression of the Infinite. I now realize every unique thread of the tapestry of life is essential for the picture to be complete. Some heartbreak right? I can still scratch the itch of the salty tears I cried in the times I felt the loss of my idealized experience as dad, though those times are dwarfed by the triumphant realization of the gifts I've received instead which is why I'm bringing them up here.

Love is without words. Love is perspective. Love is nonjudgmental. Love is accepting and kind. It's giving without strings. Love can be surprising when you observe what's beyond what's happening in form. When enlightened by the A-Ha moment, suddenly all the pieces fit together and the path you took up the mountain makes sense. As the observer, love is in and through everything and always has been. On your path of love and a return to wholeness there will be a repeated coming to know the Truth of who you are and who you are forgetting. You will find your passion and lose it over and over again. This journey to your mountaintop will take you through a repeated merging and splitting off from love. You'll experience the life and death of it but with each rebirth of love your union with the Absolute Expression animating all things is greater. The sorrows will push you into transformation. Throughout your life, you'll find closing your heart is far more detrimental than closing your mind could ever be. *At the end of life you won't be concerned with how much money you made; you'll be asking yourself, did I love well? Did I live fully?*

Self-absorbed Big Mouths

When you look into a mirror, do you really know whose reflection you see? Is it you who is looking out or are you the one who is looking in? In a previous chapter I pointed out that, in reality, you're the one who is looking at both; because, you must remember, you are the observer. Here's another mindbender for you to consider. Do you really care which one of you really represents you or are you more concerned with what's going on in your head? Do you push back your observing self in lieu of planning your response to a remark you hear? Are you attending to what is presenting itself before you or are you more interested in how you are being perceived? Do you always have to make a comment after someone says something to you? Have you ever been with someone so absorbed in their self-importance they don't see anything past the boundaries of themselves? They dominate the scene because while they believe "they care" they never stop to consider whether or not you're 'feelin' the love.

When you're living from the mystical connection of love there's no need to impose your viewpoints. When you come from love it's important to allow others to be who they are. As with my son, my love for him met him where he was coming from. If you've made a choice to remain in interaction with a self-absorbed big mouth, it's also crucial for there to be enough self-love so you can express your uniqueness and opinion. Those who continue to roll over others with their perspectives on everything will continue to find people to roll over, but you don't need to be one of them.

As you live from the mountaintop, trusting what your intuitive self sees, you'll discover vast landscapes beyond what you've been told exists. In those landscapes is an unparalleled expansiveness filled with infinite opportunity. You feel empowered there; and you are encouraged to be who you really are. On the mountaintop, you are transparent, you're known, and there's nothing to be hidden as you are honored for the gifts you have to offer. You feel appreciated for your contribution to the tapestry of life and there's a reciprocal flow. You feel healthy, vibrant, refreshed, and energized. You're prepared to walk through the physical realm with all that's necessary to fulfill what you care about and nothing can get in your way when the Infinite reservoir is moving through you. There's always enough to share and give freely.

There's so much more to your inner kingdom than has ever been written. When you're all wrapped up in what others think of you, it blocks your mountaintop view. In essence, it clogs up the calming transmission of love. My advice is to get over it. There's no scarcity of love, and expansion into this magical field is beyond control and description.

Ever been in an argument? Probably a rhetorical question.. Let's talk about what you feel and how you respond to the heat of that argument. There's no question that arguments stem from a scarcity of love. When tempers flare and you find yourself in a defensive posture needing to be right, it's time to look within to find the clog. If not both, in every argument at least one person is left beaten demonstrating ever more the scarcity of love in the situation.

Whole Body Awareness

Heightened awareness comes from the energy of the whole body rather than from the logical analytical reasoning of the mind. Yes, you have an intuitive knowledge of what's right for you and can trust what you feel in the body, mind and soul to be true. You begin to open to a new kind of integrity of your being that aligns with a harmonious vibration or what some might call love. No longer blindly operating from the previous programming of your beliefs or the dominating perspective of others, in love, you are staging your exploration from never before visited heights. Love is a return to the whole. Finding yourself congruent with what your higher self knows is the truest love affair.

This kind of behavior doesn't always come with acceptance from your clique of friends with whom you are in behavioral agreement. When you break free of servitude to the collective-think you'll start serving as an example to those around you. This kind of self-trust is a loving behavior that will save the planet once there is a tipping point of others following the same choice. For example, you know that fossil fuels pollute the environment and you know bigotry is less than loving, but if the collective-think holds a warped view of what's acceptable then sadly that is what prevails. Your knowingness and connection with a new thought can change the collective thinking. Is the hair on the back of your neck standing up at the mere thought of the collective think getting their way? It's because your ancestral connection is fueling a knowingness and that hair raising is your vibrational nudge to pay attention. It synchronizes you with the omnipresent Intelligence. The Divine expression is living amongst us and through you as you now. So once again, the observer recognizes the disconnection of those following the collective think and inspires the nudge to be one who makes a difference in the world.

When you live in alignment with your soul, loving who you truly are, you will bring your realization back into the Oneness with people, the planet and the universe. You'll live knowing an internal peace and be a loving difference-maker on the planet. Loving what's in yourself will open a mind that had the lid put on it long ago. When love opens your awareness, what comes through must enter through the filter of that love. The transformational possibilities are infinite. Life is supposed to be a gift of joy and laughter. It's not meant to be a journey of hardship and struggle. The loving view helps to remind you to be kind, freeing yourself from the way of the battle. Remember, you aren't meant to fight your way through this life unless that's your calling. Joyous laughter is a sure sign Life is present. I always remember my point of choice within my loving journey alongside my son.

One People, One Planet

When aligning with the mystical and living from the mountaintop, the fight along the false fault lines of division like race, politics and income brackets stops naturally. There's equality for all, not just for those you're in sympathetic agreement with. Celebrate diversity of perception and lifestyles by embracing the differences of others. A more loving way could not be found. The collective consciousness which continues refusing to participate in abusive systems like control over how, who or why you love is diversity in action. When the mass consciousness can say no to what we intuitively know is not love, without battle or complaint, but instead by just refusing to participate, something greater is invited to emerge. No one is born a racist; prejudice is something which has been taught. If all children who were conceived in love were taught upon arrival, love is the only currency, imagine the world we'd be living in.

From your perch on the mountaintop you'll rise to a stronger power of self-expression, transforming the density and heaviness of unexpressed love from within. Your unique path will create a more recognizable route to those who want to play in the light of your love's expression. When you welcome diversity, your world will blossom and many new possibilities will be introduced into your life. A sense of separation is the cause of all disease and war. When you're able to embrace the differences of life, healing happens. You *want* to heal the sense of separation from Life, so there will be no otherness. Where life flows, there is wholeness. Where Life doesn't flow, everything less than wholeness becomes an option and therein lies the potential for great heartbreak, grief, loss and sorrow. Whether it's the media, culture, science, religion, or medicine there is no buckling to the oppressive images. Yes, do follow your heart, but not at the expense of hurting others.

Becoming comfortable with differences removes you from being a slave to the fear of being judged yourself. When you allow the world to be what it is instead of attempting to create conformity, you choose trust and love over fear. Difference isn't bad, it's just different. When you don't know love in the midst of difference, it can bring up an uneasiness which is actually familiar. You must step through your discomfort rather than retreat from it. On the other side of that decision, you'll find Spirit of Life waiting for you. Otherwise, your thoughts will go into overdrive building a whole structure rationalizing why you're right in your cultural belief and others are wrong in theirs. If someone else is not inflicting pain or their will upon others, then open your awareness to a new aspect of the Infinite. To be able to experience more of the Infinite you must go beyond what you already know. Get familiar with your discomfort so you can be fully present in the disruption of the old behavior. To be unique and beautiful, life must be a tapestry of diverse colors and textures.

Love frees you to be who you truly are. But, you learned early that approval came easier when you did what others wanted you to do. So now, when you feel love, you express and accomplish more than when you were being criticized. *Aren't you more candid in your creative expression when it's welcomed and more restricted when it's not?* Always needing to be right rather than creating space for what's best is a sure way to shut out love and newness. If you aren't happy, there's something wanting to be known in your life.

You know the cliché it's better to be happy than to be right? I'm so blessed to have the opportunity to work daily with passionate volunteers in my community. They offer good intentions and smart ideas that, in some cases, have previously not panned out. In spite of my knowing the potential for a different outcome, their joy and love adds to the collective consciousness and uplifts everything and everyone, no matter the outcome. So, I choose joy and happiness over being right - which is really the right choice.

Alternatively, there's not much space in a healthy relationship for "I'm right. You're wrong." Who does that make happy?

A Generation of Clones

Children who are left to be babysat by the screen begin to lose their uniqueness as they align with the mentality of someone else's programming. Add the factory approach to education, which is memorization and loss of free thinking to match the common core curriculum, and we've got a cooperative piece to the collective puzzle who thinks they're different, but aren't. In fact, it's a generation of clones we risk creating. When our children develop a unique and diverse expression, they become difference-makers bringing to the planet new pieces of the tapestry from their remembrance of the mountaintop. Embracing rather than just tolerating diversity becomes important for evolution. The centralizing uniformity doesn't want difference. Instead, it works toward creating a hive mentality to support the one-reality agenda. Love is unconditional in its embrace of the vast range of expression. Your transformation frees you by lifting you to a higher view. When things are different they can sometimes irritate and rub others the wrong way. After all, the complacent don't want their 'way' disturbed. You must risk being a trend-setter and messenger of the greater possibility and be willing to deflect the ridicule that will inevitably come on the heels of that.

People are willing to express more when they feel loved and safe in a non-judgmental space, as opposed to being in the presence of upset and anger. Anger will never produce love. It may get what it wants but anger will never earn the heart of others because it leaves an energetic wound and scar. If you've been criticized for a long time, unconditional acceptance may seem unattainable. There's a big difference between not being upset and truly caring for another person's well-being. The world is infinitely more beautiful when you see it clearly from the mountaintop and realize everyone has their flaws, mistakes, fears, hopes and dreams.

When understanding is present, resentment and anger make no sense. The world becomes a friendlier place when you pause long enough to clearly see the people who live in it. The world you believe in is the world you see, and the world you see is the world you live in.

As a weary traveler approached the outskirts of a town he'd never entered, he asked the old sage sitting on the side of the road, "Hey, old man, what kind of town is this?" The wise man looked up at him, shaded his eyes from the sun and asked in return, "What kind of town did you come from?" The traveler thought for a moment and answered with a heavy sigh, "Oh, it was terrible. It was a violent sort of place with a lot of corruption and theft." The sage didn't have to think long before answering, "Well, son, I'm sorry to say this town is much the same." The weary traveler picked up his bags and made his way down the road.

As he disappeared into the distance, a new traveler approached the sage. "Excuse me, kind sir, can you tell me what kind of town this is?" The sage removed his cap, scratched his head, and placed the cap back on as he turned to ask in return, "Well, son, what kind of town are you coming from?" "Well, sir," said the rosey-cheeked traveler, "It was a beautiful town. Everyone was kind and loving and generous." The sage thought for a moment and raised his eyes to the sky, "Well, son," he said, "I'm happy to tell you that you've come upon another town just like the one you left."

Learn to celebrate and welcome diversity of thought and lifestyle instead of condemning it. Discontent flourishes where there is no love. Be wary of the pseudo love you'll resort to as you avert the feelings of discomfort where there's a dearth of love. Too often people will stick with the familiar despite a lack of love to keep from any more anguish in their lives. That familiar can resemble a stagnant relationship, unrewarding career, personally irrelevant religious philosophy or predictable but boring patterns that can make the human experience dull and lifeless.

Twisted Perspective

Have you ever attended a seminar and thought it was wonderful until after the last break when the facilitator came down hard with a sales pitch to purchase their weekend workshop or products? Despite enjoying the seminar, you were left with a total sense of being used as a pawn to someone else's hidden agenda. What about going to visit a new acquaintance? Have you ever spent some time with someone you barely knew and everything was fine until the last few minutes of your time together, during which they suddenly assaulted you with their finely detailed manifesto of hatred? Even though the majority of time you spent with your new friend was enjoyable, the last few minutes were horrible. What memory and feeling did you leave with? You don't want to go back into that situation. Watch out for a person who defends their actions by saying, "Well, it was mostly good." When violence enters the scene, the good is quickly erased. After the damage is done, the lingering memory from the interaction isn't a pleasant one despite how the perpetrator will try to twist your perspective. The remembrance from the first part of the encounter is quickly trumped by the overwhelming negative energy exchanged towards the end.

Lack of love in life can cause disgust, prejudice, racism and hatred in the world. Diversity of cultures is being swept up by the images of western influence. When the bright colors give way and emulate the bland dark suit of uniformity, there's another type of extinction going on. As diversity is stymied, uniformity and the desire to fit in takes hold.

Some people get offended by different thinking. There's a simple way beyond being offended and this is to choose not to be offended. When circumstances get tough; love and trust will support you through turbulent times.

Affinity Bias

It can be painful not having a self that fits in, but who were you before you were somebody else? Are you acting like someone you are not? What seems real can feel like separateness. The beauty of diversity is inclusivity. Don't get caught up in what you're told you should be. Instead, be who you really are. Live from your essence; let any shames of self, go. Know your self-worth above all other selves. There is no recrimination in your loving truthful self.

There seems to be an affinity bias, where one likes to be

around people of similarities. These unconscious biases impact decisions and without an overriding consciousness for inclusivity, there's a painful indifference to those in the out crowd. Omission and exclusion are your blind spots. Open your eyes and heart and recognize organic diversity throughout life and nature starting with you. You are more than your distinctions. It doesn't matter whether you are male, female, LGBTQ, or disabled; no matter your race, age, religion, geographical location, financial status or whether you are a veteran, vegetarian, elder, extrovert, introvert, boomer, millennium, mother, or single dad. When you put a couple of the combinations together it can either create more welcoming opportunities or more rejections.

As an example, someone who falls into the category of elder, single parent might not be welcome in with the young crowd at the tot lot where alternatively, the same single parent might be the warmly embraced by the local parenting community.

What's interesting about physiological prejudices is the science behind it. Statistical examination of the human species has proven we're all genetically linked having evolved from "Mitochondrial Eve". This maternal ancestor, who is known to have come out of Africa, is the ground zero for all living humans.

Diversity is our unfinished business. If we can't acknowledge what's going on with diversity, then we can't address the issue of exclusion that comes from a lack of love and acceptance. *Where are you closed down to extending love?* Some commercial trucks have a sign on the back of their trailer that reads, 'If you can't see my mirrors I can't see you'. If you can't see your biases you'll be acting unconsciously in a less than loving way. Until we learn to live with each other there will be an epidemic of disconnect that plagues our planet. Appreciate the marvels of the diverse tapestry we call life on earth.

Giving Your Power Away

It's through contemplation you come to know Spirit right. It's the true realization beyond description that allows love in, thus eliminating the sense of emptiness in your soul. When you believe the world is harsh, you'll find evidence to support that belief. You'll feel attacked where there's no assault. Shrinking or being intimidated when around important people of power, position or influence doesn't serve you. Love who you are enough to release the magnificence inside so you can bring your greatness to the experience.

When you find yourself ill at ease, it's your clue there is something that needs to be known. Don't let it stifle you, instead pause and allow the awareness of your observing self to review the situation from a higher place. Don't give your power away to blame and bitterness. Drop the blame statements like, "You make me so angry!" Turning others into scapegoats for your lack of responsibility will only give away your power to choose differently. If you give your power away to another person through disappointment, you've set conditions on your love. You'll have severed the mystical connection by your earthly expectations. Simply put, you'll regain your freedom the moment you stop the blame game.

If you withdraw your love based on behavior then there are conditions on your love. Life loves unconditionally. The rain falls on the just and the unjust. Your defensiveness is a reaction to feelings often coming from a lifetime of attempting to survive on your own. In that resistance your true nature, which is connected to the whole, is hidden. Living from the mountaintop helps you to see the many streams of Source pouring into the core of your being. When loving is not the first choice it's because it isn't seen as a choice at all. Your higher awareness is clearly not operational when you are defensive because you're too far down on the side of the mountain.

People's upsets are disturbing only because you've lost your connection with Life. Without love you're empty, because there's a hole where everything pours out. When you attempt to plug up the hole with the things of this world, quickly you realize you can't. The hole feels like a bottomless pit because it can only be filled with the love from within. The Buddhists tell the story of the hungry ghosts with their pinhole mouths and necks so thin that there's no room to swallow. As a result, they can never get enough food down to satiate their hunger. It's said these hungry ghosts are incarnated from beings who were greedy, envious and jealous in their lives as humans with bottomless soul needs that couldn't be filled from outside.

Manipulating people to get what you want shows you're primarily concerned for yourself and only yourself. When love or any currency for that matter is earned this way, it'll never feel like it was freely given even if that was the original intention. It definitely can't be freely received in love since there was an intention to attain it at the get-go.

When I was a kid I pined for a Kiss CD. Wait, tape. Ok, now I'm dating myself, it was an 8-track. I'd gone to one of the pyrotechnic concerts and I was really hot on the sound. I started noodging my mom months in advance of the holidays and knew she would have delighted in giving me this gift had I done more than casually mention it a hundred times. Instead, she bought it for another kid in the neighborhood thinking it was the perfect gift for a teenage boy. So, in spite of the fact that my parents had given me a van earlier that year, I was a bit burned that not only didn't I get what I wanted but that some other kid got what I wanted. Why do I tell you this story?

In the end, I got the 8-Track because I manipulated her with guilt. But did I get it as a joyful gift from my mother? Not really. So what's the difference? I got the8-Track. The difference is big because she felt bad and I still remember acting like a spoiled brat. I got what I wanted, but I didn't feel her love in the gift because I didn't allow her to give it to me with love. When you manipulate, rather than wait to see what the universe has for you without expectation, you miss the boat on the most important part of the gift.

Don't delude yourself. You may get what you want through manipulation, but it's not love. The short term gain can be damaging in the long run and never fulfill you or fill the seemingly bottomless hole inside. Don't be a hungry ghost. When people behave poorly, it's because they don't know any better. It's an opportunity for you to give them unconditional love right when they need your love most. Heaping on more garbage with your looks, sarcasm or critical words is not the mystic's way. Anger, resentment and manipulation don't make for happy people – period. Being an expression of mystical love is being a conduit for caring about the wellbeing of another person more than caring about how they make you feel in their presence. When you're a conduit for love to express you merge with the inexhaustible Life Flow and experience your union with the Whole.

Lake Meditation

When leaving the body behind, it's always a good idea to know how blessed you are in this field of grace in which you play. Before meditation, take a moment to state:

I know all is well and wherever I go in my expanding awareness, all is good and I am safe. I'm surrounded by and live in an Omni Dimensional Life Force that can never be violated, because there is nothing opposed to it. I move on the very currents of Life Itself and I'm free to notice all things without attachment to anything. Free to move beyond any image at any time and courageous enough to remain in it. I open to a graceful guidance on my soul's adventure, surrender my demands to logical understandings, and welcome new and unknown states of consciousness for my soul's evolution.

Take a few breaths to bring your attention back to the center of your body. Find a natural rhythm for your breath to fall into. See if you can follow your in-breath into your body . . . Exhale. Take with it any tension, worries, or concerns while creating more internal room. Find a natural rhythm to your breathing and follow your next breath letting it take you deeper into the space beyond your body temple, where past and future dissolve into the present. Your inner awareness becomes the threshold you move across, where now your exhale *propels* you further into the openness of the void. Allow yourself to become available and receptive to a deep hearing and heightened awareness to move you to greater good.

Notice you are in a vast expanse with infinite points of light as if you are in a galaxy of stars . . . Allow your awareness to be drawn to a beautiful blue orb that is calling you home . . . feel an attraction and relational remembrance to the vibrancy of this world. You move in closer and when you do, you see the pristine snowcapped mountains, the wooded forests, the lush green jungles, the expansive deserts, deep canyons, still lakes, running rivers, and the all-embracing blue ocean . . . Your soul is deeply moved by the physical beauty. As your awareness of the magnificence of this place is heightened, you feel the call of this earth for the gift you have to bring. You return to your perfect mountaintop . . .

It feels good to return to your familiar sacred place. Look around and notice your surroundings. As you look out from your elevated mountaintop view you feel a connection to a valley below and the river that cuts through it, you remember your adventure in the canyon and exploration of the cave . . . You can see a sparkling lake in the distance and feel the pull of its beauty. Pick one of your paths and lucidly head down under the canopy of trees. Feel the shade and hear the sounds as you make your way to finding a tranquil setting along the lake to sit for a while . . . Sense the calm and quiet of this setting. Listen to the stillness - What do you hear in the whispering from nature?

Gaze out upon the glassy lake mirroring the Caribbean blue sky with its puffy white clouds . . . Visualize your heart opening like the petals of a flower, letting go of any sacred wounds and filling with light and love pouring into this magical spot . . . Feel this love expanding and radiating through every cell of your body. Allow your witnessing self to just observe any emotions coming to the surface. No need to do anything but breathe through them, releasing them . . . Allow the love to fill your heart space.

You are a channel through which this mystical love flows to the world from the Cosmic Realm. There's a harmonious blending of wisdom and love presenting answers from your knowing of the heart.

It's easy to love those you hold dear but you are being called to love those who have been exiled from your heart. You no longer are attempting to love - you *are* love.

Dive into the heart of love, dive beyond the surface, dive into the depths of love as you now dive into the lake before you . . . feel the initial shock then the ahhhhh of how good it feels to move freely, weightlessly and unburdened. You left the conscious world above the surface and now move in a whole other world where you are totally immersed. Move in and have your being in this sweetness, the ecstasy and glory of being pure love . . . You are engulfed in the essence and you feel more alive than ever. You die to the previous conscious realm of struggle only to suddenly be alive and free in the essence of Love Itself. Through this portal you realize you are eternity forever creating. There are no words of any language to define this joy you are . . .

It's time to return from this dimension to your mountaintop. You must leave behind everything, including your blissful visions. As you move from one realm of awareness to the next you'll find your heart opening to the mystery of your new realization from your mountaintop . . . You understand your immersion wasn't to escape from humanity but to prepare you for your return to be who you truly are . . . Allow this experience to resonate without description in the vibrational level of your body as you step out of the lake onto the shore and find yourself standing on your sacred mountaintop . . .

You return to your world of activity refreshed and

renewed. Know once you've been somewhere you can easily return to that somewhere by simply calling it back to your awareness. There is always more work to be done, but for now, pull yourself back into your body permitting gratitude for your discoveries to fill your field of awareness. Feel a joy knowing you'll be consistently returning to your sacred space, but for now, choose a path down the mountain . . . Familiarize yourself with this trail back into the world of form. Know there is always this corridor, this passage back to the elevated perspective of your world. Touch some of the trees as you pass by them and feel the earth move beneath your feet. As what you saw in the distance comes more into focus returning your attention to the breath. Breathe . . . And, when you're ready, slowly move your fingers and toes, stretch, and then gently open your eyes and sit for a moment to readjust to your physical world. Take your pen and take some time to write out your experience. It doesn't matter if it was memorable and you are certain you'll never forget it, you should still capture it on paper – later, you'll be glad you did.

Soulful Adventures

- Where do you have a self-absorbed big mouth in your life whose lack of sensitivity is so out of touch that they pollute the emotional environment they're in? Why do you continue to interact with this person? Where have you been or are being the big mouth? Do you want to continue that self- expression?
- Do you recall a time of pain when you were heartbroken? Have you since come to understand the gifts it offered? What are they?
- What twisted perception has someone attempted to get you to buy to accept their poor behavior? What twisted perspectives have you attempted to convey for your inappropriate behavior?
- Loving what's in you will open your heart to your true

self. Do you remember putting a lid on your creative expression? What did you seal off and what prompted you to close off your self-expression? Where is it time to take the lid off and how can you accomplish that now that your awareness has shifted?

- Where are you feeling stuck with the familiar? Do you have a sense of discontent even if latent; that could possibly be in any of your relationships, unrewarding career, poor eating and exercising habits?

- Diversity is our unfinished business. If we can't acknowledge what's going on with diversity then we can't address the issue of exclusion that comes from a lack of love and acceptance. Where are your blind spots when it comes to affinity biases? Where are you closed down to extending love? Where is the edge of your comfort zone when it comes to conversation about diversity?

- How do you give your power away creating issues of the heart like grief, hatred, anger, jealousy, fears of betrayal, or loneliness? The middle of your chest is the balance between your body and spirit. Unconditional love is centered here and is the creative and powerful energy best used to guide and help you through the most difficult times.

- What relationship memories both present and past are in need of some healing? What emotional memories do you need to heal? What emotional wounds have taken over your life leaving you with a lack of trust and keeping you from experiencing greater love?

Body and Soul Practice for Connecting

Body Connection to Open Your Heart Center

To physically activate your heart center try this practice for a few minutes. Sit up straight with your legs crossed or in a chair with your feet touching the ground. Bring your arms out to your sides with the palms facing forward. Your arms will be parallel to the ground. Then, exhale as you rotate your arms forward, keeping them straight almost to the point where the palms meet (but don't clap). You will feel your pectoral chest muscles contract. Now, rotate your arms back as you inhale thus expanding and stretching your chest area. Start this practice off slowly at first to stretch and warm up your shoulders, then find a good rhythm and continue at a comfortable pace.

If that's too much work, just try hugging yourself for a while. Some good belly laughter will heal all things.

Soul Connection to Open Your Heart Center

Find a place to sit with a straight spine and with your hands on your lap, breath in through your nose and exhale making a *ha* sound out your mouth. Let your *ha* exhale be twice as long as your inhale. Do this for a few minutes extending the time when comfortable while focusing on your heart center. Bring into your heart images that have brought pain to it. Surround that time, place and person with love, while embracing any soul lessons offered through those experiences. Continue until the images stop presenting themselves. Close this time with a few more minutes of *ha* breathing. Then move your hands into a prayer position with your palms touching and lift your hands over your heart with your fingers pointing up and your thumbs pressed against your heart. Tap your heart a few times with the base of your thumbs releasing and contributing love into the flow of Life ~ Namaste

Mystical Writing

People are often unreasonable, irrational, and self-centered.
Forgive them anyway.
If you are kind, people may accuse you of selfish, ulterior motives.
Be kind anyway.
If you are successful, you will win some unfaithful friends and some genuine enemies.
Succeed anyway.
If you are honest and sincere people may deceive you.
Be honest and sincere anyway.
What you spend years creating, others could destroy overnight.
Create anyway.
If you find serenity and happiness, some may be jealous.
Be happy anyway.
The good you do today, will often be forgotten.
Do good anyway.
Give the best you have, and it will never be enough.
Give your best anyway.
In the final analysis, it is between you and God.
It was never between you and them anyway.

This writing was found written on the wall in Mother Teresa's home for children in Calcutta

Chapter 6: Flow

Not what we have but what we enjoy constitutes our abundance.
~ Epicurus

What Does Abundance Look Like?

What could possibly be more magical than coming together with your clan, whether it's over a meal, in a home, with your birth family or a chosen tribe of friends? Finding yourself in a setting with those who see you for who you are, sharing your dreams without pretense, and laughing till the sun rises is as rich as it gets. Feeling unconditionally loved is an abundance that enriches the soul. And let's face it, it just feels really good.

It's right for you to live an abundant life because you're an avenue through which Life flows. You can be both spiritual and successful because one does not preclude the other. You don't have to make a choice between the two. As a transformer of Infinite Undifferentiated Potential the reservoir of abundant good awaiting your recognition is ripe for the tapping. Life wants to come into form through you. Your joy is found by doing what you love with ease and grace rather than escaping to some secret secluded hideaway and staying there the rest of your days. A sense of abundance will support your walk in this world as an expression of joy leaving a current of happiness in its wake. It's in following your calling while remaining peacefully mindful that makes you a conduit of Life.

There's a dichotomy between things above and below the surface as it relates to abundance. Those with an eye for subtle differences will sense a feeling of either abundance or scarcity almost immediately. A great story illustrating this comes from a personal observation I had when visiting Tibet. In counterfeit cultures, like the one the Chinese tried to replicate in Lhasa, I visited what remained of some of the original buildings but found the spirit behind their creation was gone and the city was a shadow of what it once was when the Tibetan culture thrived there. All around the original Norbulingka, which now looks like Chinatown, the handicrafts of the Tibetan artists were both missing their details and merely being hocked by those sellers looking to take the most tourist dollars home in their pockets. My heart sank as I felt the emptiness in the experience I had dreamed of having for much of my life. Thank goodness I made my way to the Tibetan re-creation of the Dalai Lama's Norbulingka palace in Dharamsala, India, where the fine detail and the pride and spirit of the Tibetan culture flowed in abundance. In all of this, the richness that goes beyond words was placed somewhere else. I witnessed that the richness doesn't go away, it just finds a way to express itself through another open channel.

The magnetism of the western culture is filled with the attraction of glamour and the arousal of our senses for more worldly ambitions. It's right to be able to enjoy the fullness of this world without exploitation, but when the pursuit of form eclipses your desire to reveal your soul's expression and your connection with Life Itself, you'll lose your peace. When the traditional media venues brilliantly feed you images to provoke wanting and envy, it's time to listen to a new station and embrace a new thought. Going forward with a sense of confidence and self-assurance, loving who you are and what you've got to share is a sure sign of an abundant life. Yes, it's your right to have a healthy body, abundant cash flow, the freedom to live where you desire, and share what your heart wants to give, at the same time as expressing what you came into this world to do.

A sense of scarcity sucks your alive-ness away like a vampire. It doesn't feel good because it isn't good or natural. Lack, fueled by misguided beliefs, is an unnatural disease inflicted on the human consciousness.

The Wants

There's an anxiety and tension that's physically uncomfortable when you are focused on the wants. Sad to say, the truth is, you'll never satiate the insatiable. You were born perfect, whole and complete. This is your truth. Where there's a sense of lack the affluent flow of creation is redirected to living in want. For example, if you want a car, and all your energy goes to wanting the car, then the manifestation of the car itself is postponed to living in want. It takes a lot of effort to suppress wants and concerns. This exertion would be a lot healthier if it were spent on making your vision a reality rather than wanting it to be true. When you're living your soul's purpose, abundant joy is a constant. Life is rich when your days are full of what you love to be expressing.

There's enough in this world to support the expression of what you love. What's detrimental is when you want more than enough. You're listening to a fear of lack when you disregard your sense of balance to stockpile more stuff. Worse, when this occurs, you'll disconnect from your inner guidance. The challenge to the addiction of fulfilling the wants is that it often results in a never ending cycle of wanting more. When you're all wrapped up tightly in the wants, what you've already got won't satisfy you for very long. When this overindulgent energy begins to dominate your field of awareness, it's time to return to your mountaintop. Go ahead and look out upon the abundant vistas and remember to re-align and re-unite with this view. Know you don't have to own everything in front of you to enjoy it. The wants are just part of the cultural trance. Don't buy into a definition of yourself as a needy hoarder.

Life is best described by the word flow but acquiring and storing like a squirrel tends to be the opposite of that definition. Many people have difficulty letting go of their collections of, as George Carlin used to say, "stuff". Unless you own a storage warehouse and create space to hold other people's stuff they never visit, it's a good idea to get comfortable with untethering. Letting go of "stuff" and "things" will support flow and movement in your life. When you let go you'll be free to merge with new ideas. Life will introduce a blank palette with infinite possibilities raising you to a new level of aliveness, through which you can create.

The more alive you feel, the more present you are. The more present you are the more available you are to your creative connection to the Infinite. Being excited about your vision and passion increases the Life flow bringing meaning and fulfillment to your daily activity. The flow of abundance is not just about getting and holding, it's about giving and circulating.

You're already in the flow of abundance. Your place at the table has been set. When you're caught in the wants for anything, that longing arises from a sense of separation. When you're in that state of desire, it's how you focus on the imagined outcome that pushes away your vision. In wanting, you concentrate and try harder, paradoxically confirming what you don't have and won't get. When you can rest in confidently knowing without anxiety or doubt what's rightfully yours, you'll find it's yours now. You'll move boldly with assurance in the direction of your dream creating it as you gain momentum. You don't attract what you want, you attract what you expect.

Who hasn't been involved with sales at some point in life? Whether face to face or on the phone, I'm sure there are many of us who've grumbled a post-mortem when we didn't get what we wanted. Doesn't really matter what it was, if we were left disgruntled in disappointment, there are few of us who'd deny that no sooner than we hung up or turned on our heels, that we mumbled a well-placed expletive directed at our prospect. We had the wants; they said no, we got angry. What manifests? The anger and disappointment manifests unconsciously in a string of similar negativity until the consciousness changes. You might wonder how this is even possible when you're tirelessly visioning and affirming the positive, but the energy of abundance is hidden in the quiet lessons and objections of the "no's" you receive. Those no's are always full of infinite possibility if you embrace them for the potential they bring and change your attitudinal approach slightly. Stand back though, because when you make this paradigm shift, the floodgates will open.

Abundance doesn't only refer to money or things; it's an inner state of being that shows up in all areas of your life, including money, ease, health and fulfillment. Your good comes to you from untold regenerative possibilities because you live in an Abundant Universe. What you're motivated to do on the outside comes from your inner connection to the emerging desire to express. When petty controlling fears worm their way into your field of awareness, your high soul qualities of trust, gratitude and generosity seem to get squeezed out of the picture. A sense of lack constricts your ability to live in the flow- which if you'd have had your druthers; I bet I could guess which way you'd prefer to go.

Your Spending Talks

Money is just a tool. Currency is a current for your expressions, because dollars are a powerful way to reveal what's important to you. Money becomes an expression of your consciousness. Being conscious of your spending with your Spirit brings you more into the concurrent experience of wholeness.

At first, conscious consumerism takes a bit of extra energy to ramp up in your life, but then it will soon become easier to stay aware of when issues of meaning crop up.

Consider finding out which companies exploit children in sweatshops so you can have cheap consumables whether they be jeans or electronics. If you discovered that your favorite bargain brand was manufactured under inhumane factory conditions with non-livable wages, would you feel the same satisfaction at the cash register despite getting a bargain? Have you ever wondered where the furniture you purchased for your last home came from and how it got to your living room? Did it take decimating and exploiting our natural resources to get it there? Have you considered the destruction of farmland that's occurring to support corporately-manipulated, genetically modified seeds being forced upon you needing untold chemicals that bleach the land and poison the water tables when you purchase something? I've yet to mention the laborers, who were once called farmers, working in toxic conditions with substandard insurance and below minimum wage pay to bring you perfect looking produce. Those who live from the mountaintop look from a broader, more elevated perspective and see what's downstream and what's being passed on to our children. Pay attention and make the extra effort to integrate what's in your heart with your actions in this world. I'm not here to chastise you, instead I just want to encourage you to maintain an awareness to your actions. In the mystical place there is no separation between the two.

To live in integrity requires alignment in all areas of your life. Are you always attempting to get service people to cut their prices and cut you a deal on their products? Are your conversations about how you got such a good deal pretending that it wasn't at the expense of someone else? If yes on either question, then you're living in an atmosphere of getting less than you ask for in life. Watch out as it will be reciprocated in your world being less full than you'd like it to be. To live life by joyous design, rather than by just getting by, you must be a conduit of flow rather than constriction. It's always alright to say no to what someone offers you; what's questionable is when you expect that same someone to be less than who they are to please you.

I once put a row of twenty-five palm trees in the ground at my home. I purchased them in a neighborhood where homes had large enough properties that it was not unusual for homeowners to have small private nurseries in their backyards. I understand the art of negotiation is part of business, but pushing individuals beyond what's right and taking advantage of them is not a kind way to walk in partnership on this planet. I got my twenty-five, fifteen gallon queen palms at a ridiculously discounted price at the true pain of this gentleman who wanted the money more than the palms he'd been nursing along. For years, whether I was a blessing to him or not, every time I looked down that row of palm trees my thought was never what an awesome deal I got. Rather, what a cheapskate I was for taking advantage of his situation. Just because you can get away with something doesn't make it right. Living in integrity with your spirit is doing what's right above and beyond what you can get away with.

Living in integrity is being true to the abundance of who you are, not the littleness of who you are not. You can play the little games when the stakes are low and you know you can win or if losing doesn't really matter. It's when the stakes are high and you're really attached to an outcome that you draw from your core being. You'll come to discover your past behaviors are the first to come to the surface of your awareness. It's getting something for far less than its known value that you need to move through. *Are there any financial areas in your life which come to mind that could use some cleaning up?* Your true character is revealed in times of difficulty. Will you be coming from a generous spirit or one of limitation? Life returns what you cast out. Remember to allow your observer to weigh in on your behavior and thoughts, because at any moment you can choose a new thought creating a new causative pulse in your world.

Battling Your Way through Life

You can battle your way to success, but it's not by might that you'll find your peace and assurance for a good that lasts forever. The act of moving joyously and harmoniously within the flow of Life will help you develop a deep trust in something greater than what is in your control. Your world is a mirror of your consciousness. Is it a friendly reflection coming from within, or is a hostile and anxiety-ridden duel inside your head reflecting itself in your world? You have a right to live in an abundant state of flow and this is best accomplished through appreciation and enjoying what you have. It's a matter of living on purpose to feel the soul satisfaction of being fulfilled.

The battle comes from your attachment to the outcome. It's a matter of going full out as you follow your inner urging yet not being attached to how it has to look in the end. Hanging on to how it has to turn out will only annoy your mind and impact your actions thus pushing your awareness away from what's presenting itself in the moment. When you allow yourself to be used by Life, you trust the moment more than you would have if you had followed your mind's picture of what that moment was supposed to look like.

Saying Yes to the Call

At the age of 19, I stepped away from student life at a University and a relationship with my girlfriend to run off to New Zealand on my own to surf and ski with no intention of returning. I met a young woman on the plane who, within hours, had designs on walking down the aisle with me (and I don't mean the aisle of the aircraft). After a year in Europe as a nanny, she thought it would be fun to bring her parents an American guy as a souvenir from her adventures. Since I had nowhere to go when I got off the plane I followed the abundant flow of life taking care of me. Heck, I was 19. What would you have done? While I was well cared for by this young woman's family in the town of Tepokki and embraced the graciousness of her clan, they soon recognized my greater purpose and arranged a ride to the ferry to the South Island. Upon arriving at an isolated youth hostel at Mount Cook, I was left waiting for storms to clear off the nearest Glacier so I could ski. But something life-changing and extraordinary happened to me there in the interim.

While meditating under the protection of an outcropping of rocks shielding me from gale-force winds, I saw the light at the end of the tunnel and my future life unfolded in front of me. I guess I could say it was a vision, but it felt more like I had entered a space where I saw myself at a spiritual center of healing and service. I was observing myself, on a stage looking out from under the lights, at me meditating under this outcropping of rocks in the midst of a storm. Did time dissolve? Was my future-self communicating with my younger-adult self?

In the great mystical book, Cloud of Unknowing, an unknown monk wrote, "Yet it is not a will or a desire, but something which you are at a loss to describe, which moves you to desire you know not what." Truly, I've never had words for this experience, but my life was forever changed after that moment. I rushed home to enroll in the right program to support my vision of spiritual leadership. I fell in love with the vision Life had for me. There was a sense of familiarity, and with my vision from under that gigantic boulder sheltering me from the storm I recognized and remembered what I came here to do. All I wanted to do was be used as a conduit to bring it into expression. Since that moment, my life's journey has been magical and filled with incredible and continuous demonstrations of the healing power from beyond. Life has used me to inspire, uplift and deliver a practical approach to the use of the universal spiritual truths as applied to the individual needs of whomever I am serving.

By saying yes to that not-so-subtle tap on the shoulder, my soul's curriculum was rearranged, bringing forth my life lessons and insights in ways I never would have expected. I've grown, stretched and had the opportunity to enjoy a fulfilling and blessed life of enough while surrounded by an abundance of love. Yes, I've had my challenges and concerns but I've been able to face them with a deep knowingness that I'm on my right path. That path is my home while I walk this world so I don't ever feel the need to hide. There's so much more for me to do here which is why I get so excited when I hop out of bed every day. I couldn't wish for a greater abundance than to know the joy I have in my life.

Living your passion is living in grace. Doing your dharma and following your purpose will give you an inexhaustible, synchronistic string of energy. Whether you're called to champion a cause that'll save the planet or work one-on-one as a caregiver, do what fills your heart and fulfills your purpose. Whether you're a warrior or a lover, when you've found your connection to Source your gift will be a light for the world. When you are a conduit for Spirit you can give more than you ever knew you had in you and feel richer for it. You'll discover resources in times of doubt and learn to trust the truth of your inner voice. And, if you blow it doing what you were called to do, it's far more rewarding than going through life on autopilot doing "the right thing" that someone else thought was best for you to do. You must be authentic to be mystical.

Perhaps you've forgotten what your gift to give this world is? There's always a chance but I also know there's always a spark of that gift within you. Just for fun let's call it your pilot light. That pilot light is always on, always remembers and can't be extinguished. When you fan the flame it heats up. Returning to your mountaintop allows you the opportunity to remove yourself from the gale-force commotion of your world to check in to see if your life is working. Working doesn't mean you aren't coming up against challenges and rejections. It means, assessing if your effort is still effortless. Is there still a fire inside for what you are called to do? Your genius cannot and will not come to full bloom until it is understood. When you say yes and align your actions to the stirring of your soul you'll find an abundance of energy accumulating to direct you as you follow your call. Your spirit will know when it's time to act. The yes to your subtle tap will bring you an abundance of astonishing gratification.

When you make a commitment to your calling it allows the abundant energy of Life to source you as its delivery vehicle. *Does your commitment afford you freedom and clarity where ambiguity once kept you incapacitated? Or does the fear of that commitment leave you wondering if what comes along next might be better?* Saying yes to your dharma will help you to eliminate self-doubt. Trust your inspiration more than your frustration. Little wins on your path become signs and confirmations that exponentially increase your abundant energy flow. All the good that energy flow brings with it allows you to connect with your Life Force, becoming the nexus from which your actions emerge. You must trust that something inside of you has a greater vision for your life. As you open to that trust and listen to the 'you' who sees your life as the observer, time will vanish as a deeper listening and feeling fuses with your expression. The funny thing is the more you act upon your intuitive tugs the more you'll come to trust them. Like most things, the more you practice the better you'll become. That said, when your mother said, "practice makes perfect" as you pained over the piano keys she knew what she was talking about. When you have a gift and you put time into honing that gift, what you deliver is out-of-this-world.

Gratitude

Gratitude is a quality of Love. What you appreciate appreciates and to the mystic, every day is thanksgiving. Gratitude deepens your delight with life and sweetens everything you receive through it. There's no doubt it's easy to feel gratitude when the gifts of life are flowing and the circumstances are bright, but when there's tightness and constriction, it's quite a bit more challenging. The irony is the most perfect time for the multiplying factor of gratitude to be called into action is when it's hardest to find anchors for that thanksgiving. Looking for the good in difficult times is not always easy. Indeed, you might have to dig deeper than usual, but I'm certain you'll find it and when you do, praise it, over and over.

Gratitude is the alchemy that can turn anything into a gift. It and it alone can lift your focus to the mountaintop allowing you to shift from difficulty to understanding. This appreciative inquiry allows you to transfer your focus from what's not working to dwelling in a sense of fulfillment from what is present now. Take away your daily doses of thanksgiving and life quickly shrivels up from a lack of vitality. Things that were once awe-inspiring like your home, travel, friends, health, freedom, fresh air and water when taken as entitlements will quickly lose their charm. When you fail to notice the gifts in your life those gifts will stop appearing. *No one enjoys giving to an unappreciative person with a sense of entitlement, do they?*

Do you pause to say grace before meals giving thanks for what you are about to partake? Or do you consume mindlessly without a moment of appreciation? Go back and review the mindful eating meditation in chapter three. Thanksgiving is a recognition and acknowledgment of the spiritual source and activity of all. It allows your eyes to see some form of beauty and your supply before the fullness of its creation. Give up the concept that your wellspring of good is being withheld from you, because all has already been given. The mountaintop view allows you to see what you want to align with and the path to get you there. Gratitude is what cleans the lens for your greater vision. The very substance of life is always ever available.

Gratitude is a generative energy that acknowledges your connectedness to the generosity of Life. Do you remember your parents teaching you about the obligation of saying thank you? Think for a moment about the kind of gratitude that leaves you feeling some kind of debt, as if this form of gratitude carries the burden of having a pay back. True gratitude comes from a sense of wonder and astonishment. Gratitude moves you away from the chase for more and appreciates what you have right where you are now. Your interaction is not with fear or obligation but with enjoyment and a conscious mountaintop experience of bountiful resources is already available to your creative expanding awareness.

Praise is the language of Life that wakes you up to the magical gifts that are now all around you. To live life praising will have you dancing in a vibrational match with the good of the cosmos. It's a conscious act that keeps you in a state of thanksgiving. Look at the blessings around you and praise them. That praise will awaken activation in your awareness of the field of grace. You praise it and you'll raise it!

Giving

Everything rises out of the formless coming from the void, returning to the nothingness it originated from. The challenge lies in your belief system training you to think joy and abundance comes of getting the goodies and being the collector, when in truth you are here for Life to pour forth its blessings to the world through you. It's not about ownership because you don't need to own the goods to enjoy them. It's you that's the distribution point for good to flow. It's not about being a receiver but rather a giver. Give it a whirl and watch as your personal life is blessed beyond measure. You're a finely tuned instrument through which grace flows but all of your gifts must be utilized for that grace to flow and live in thanksgiving. What you hold back becomes a block to your abundance.

Generosity is an expression of love. True giving has no strings attached or expectation of getting anything back as the overflow from the heart has no obligations. The generous that walk among us find a great deal of pleasure in sharing their gifts. They find it's regenerative and doesn't flow with the concern of running out, there's just too much joy in the giving. There's also an amazing expansion of time and satisfaction that comes of giving in this truly unconditional way. You come to experience that you aren't diminished in the giving but expanded in all ways. The more you spread the blessing the more blessed you are. There's no bartering in giving. That would be akin to deal-making like, I give you this and you give me that. You give purely because it feels good. Your contribution expresses what is near to your heart and soul. You're a channel through which the Inexhaustible Blessings flow. Say goodbye to the consumptive consumer compelled by cravings of lack because you'll be coming from an abundant flow.

You just become more alive when you give to the things you care about. I'm not talking only of giving money, here. I'm talking about your time, talents, your heart and soul, love, knowledge, attention, and compassion. What you support is a clear statement of what you value in your life. If you want to know what's important to you or anyone, take a look at the checkbook register or credit card statements and you'll discover where your dollars go is where your value lies.

When you move on from this world you'll be remembered not for what you accumulated but for what you gave. And, if you haven't always practiced this mindset, no worries. It just doesn't matter what happened to you in the past, it's what you are giving to the present moment that matters. You can live an abundant life not because you are a chosen one, but because you have chosen to put yourself into the affluent flow of Life. It's great to be the cause of the ever expanding wealth of your life. Of coursefor this to happen, you must move from thought to action. What good is it to have a nice car in the garage and never take it out for a spin? How does it help you and others to know about the prospering power of circulation and not participate in the sharing?

You have to dig the well before you can drink water from it. The meal must be prepared before it can be eaten and enjoyed. Too many people come from the opposite way; they'll give after they assess the value they received. They've forgotten how richly blessed they already are. You'll be pulled down a slippery slope if you look for reasons not to give. If you take this commonly mistaken approach to giving, the law of attraction tightens and restricts the flow of good for you so you have validation to *not* be in the flow. Not just in monetary ways but in all ways and in every area of your life.

When experiencing a recession in your world, it's crucial to your abundant well-being to start giving more to all areas of your life. Find what brings you joy and reminds you of your spiritual connection to Life. You know what inspires and uplifts you to want to make a difference; give there and give there generously. Giving back returns you into the current immediately. But you mustn't do it with a neediness and deal-making expectation for return. And you mustn't do it just because I'm telling you it will work to bring more currency into your life, because then you'll have an underlying expectation rather than an unconditional giving-ness.

Let your giving-ness be an extension of your consciousness because you come from appreciation. Is it more blessed to give than to receive? What's more important, your right or your left hand? They are both equally important for the whole expression of You. They are both valuable and necessary just as both the acts of giving and receiving are necessary. Be the activity Life is abundantly having through you with no strings attached and watch all the relevant areas of your life be blessed because you are modeling the blessing you wish to see.

Just a Reflection

Life's like the reflection of a glassy mountain lake. It reflects all things, yet remains bright and shiny, unaffected by whatever beautiful or appalling images which may appear upon it. You can get so caught up in the remarkable images playing out that it's easy to forget what you are seeing is just life mirroring back what's in front of it.

You must embrace that making a living is not about

proving what you deserve is as a result of how hard you work. If you hold that to be true, your life will reflect only opportunities to work hard. It's never been about how many hours you can put into a day to accomplish everything. *Does it make sense to experience burn-out as evidence of how deserving you are?* Do you feel entitled to how much you earn purely by how tired it leaves you? Let your ideas and dollars work hard for you. You'll never find freedom in billable hours. You must discover how you can be more valuable in the market place. This is not always as easy and quick as it sounds. In the preparation comes the unparalleled value you will bring to the outcome.

Here's a paradigm shift for you. Is your job making you poor? Do the things you own own you? *Are your thoughts or habits making you poor?* You must move from your attachment to loving things to appreciating them, enjoying them, sharing them but not allowing yourself to be possessed by them. The love of anything over your mystical connection with Life is the surest route to a rough lesson in detachment. See all the good in your world not as something you possess, rather, see that it flows through your life. You have infinite accessibility to all that Is!

One of the biggest challenges you'll face is the lure to settle for less than what you are entitled. There are untold stories of people who've sold out. For the love of money, they became someone they didn't like anymore, enslaved by their responsibilities, and overtaxed by obligation of running a business, managing employees or just funding the family budget. Money won't save you from the anguish of these kinds of soul compromises. Allow your relationship with abundance to be one of exhilarating opportunities rather than fear based on loss.

You either realize freedom or constriction in your life. Your life regularly demonstrates one or the other. It's the reflection of your consciousness, just like the mountain lake's reflection of the sky and clouds that pass over it. The proof in the pudding is in the taste. Multitudes of people are running around espousing all of the new age clichés in defense of their stuck-ness. Whether it's all good, I must have done something horrible in my past life, or it's in my DNA there's a void of self-introspection and it's all just rhetoric without heart. They don't know how to manifest freedom so they justify their unhappiness with phony spiritualizing of their issues. It's all just a delusion that creates even greater separation from the Infinite Source, while the physical experience remains unhappiness. Get to the mountaintop for a greater view so you can see how it can play out for your greater good and happiness. In this life, there are no rules that say you must be miserable or struggle for your art.

When you know the abundant feeling of freedom, it becomes something you wish for everyone you love. The path to freedom begins with self-awareness. Honestly, don't you just feel better when you have a sense of clarity? But, just because you become aware of a poor habit doesn't mean you choose to quit it right then and there. An addict may hate themselves every time they partake, swearing it's the last time they'll do it as they indulge. But if that part of you who's witnessing the behavior is allowed to be heard there can be a cumulative effect resulting in the release of the poor habit without self-inflicted mental abuse.

Your addiction to superstitions has power over you and your belief that there isn't enough is a lie. All of it feeds into a place inside you that has you playing musical chairs not wanting to be the one left without a place to sit. The more-is-better philosophy of life will make you fat and lethargic. Your distorted perspective will keep you in the human game of struggle and playing into the hands of the ones you think are your source for good. You might blame and complain but you won't question and that's where the error of your ways begins. The power returns when your curiosity does. Blessed are those who are curious for they shall live an exciting life. Maybe you grumble a bit but stay put and miserable. Perhaps you are feeling stuck and unhappy but rarely move past it. Knowing your Source is not reliant on people, places or things but avenues through which the Infinite Source pours into your life alleviates so much tension if one channel dries up. When Source is present, so are incalculable streams of good seeking to move through your world.

Abundance isn't an amount. It's a state of being. In your pursuit for more, you miss the richness and completeness that's already anticipating discovery within you now. It's a frame of mind to live from. Abundance is a declaration and a knowingness that there is always enough. It's living inside of you just waiting to be called forth. Your struggle has nothing to do with the amount of money you have. No, rather your struggle is all about your relationship with the Infinite flow.

My dog Sage loved to chase rabbits. He couldn't wait for morning to arrive so he could go on the hunt for those furry little cotton-tailed critters. He never caught one in his life nor did he even come close, but those facts never denied him the extreme pleasure he derived from the chase. His muscles would start twitching with excitement the moment we'd approach the door in the morning. Once outside, he'd run alongside the road sniffing the air in search of a scent to catch. There was no doubt when he caught a scent because he was off with an explosive surge of focused energy. In that moment, there was nothing else in his world. He was alive, on purpose expressing an abundance of energy that came from the depths of his dog being. There was a total alignment with his passion and actions as expressed through his effortless pursuit in his fine-tuned hunt. Sage returned empty-joweled every time, but he was always full of joy and panting with excitement. He'd head home, devour his breakfast like there was no tomorrow, drink his water with the same gusto and then stretch out in the sun for a morning nap with the same kind of abandonment and commitment to his closed-eye adventure as he'd had with his bunny hunt.

The more you feel the more alive you are. When you play in any mode but full out, the flow trickles and eventually shuts down entirely. When you make an authentic commitment your purposeful position picks up momentum and opens the channel making you a conduit for the unrestricted supply of energy. Abundance thrives on flow. Too much decorum for how your good is supposed to show will rob you of the joy as to how it actually shows up.

Tree Meditation

When leaving the body behind, it's always a good idea to know how blessed you are in this field of grace in which you play. Before meditation, take a moment to state:

I know all is well and wherever I go in my expanding awareness, all is good and I am safe. I'm surrounded by and live in an Omni Dimensional Life Force that can never be violated, because there is nothing opposed to it. I move on the very currents of Life Itself and I'm free to notice all things without attachment to anything. Free to move beyond any image at any time and courageous enough to remain in it. I open to a graceful guidance on my soul's adventure, surrender my demands to logical understandings, and welcome new and unknown states of consciousness for my soul's evolution.

Take a few breaths to bring your attention back to the center of your body. Find a natural rhythm for your breath to fall into. See if you can follow your in-breath into your body . . . Exhale. Take with it any tension, worries, or concerns while creating more internal room. Find a natural rhythm to your breathing and following your next breath, let it take you deeper into the space beyond your body temple, where past and future dissolve into the present. Your inner awareness becomes the threshold you move across, where now your exhale *propels* you further into the openness of the void. Allow yourself to become available and receptive to a deep hearing and heightened awareness to move you to greater good.

Notice you are in a vast expanse with infinite points of light as if you are in a galaxy of stars . . . Allow your awareness to be drawn to a beautiful blue orb that is calling you home . . .

feel an attraction and relational remembrance to the vibrancy of this world. You move in closer and when you do, you see the pristine snowcapped mountains, the wooded forests, the lush green jungles, the expansive deserts, deep canyons, still lakes, running rivers, and the all-embracing blue ocean . . . Your soul is deeply moved by the physical beauty. As your awareness of the magnificence of this place is heightened, you feel the call of this earth for the gift you have to bring. You return to your perfect mountaintop . . .

As you gaze out to the north your awareness is drawn to the snowcapped mountain peaks. In the strength of the north winds there is the wisdom of the ages bringing a feeling and calm which comes from having seen it all. This stillness is filled with a gratitude for timeless knowledge. There is an awakening of intellectual illumination from the furthest reaches of your memory. You are called to journey to the north, so pick a path and lucidly head to the call of the wild . . . As you maneuver through the tree line in your ascent you come to the base of the largest tree you've ever seen. It's the size of a two lane road. You just stand there and marvel at its magnificence, the abundance in its towering size, and what it must have seen throughout the millenniums as it stood in this place patiently watching humanity evolve . . .

As you begin to explore the tree you find a crevice in the bark, and as you look into it you notice a stairway that you decide to investigate further . . . As you climb you enter the behemoth's memory of nature and its passage of time inspiring your own personal reflection. You feel its memory of a fire it once survived, reminding you of the fiery times in your life and your experience coming through stronger and wiser for them . . . you can feel the time the tree lived through lush seasons with abundant rainfall and nourishment that blessed its existence reminding you of your prospering times . . . you pass through the memory of the tree's seasons of drought reawakening in you the memory of how you came through dry times like those . . . Ascending higher, you see where the tree has been attacked by petty pests and small insects who left their scars but did not bring the mighty tree down, reminding you of the nuisances that didn't stop you from what you had to deal with through the years . . . As you move higher you sense the seasons of snow and cold that this tree has endured and you are reminded of the dark night of the soul you survived.

Climbing ever higher you see branches broken by gale force winds but this tree responded by becoming stronger in its dance with nature. What gale force winds have hit your life making you stronger? . . . higher you go, knowing you are towering above all of life feeling indestructible. You come upon where the tree was struck by lightning for being the biggest expression around, and in that you realize it's humbling to know there is always something greater . . . tree's history, like yours, is left behind. It melts like an ice cube on a hot summer sidewalk. The misperceptions you once lived with of your self-worth, your value, and the gifts you had to share dissolve into their proper place in your history. Allow innate benevolence . . . and integrate it into the lumber of your life. You are no longer controlled by past limiting beliefs living in the cemetery of memories. You are lifted ever higher by your life experience up until this moment. It has all been perfect for your soul's growth. You are free in the present moment to step onto an elevator that takes you to the top branches as you no longer need the comfort of the stories from the past to be who you are now. Rest now, under the expansive blue sky and reflect . . . Perched high above the history of this giant you glean the mystical lesson that all the narrative of its past is perfectly integrated into what it is and what makes up its strengths in the now. What is now felt is its joy for all it has seen and been part of . . . Beyond the description of the word tree, is the joy that came from those who've climbed its branches and have come to know through experience what this expression of Life really is. Who you are is beyond the roles you play in your family, what your title is, and what you do for a living? Surrender to the uplifting energy that comes from embracing and accepting all you've gone through. It's all a part of who you are but not all of who you are . . .

It's time to find your voice and speak your truth. The throat chakra can bridge the ethereal realm of thought with the physical world. Vibrations are the connectors of the subtler realm to this world. Those same vibrations are the bridge between your inner and outer self. Where have you had difficulty speaking your mind? In what instances do you find yourself tongue-tied and unable to project your voice? What emotional blocks keep you from claiming your power and speaking out? Are you willing to allow these blocks to melt away? Or, are you a people pleaser running your words through filters to assuage others? Where does this make it difficult for you to tell the truth or even hear the truth? Just as your neck bridges your torso and head, your throat is the expressing center that bridges the upper occult realms with lower vibrational world of form.

For the power of the mystical to be expressed, you must clear out the blockages . . . roar like a lion from this tree's top branches and let the world know you're back with a message to deliver . . . Ro-arrrrr. With a sense of knowing your experiences have made you stronger and more powerful in your spirit's expression on this earth. Roar knowing that you'll be courageously telling your truth wherever you are and that you're the conduit through which Life is expressing. Ro-arrrrr. Give one last roar allowing the vibration to lift you from this tree top placing you back down gently in your sacred circle on the mountaintop . . . Ro-arrrrr. Pause to reflect and integrate what you just learned from your mountaintop view.

It's time to return to your world of activity refreshed and renewed. Know once you've been somewhere you can easily return to that place by simply calling it back to your awareness. There's always more work to be done, but for now, pull yourself back into your body permitting gratitude for your discoveries to fill your field of awareness . . . Feel a joy knowing you'll be consistently returning to your sacred space, but for now, choose a path down the mountain.

Familiarize yourself with this trail back into the world of form. Know there is always this corridor, this passage back to the elevated perspective of your world. Touch some of the trees as you pass by them and feel the earth move beneath your feet. As what you saw in a distance comes more into focus return your attention to your breath. Breathe . . . When you are ready, slowly move your fingers and toes, stretch, gently open your eyes and sit for a moment to re-acclimate to your physical world. Take your pen and take some time to write out your experience. It doesn't matter if it was memorable and you are certain you'll never forget it, you should still capture it on paper – later, you'll be glad you did.

Soulful Adventures

- Energy flows where attention goes and form shows. Notice whatever you focus on becomes more real for you. When you are not paying attention you are missing signals from your life. Write out what signals your life is sending you and what their energetic vibration means to you.
  - What does your abundance feel and look like?
  - What does an abundant Universe feel and look like?
  - Put your attentions on these qualities and let them fill your field of awareness.
- Are you a conscious consumer? Do you know the statements you make with your spending? Do you support environmentally safe products or does the toxicity of the soap you send into the water not matter to you? Do your products come from the exploitation of cheap labor? Do you even care enough to ask or know? What kind of food products and production do you support with your spending? Do you invest only

for profit or also to support what you believe in?

- Take the time to investigate how the products and textiles you use come to you.
- Be aware of how your foods are processed, raised and grown.
- Where can you shift your spending practices to be more in alignment with your beliefs of the heart – or is that just too much effort? Remember, the mystical is merging your actions with your heart's beliefs, and there is no separation.

- How are your wants keeping you in lack? Where are you being a cheapskate?
- What is your calling, your dharma, your soul's purpose? When and where did the light come on for you or has it yet? When did you realize you knew what your purpose in this world was? Are you following it? How could you come into greater alignment for it to express through you in a stronger way?
- What did you love to do when you were little that gives you a glimmer of what you'd love to be doing now? What do you really want to do with your life that'd make you happy to get out of bed every morning? What gifts do you have to bring to humanity? What skills would you like to develop to support that?
- Take at least 10 minutes to write an inventory of all the gifts in your life. Include family, friends, home, health, freedom, vocation, special moments that warm your memory, an illness or accident that woke you up, chance meetings, a stranger's smile, laughter . . . Good, now go a little deeper and take another ten minutes and notice the gifts that came from the challenges in your life.
  - Write a thank you note to an obvious

blessing.

- Write a thank you note to a challenge that brought a hidden blessing.
- Make a call to someone on your list and express your appreciation.
- Spend the rest of this day consciously blessing everything you see. When you lay your head to rest this evening bask in the blessing of gratitude.

- Where do you find your spirit gets fed? What inspires you and makes you come alive. Where are you reminded the most of the Infinite Life Source? Where do you get the most connected with Life?

- Do you feel it is the responsibility of the affluent to support and help perpetuate parts of the culture they value? What sources you? How can you give more there?

- Do an expenditure evaluation by looking at your checkbook register, credit card and bank statements along with your cash purchases and ask yourself if it really reflects your spirit's values. What clear picture are you leaving the world as a statement of what's important to you, what you care most about and who you are? What do you really want to use your money for?

Body and Soul Practice for Connecting

Body Connection to Open Your Throat Center

Do some gargling with salt water. Try some singing, or even screaming.

Speak your truth where you've been holding back. Roar like a lion.

Relax in the yoga posture called camel pose. If you are unfamiliar with it, sit on your knees and lean all the way back allowing the palms of our hand to rest on your heels opening your chest and throat to the sky.

Soul Connection

Chant or hum and feel the vibration of that noise and feeling in your throat. Then move the vibration down into your torso; then, when you are ready, move it back up through your forehead and out the crown of your head. Feel the flow moving up and down your body, after a while of practicing this exercise, sense it as just one vibrating pulse. Notice how your inner thoughts move out through the vibrational waves and observe what thoughts travel into your field of awareness.

Mystical Writing

Everything you see has its roots in the unseen world.
The forms may change yet the essence remains the same.
Every wondrous sight will vanish; every sweet word will fade,
But do not be disheartened, the Source they come from is Eternal,
Growing, branching out, giving new life and new joy.
Why do you weep? The Source is within you
And this whole world is springing up from it.
The Source is full, Its waters are ever-flowing;
Do not grieve, drink your fill!
Don't think it will ever run dry, this is the endless Ocean.

Jalal ad-Dīn Muhammad Rumi
1207 – 1273

Chapter 7: As Far As the Soul Can See

Miracles happen, not in opposition to nature, but in opposition to what we know of nature.
~ St. Augustine

Try Levitation

Magnetic levitation trains are here and floating above the ground for you to ride. If you ever played with magnets you already know while one side attracts the other repels. This is the principle behind electromagnetic propulsion. Regular trains use fossil fuel in a big engine to pull typical cars along a steel track battling resistance and creating horrible pollution on the planet. Alternatively, maglev trains use the magnetic field in the guide-way walls to propel the train. The magnetized guide-way repels the large magnets of the train's undercarriage allowing the train to levitate above the guide-way. Maglev trains actually float on a cushion of air eliminating friction altogether. This lack of friction and the train's aerodynamic design allows these trains to travel in excess of 300 mph.

With a lack of friction, you too can fly through life at the speed of thought as you rise above a fixed idea. For instance, in this case, combustible engines aren't necessary for propulsion. In the new space above what you believed, there are new possibilities to be seen. You don't have to know what you're looking for, you just have to release the lower vibrations to then naturally begin to rise. When you stop thinking about what isn't possible, you begin to see what is possible and with that, you'll feel infinitely more choices for your exploration.

When you're no longer bound to the earth by what you see, feel or think, you'll lift above your current perceptions and emotions. Hear the call to a greater sense of freedom and you'll find a greater space emerging between what was and what can be your new reality.

Sometimes you don't even realize when an old reality is impeding the emergence of the new one. When I first received my private pilot's license I was so excited to take my wife for a romantic dinner in Big Bear California. We flew from our coastal home, had a scrumptious dinner at Madlon's and headed home while watching a spectacular sun as it set into the ocean from above. As that sun went down, everything got dark inside the plane, and I mean everything! I turned the lights on the instruments and nothing seemed to be getting brighter. I could no longer read the instrument panels and I was beginning to feel my internal energy rise. As it got dark outside, it got even darker inside, both literally and figuratively as my palms began to sweat and I contemplated whether or not I should tell Kalli that we had a serious issue. As the final minutes of the sunshine disappeared, I turned to let her know we were in trouble and saw she seemed to be experiencing the same thing. At that moment of recognition we both burst out laughing. We were still wearing our sunglasses. *Where are you still wearing your sunglasses?* Sunglasses relieve the strain on the eyes in bright light, but when you wear them in the dark they impede your ability see from the elevated perspective.

As you let go of the attachment to your identity, you will quite literally float out of the realm you've been operating in. A lightness will take hold of you as your sense of self dissolves and you merge into the One. Granted, tell someone a little less conscious about this experiment and you might find yourself branded a heretic or labeled unpatriotic from the political arena. Belittling comments targeted at those who think outside the preferred opinion of the day are actually a good sign. They mean you're pushing the envelope. So rather than inspiring a dynamic, thought-provoking and explorative conversation bound to lift everyone in the room beyond the present vista, expanding what's possible, your character and motivation will get called into question and you'll get judged.

If you are one who has a deep knowing, you shouldn't care if people say you're crazy. In fact, embrace it! It will further distinguish you from the herd. Mark Twain was known for saying, "Keep away from people who try to belittle your ambitions. Small people always do that, but the really great make you feel that you, too, can become great."

You'll witness many mutually agreed-upon perspectives left behind in your rear view mirror when your intuition lifts you higher. It's almost as if you're deprogramming your operational belief systems for a greater knowing. When the expanded awareness is renewed, the new view of the possible becomes the renovated observation deck for your visionary life to manifest. You are not your little concerns; you are an evolving spiritual expression of Life Itself.

Embracing the Difficulty

So many people on this planet seem more concerned with changing the condition of what's around them rather than nurturing the spiritual truth of their own being. The substance of form is the mind made visible. That said, sometimes illness or a particular challenge is part of a person's destiny and not a consequence of ill thinking. *Who are you to know what someone else's path has in store for them? How do you know what is for their highest and best good?* Other people's commotion is part of their story and their path. Let them have it and don't become a victim to their drama.

Oftentimes when difficulties arise, the first reaction is to fight it, hate it, numb it and do whatever battle is necessary to keep the unpleasant conditions at bay. But, there's also the option of embracing it as a gift from Life. I know it's a stretch when you've spent your whole life blocking out what got in the way of your version of happiness. This gift of an obstacle just might be your soul lesson awaiting you in this very condition showing you your new calling. Even if science discovers cures for every human ailment, it still can't and won't heal the spirit. I'm all for getting rid of physical pain but, the disruption the pain creates will still find its way back into your life as an opportunity for growth. You're here to live in joy. When you live your purpose your dis-ease will help you stretch to get back home to wholeness.

Your wholeness has been the truth from the beginning. Two plus two is always going to equal four; it has been from before the beginning and will be forever more. From the day you incarnated into who you are now, your wholeness has always been there as a choice of yours.

Yes, just as proper use of math is an option, so is yours to always be whole. But, and it's a big *but* followed by an even bigger *if*, it only becomes your reality and has meaning in relation to its application in your life if you use it. Your well-being may be masked or forgotten but, it's still here for you now. And by the way, you don't make anything happen; the answers to your prayers are complete when you can align with the truth of who you already are.

Lifting above typical and acceptable means and time frames for healing requires you to surrender your need for an explanation as to how the healing is to happen. Living life from a higher frequency means unfoldment doesn't have to operate through your rational ways of understanding. Sometimes you just have to follow the irrational side of logic. Your spirit is so much more incredibly powerful in its ability to heal than the knowledge of science ever was or will be. Yet the governing bodies in the medical world will defend their hierarchical position to the death. The western approach to medicine has brought great benefits to the healing process but defends itself by doing everything in its power to eliminate any viable alternative approaches.

Where a holistic approach may present many different options, competition for the market of healing by standard approach is compromised and thus must be neutralized by those in the readily accepted sciences. Most medical doctors enter into the healing profession impassioned by a desire in their hearts to make a difference. Yet, after years of practice, it's not unusual to hear conversation of discouragement from them about the abusive system they're required to operate within to keep their license.

A Conscious Union with Life

Your higher life force can enter into the healing equation to re-pattern the whole physical being at any time. Can a body, which is beyond apparent physical recovery in the perspective of today's medical world, really experience a sudden turnaround and be perfectly whole once again? The case studies of miraculous healings are many.

Anita Moorjani's well documented case in her book titled; *"Dying to Be Me"* described her body as riddled with cancer. She was exhausted from fighting the disease for four years and her body began to shut down, overwhelmed by malignant cells spreading throughout her system. She slipped into a coma as her organs failed one at a time and, at one point, even flat-lined. Pulled away into a bigger picture, and away from her attachment to her body and life, Moorjani's tumors began to shrink at a remarkable pace. Within weeks she was cancer-free, and walking away from the hospital where her deep lacerations healed and organs began working again right in front of the amazed medical staff. She said, "I personally don't feel the need to pray to an external God that's separate from me, because I know that I'm always one with the Universe, 100 percent of the time." Healing comes from a vibration higher than the manipulation of the physical laws we know. I am a true believer having witnessed it time and time again.

Apollo 14 astronaut, Edgar Mitchell said, "It's just our ignorance that causes it to seem supernatural." The shape-shifting of vibrational healing, when you move from sick to well, is the energetic fluidity taking on a new mold. A mystic is not necessarily a healer; they just have a conscious union with Life Itself. In that accepted and realized oneness they are

100 percent connected with the Universe. When you live from the mountaintop perspective and an inner connection to the Universe, things of this world are no longer as attractive as they once were. This direct inner communication is far more powerful with its imagery than words could ever be. These images that implant themselves in your field of awareness allow you to see beyond intellectual blindness thus lifting you out of any previously held cultural indoctrination. This is where healing happens. Yes, healing occurs beyond the normal pathology.

It's easy to get pulled down into the argument of the world's positions taking one side or the other. As an example, both the political left and the right fight over how to spend taxes or which direction interest rates should move, but no one questions how the whole monetary system is set up. It's just one of those generally accepted operating systems that isn't ever explored in this culture. You must lift above the paradigm of the conflict of opposites if you want to experience a healing. From your vantage point atop the mountain, you suddenly recognize how small the battle below is compared to the whole picture laying itself spread out before you.

Another illustration of this is the belief that your body has been programmed from birth and your heredity is what determines your physiological outcome. Doctors may debate whether to use one medical approach over another, but few will talk about the life which animates the body itself. *How can the life that animates you be activated so your own internal healing system creates a "supernatural "outcome?* When you rise above the normal and accepted operating beliefs that the rest of the world seems to follow, the mountaintops' perspective will give you visual impressions beyond the closed- minded norm. These images of wholeness are always looking for an open door. When you find them, they'll lift you higher enabling you to see expanded images of possibilities that aren't even a part of the cultural conversation.

The choice is always yours. Do you hold on to old illusory ideas and convictions in an attempt to feel secure in the known? Or, do you allow yourself to be lifted above those outdated restricted notions? Most don't experience reality as it is. Instead they experience their belief about reality. It's once removed from the real reality. The invitation of new images, which paradoxically were there from the beginning, has always been available for your application.

Your body was created as a magnificent channel through which "Heaven could be brought to Earth" by transmuting the Absolute into form. The controlling mind doesn't appreciate perceptions beyond its control and will systematically shut down access to beyond. You hear constricting phrases like, you can't do that, you've got to be responsible, it doesn't make sense, what will the neighbors think, and you respond with fear and paralysis. And in doing so, you stay with what is. But, if you listen deeply you'll hear a voice within that's no longer comfortable being comfortable with the little self's control. It's the observer of your life telling you there are other life-affirming options beyond what you perceive as discomfort.

A Grandmother's Love

When I was a kid my Grandmother would often come over for dinner. One evening when I was about twelve, a cranky version of Grandma sat uncomfortably in our living room. Challenged with chronic back pain the medical world told her could only be alleviated by surgery, Grandma had grown frustrated. Even after seeing multitudes of chiropractors and osteopaths her discomfort was still barely reduced. This particular evening my mom asked me to put my hand on my grandmother's back while reading a prayer she handed me. I really didn't know what she was talking about or what effect it would have, but I was quite aware if my mom told me to do something I'd better do it and with some speed. So I did exactly what she asked and promptly ran out the front door to play. The next time my Grandma came to dinner, she handed me a buck and thanked me for the healing. I turned to her and said, "That's great Grandma, got anything else you want me to heal?"

My mom was quick to call me over, and I was certain it was to split the money with her, but I was way off base. She wanted me to know, and in no uncertain terms, that I didn't heal a thing. That day she explained to me that there's a Life Force moving through us all and It is what does the healing. I could be a channel for it, and I could be paid for my time but it was imperative that I know that I wasn't the one who did the healing. Later in life I realized it was the love of a Grandmother not wanting to disappoint her grandchild that opened her up to something the medical world denies. Doctors would later shake their heads in disbelief as they couldn't digest the concept that a 12-year-old was usurping their game; or bigger yet, that a spirit within a body could regenerate that body without medical intervention.

Since then, I've seen bones fuse instantaneously while onlookers with wide eyes watched as I prayed over their teacher who'd fallen down a flight of stairs. I can remember in the early days of AIDS meeting with friends who, when they were first diagnosed with the HIV virus, were met only by masked medical professionals. HIV, which was once considered a death sentence, is now considered a chronic disease and in some cases, people having been diagnosed with it are fully healed. Stories of tumors disappearing are frequent occurrences and instances like my mom who needed insulin injections for years reaching a point when they were no longer necessary have become commonplace. I've even read accounts of individuals with split personalities whose eye color changes, along with other physiological conditions, based on what personality is controlling the physical vehicle.

Great examples of those who are able to lift beyond the physical perception are shamans, elders, medicine women, men and wise ones of the indigenous people. Those of the first nation have always been more attuned to their internal guidance systems than we are in this day and age. When you lean into your intuition, you'll find your life is suddenly filled with serendipitous occurrences. That is because there, in your intuitive state, you are operating in the All Knowing field of grace where all is part of the Whole. You'll move beyond the sequential law of attraction and into the powers that jump the linear line of the standard operating systems, like synchronicity and quantum action.

In the state of being part of the Whole, you'll find yourself walking around with more compassion than anxiety. You'll connect more with Spirit than with the material realm. The push of pain diminishes being overly concerned with what others think. The punches this world throws at you will no longer connect with your form. Instead, like air guitar, those punches will find only vacant space as you've been lifted above the bother of all of that. The motivating energetics from where people speak will be so much clearer. You'll see with such a remarkable compassion and non-judgmental clarity that it will look and feel like a completely different existence. That's just the way it is from a lifted vision. It's not about attempting to see and working to feel this intuitive awareness; it just happens. It's a knowing over belief.

The Excavation Site of Pain

Where you're out of balance, the places where you feel dis-ease or experience pain become the excavation sites to a greater discovery of wisdom and personal revelation in your life. A well-lived life doesn't avoid conflict but awakens a new kind of insight that will change the trajectory of your unfoldment. Take back the power you've given away to blame, discouragement and rehashing old wounds in an attempt to figure out the discomfort. Your crisis is a summons for a higher realization. *How big does a crisis need to be before it grabs your attention?* Is global warming/climate change big enough for you to realize we must live in balance with the earth? There are answers that are available for our planet right now, but if no one believes there is a crisis then there will be no call to action. When people are in too much pain, they don't have the energy to direct any issue outside of their own discomfort. Or, when they are too comfortable, the why-bothers kick in and the resulting complacency supports nothing.

How many cities need to be submerged before we believe the polar ice caps are melting? How many mammals like polar bears, tigers and elephants need to meet extinction before we pay attention since we're not noticing amphibians, birds and insects that are simply disappearing from our planet? Are you aware of how few bumble bees and monarch butterflies are left to pollinate our food, flowers and future? Einstein said, "If the bee disappeared off the surface of the globe then man would only have four years of life left. No more bees, no more pollination, no more plants, no more animals, no more man." *What does it take to lift above the crisis high enough to see the gifts and the potential for healing our planet?* Your consciousness must lift above the smog-covered drama to hear the insights of the observer. Once again, your witness will open access to the Infinite, seeing possibilities that are beyond the conflict of opposites.

When you rest in your wholeness you'll recognize the wholeness in others. The healing journey from any health challenge is a homecoming when the body returns back to being a balanced system. The Huna philosophy professes healing happens when there is a restoration of wholeness or recovery of the uninhibited flow of your energy system as it was meant to be. We also mustn't forget mental health and how integral it is in a state of whole body health. Balanced mental states create a balanced mind and body. Out-of-balanced states of mind fuel grief and anguish, among other low vibration energies. It's helpful to check in on where your thoughts are on a daily basis. *Which thoughts do you want to keep and which ones are out of balance with your higher self?* No doubt, you regularly check in on your finances so they stay in balance and healthy. Why wouldn't you dedicate at least that amount of mindful time to your inner kingdom? When you're unaware of your inner state of mind, the outer state can seem to be the governor of your affairs.

I've got beautiful peach, plum, pear, apple, and apricot trees in my garden. I feel so blessed by them in so many ways, not the least of which is by what they've all taught me. I've learned that I'm welcome to eat the green or rotten fruit if I want to pay the price of a sour stomach, but why choose the ones that make me sick when I have full opportunity to eat the delicious ones? The tree doesn't care, but my experience comes as a result of the choices I make. I can point at the rotten fruit and blame it for my stomach ailment, but it still comes down to me having made the choice and hence having the natural consequence as a result. Your life, like mine, is the outcropping (sorry for the pun) of the mental pictures you entertain. Why are you choosing the rotten fruit when you can mystically align at any time with the ripe, naturally delicious fruit? You mustn't forget for a minute that it's you that you determines whether or not you choose sweetness in your life.

Being the determining factor means you get to choose what you are aligning with and what fruit you're going to ingest. That's a huge responsibility that must be taken with great care. Meditation helps by quieting the external chaos so it doesn't interfere with the field of awareness in a detrimental way. Mindfulness gently allows you to connect with the stillness of your own inner being which doesn't know the pain of separateness because it is Whole. You'll come to know it's a waste of time to ask Life for anything, because nothing has been withheld. Everything you could ask for has already been given and has been since the beginning. Your health, wealth, or grace is not something you need to ask for, but rather something to come to know from within. It's in this realization there is healing. When you've seen it from the mountaintop - whether it's your health, wealth or answer to your relationship problems - you'll come to recognize it when it shows up in your life. It doesn't matter whether it's perfectly clear or disguised, you'll feel Spirit in the moment and know healing has taken place. It's entering into the vibrations of Oneness with the Wholeness that dissolves anything unlike Itself. And in that new frequency, the challenges and obstacles just fall away.

In truth, there's nothing that needs to be healed in life even when it feels awful, but in order to embrace that, your experience of wholeness or bliss must shift. It's in the silence where you witness all of the multifaceted expressions of life making sense at the soul level. What you might forget is that fighting disease actually perpetuates it. Battling disease prevents its cure. Praying for it to be gone means loving it enough for it to stay.

Acknowledging what you don't want rather than what you do is enough attention to continue to nurture it. When an issue in your life yearns for transformation, lift your gaze to the mountaintop and align with the wholeness of your being. Trust me; it's ever available no matter how horrendous the physical condition may be. Your regular meditation will have you witnessing self and in doing so will lift you out of the immediately painful experience but only when you're ready and receptive to the mountaintop view.

Time for a New Kind of Healing

If standard praying and asking for things from some archetypal source up in the heavens worked, wars would only be found in history books. For millenniums people have prayed fervently, beseeching with everything they have for their children to be well and safe. Has it worked to remove or even reduce the reasons people pray so intensely? Not really, but what continues to happen is a creation of bigger tools for dominance. Rocks gave way to spears, which gave way to bullets, grenades, bombs, lasers and finally atomic and nuclear weaponry. Something is not right with domination whether it's over nations, our physical bodies or even our planet. If anyone is paying attention, the 'my-stick-is-bigger-than-yours' approach isn't working. Killing is killing whether it's done cleanly or barbarically. It still creates horrendous pain that must be cleared up. It's time for a new kind of healing which will only come with a new kind of thought and response!

Maybe the Life Force, the Order and Intelligence that guides the universe, isn't reliant on you telling It what's needed. Healing is dependent on listening to a Greater Wisdom than what brought you the challenge in the first place. There's no solution to the problem only an experience of Wholeness. When physical and mental muscles interact with the spiritual, the laws of both matter and mind are neutralized. When this new dimension of awareness becomes yours, everything else loses its grip. It isn't a matter of a good power over a bad one, it's just that there is only One Power and there's nothing for It to overcome.

An attack, whether it's upon your body or a nation, is a cry for understanding. What's going on that its action has to be so violent to get your attention? You must surrender your way and what you think is best and become a place for a new thought to emerge. Remember the old saying, stop doing the same thing and expecting different results? Stop attempting to influence the Infinite with your limiting perspective. Get to your mountaintop when your observing-self points out this behavior. When there's a true invitation and opening beyond retaliation and pain, something new can and will happen. If you pray, let it not be for things. Rather, let it be only for your sense of oneness with the Whole of Life. It's in this mystical union all is known, revealed, healed and provided. You are the conduit for Its expression and It will forever pour Itself into visible manifestation through you. Just as if when you want sun, you go outside and allow it to pour over you. You bathe in what is. You don't make it happen. Open your third eye and see the light that is already shining upon you and has been available from the beginning.

It's compassion, not anger, that helps soothe human struggles. Fear and aggression are not the healers of hurt. They'll pull you down and strangle you, shutting down the healing that begs to flow. You must lift above this low density energy. When you see the mortal state properly, caring lifts you. There's no need to feel trepidation, instead, just clarify your misperceptions. One of the reasons people become stubborn about letting go of their misperceptions is because then they'll be left with having to face the truth.

Unresolved Soul Issues

Many cultures embrace a philosophy they call soul retrieval. Folklore tells of an only child and beloved daughter of a single dad. She was his everything. She matured into a beautiful young woman and when it was time for her to marry, all the most eligible suitors came around. Her father picked the most successful and handsome one and promised him his daughter's hand in marriage. But his daughter had already fallen in love with the childhood playmate she'd grown up alongside. They'd committed their spirits to one another, so when she found out what her father had done, she ran off. Her true love contemplated taking his own life when he found out she'd been committed to another groom, but instead decided he would run away, too. Their two hearts were so connected that they ran into each other in a field as they were both slipping out of town separately. Something inside their souls knew of the other's plan despite not really being consciously aware of it.

They ran off together and began a wonderful new life of a young fearless couple. They created a loving, peaceful home and had two beautiful children. But after several years, the young bride's life weighed heavy having left her father alone, so she asked her husband to go back with her. He agreed and they packed up their family and returned to the town of their birth. The young man went to his father-in-law's door and knocked and when he answered the door he shared with him what had transpired and asked for his forgiveness. He shared how he and his beloved had two children in the carriage waiting to meet their grandpa. The father turned ashen and explained how it was all impossible because his daughter laid despondent and brokenhearted in bed since the day her true love had left. Not true, insisted the young man. "Your daughter," he told him, "is in the carriage waiting to see if she'd be welcomed back by you." The father asked his servant to go check and soon he returned to report it was all true. The father went to his daughter who lay lifeless in bed and shared the story with her and as he finished, she got up and walked out the door. As the weakened half approached the path, she began running towards her other half who was just then getting out of the carriage. They met, and as the two came together they embraced and while they hugged, they merged and the two became one again. The healing was complete.

I love that story as it demonstrates how a trauma in life can really split your person from your spirit. You can't go through a major trauma and pretend nothing happened. You can't leave half of yourself behind in hopes of not having to deal with the pain. Cutting yourself into pieces only incapacitates you because you are no longer whole. Unresolved soul issues will come back for your attention and eventually you'll wake up from walking around in a daze and realize there's another part of you that was left behind. And truthfully, neither half is fully alive or happy.

This is why it's important to listen to your soul's urging to lift up to the mountaintop and check out the unhealed fragments that are still alive and calling for your attention. If they go unheeded, they can show up in your body or life nudging for your attention. Sometimes healing may not resemble getting physically better but instead gaining soul lessons and insights. Sometimes even death can be considered the answer to prayer and a perfect healing. *Can you get your perspective of how you wanted it out of the way for the true healing to unfold?* Neither of those outcomes are what the mind thinks it wants for resolution, yet it could just be the perfect healing for your soul's lesson this time around. When you accept your immortality and the fear of death is gone, your awareness isn't split rather, it's fully present for the wonderful gifts this moment brings.

Your emotions are a powerful force impacting your body. Pretending they're not there, repressing or denying them won't liberate you from their control. You are going to have to deal with them at some point and an invitation into your awareness is the way back to wholeness. The truth is, there's no power other than Wholeness and it takes your personal energy, which eventually depletes itself, in its attempt to keep the façade of separation going. You don't need to save yourself, or anyone else for that matter, because the Wholeness has no relationship with the human sense of separation that creates the physical impairment. What you must do is lift yourself out of the heaviness of the human condition to where you can say with conviction, "I have overcome this world."

When your awareness is focused on Wholeness, you'll find peace and calm in the midst of any storm. What's within you is greater than what is outside of you. Your aim is not to change anything in your body or world of affairs; it's to know the Truth of Wholeness so you can have the benefit of that Truth operating as you. Lean not on your own understanding. Do not allow your healing meditation to be about healing dis-ease or getting more goodies. Most seek healing in the physical, mental, financial or human realms. Rather, allow your connection with Source to be for the sole purpose of developing a conscious contact with Life Itself. Embrace the Wholeness of who you truly are and all that follows will be perfect for your journey through this frame of life. As your experience of Wholeness deepens, more and more healing experiences occur with a natural ease and grace.

When I first started riding horses I was at the whim of the horse to take me where it wanted to go. It was as if my controlling mind had an idea and was going to take me there.

As I gained the riding prowess I needed to direct the powerful steed, I was able to take charge and go where I wanted to go. I held the power despite being the smaller of the two of us. It didn't stop there though, because next came the magical moment when the horse and I became one. In that graceful time in space we fluidly listened to the same call and moved as one jumping over creeks and logs on our way up the mountain. Together we moved in the direction of something greater. There comes a time when you stop attempting to dominate the Power within your speaking mind and you start listening with your heart. *Can you relinquish your will, your opinion, and your conviction to accept grace?* Forget what you've been told about the prognosis and be lifted above the pair of opposites and you'll find the world of form no longer has power over you.

Forgiveness is the Grand Transformer of your spirit

It's been said, "Forgiveness is the fragrance the flower leaves on the heel of the one who crushed it." I don't need to think long and hard to share a story of forgiveness that's close to my heart. Recently, Kalli and I returned from a ski trip to find things askew in our home. The lights were on as we pulled into the driveway and the hair on the back of my neck stood at attention as I turned the key in the lock. Have you ever walked into a familiar space that felt disarmingly foreign in the moment you had to take a deep breath just to step inside? As I did, pieces of the picture in front of me came together like a Rubik's ™ cube.

I digested unfamiliar sights punctuated by holes in the staircase wall leading from upstairs all the way down to the entrance. As I flew up the steps two at a time, suddenly filled with adrenaline, the obvious trail of trouble led from our master bedroom- our closet to be specific- and I knew. Our home had been robbed. The thieves had taken our safe and rolled it down the steps in hopes of it bursting open on its own.

In the moments I pieced together the story that had taken place in our absence; I took stock of the feelings coursing through my body. I felt so violated. Not just for myself but for my beloved family. And angry; man was I ticked when I realized all of the personal mementos that no one else could possibly hold as dear as I did were gone. As my brain went to work on assessing the damage, the shock of disbelief kicked in while Kalli spoke to the Sheriff on the phone. By the middle of the same night we were sitting with a uniformed officer in our kitchen taking inventory of our lost possessions. Weren't we just on the slopes laughing? Talk about a contrast of feelings. Wasn't I just walking through security and complaining about the inconvenience of the line? I was engulfed in such a paradox of thoughts and feelings, both grateful to be back in our San Diego home and at the same time feeling like I'd been sucker-punched in the gut.

The inventory list read like a legacy of our family. My parent's and our wedding rings, stock certificates, rare coins from our grandparent's worldly travels, our marriage license, cash, and Trevor's birth certificate - they were all in there. But the possession I most treasured, and the only one I really wanted back was a journal I had been keeping of Trevor's life since his birth. Every month for the first decade of his life I had a rendezvous with the lined pages of that beautiful Italian leather-bound journal from Assisi. In it I recounted my evolution into parenthood by my master teacher. His every milestone recorded down to his favorite toy, all of his firsts, and the surge of reverence I had watching it all happen before me. Gone. Despite the overwhelming feelings of loss and grief, Kalli and I made a conscious choice we needed to let it go before the sun rose. We wouldn't allow this violation to seep into yet another day of our lives.

As for the journal, I had a lot of energy invested in my expectations with my full intention of sharing those precious memories with Kalli and Trevor in the future. What was stolen from me was the expectancy I built into my future when I'd share the writings with my loved ones; though I still have a fantasy that my beautiful journal will find me someday. The gift of the experience was recognizing that while the thieves could take the possessions, they could never take the memories of my heart and soul and in that, I realized the ultimate forgiveness.

During my life as a Minister, I've heard enough victim stories to realize that most if not all, at one time or another, have blamed someone else for their pain. Whether it was a minor or major incident, I've watched people try to forgive while still holding on to their story. Those stories are usually dramatic, intricately detailed and heart-breaking, but you can't hold onto your story and be free. Your story is the wedge that creates the canyon between you and trust of your connection with the Oneness of Life. Forgiveness is a transformative healing power that alters acute physical and mental health issues. It's a process of the heart and not the mind, and most importantly, it's the intervention of grace that activates the heart to heal.

On the path up the mountain, the urge to bounce right over deep hurts in avoidance of dealing with them can often be the preferred option. The Pollyanna spiritual bypass of "it's all good" when it's not, won't transform your life. And. if you think a life of being connected to the One will eliminate all of the soul work needing to be addressed, you will be sorely disappointed. All of life's experiences on your path are meant to be integrated into your spirit's curriculum with the ultimate goal of a full emergence of your whole self. Without release, the painful experiences are suppressed and their toxic effects begin to eat away at your body. There's only so much room in the swamp of your mind before it starts oozing over into the good areas of your life.

Forgiveness is a mystical catalyst that challenges the belief system of the one who's stuck in their victim story. Once, when I spoke at the United Nations, there were in attendance a group of children from several war torn countries. They had been asked to share a word or two about what they had lost as a result of the war. As each one spoke, their profound losses one after another, the room flooded with tears. Laughter, my dad, my brother, my innocence, my peace of mind, the ability to sleep without waking in fear, my friends, my home, my mom, my language and the words continued until there was no more room for another word in the silence that remained in the depth of grief and loss. You must always make a conscious choice. I had to decide whether I'd get sucked into the quagmire of the inability to forgive the thieves that took something from both my present and my future. I made the choice to forgive from my spirit, heart and soul. Had I made it from my head, it would not have been graceful or possible. Forgiveness makes no logical sense to the mind that has evidence of an injustice and wants vindication for the pain inflicted. At the very least, the mind wants the perpetrator to understand the trauma they caused. Oh, and then there's revenge - a game the mind plays that tells you it's sweeter when pain is caused to the perpetrator of your woe. It's as if the mind is pouring gasoline on the fire of the pain with its continual pictures of violation.

Forgiveness is an act of the heart and soul and comes not of your earthly mind. As long as your heart is closed down with the weight of previous pains, you'll be a hostage to your history and unable to fully trust Life. *How can you merge into Oneness with that which you don't trust?* In order to quiet the rampage of the rehashing mind and certainly if you ever want to live in peace again, your higher observing self must be heard. The mysterious power of Forgiveness must be allowed to enter into your field of awareness.

Forgiveness isn't about excusing or making right a wrong that someone did to you. It's not even about speaking your mind so you can move on. What it portrays is an act of compassion that frees your spirit and thus pardons the incarcerated aggressor from the jail of your awareness. No matter how inexcusable the acts of violation have been against you, life is too brief to live filled with hatred. Forgiveness invites grace into your life neutralizing hate. It isn't always easy and may open you to a repeated journey through suffering, sorrow, heartache and nightmarish memories, but if you're willing to view it from a higher observing place, the transmutation to wholeness can happen. Be kind to yourself. Forgiveness is a process in which you might go through stages of rage, grief, pain, shame and misperceptions.

Your patient willingness to heal along with a dedicated resolve to a reintegration with Life is possible in all cases. The tears of healing and forgiveness will come in time. Grace frees you from the weight of victimhood returning you to your mountaintop with a peaceful ability to freely see a new story. Things will be different, not on your terms, but by the breath of Grace.

The biggest catch is, as long as your mind desires an explanation, the cleansing relief of Grace can't enter your awareness. There can never be a reasonable justification for an analytical mind that has been traumatized. Nothing will ever fit the bill. Your transformative healing rests fully on your ability to surrender the need to know why this happened to you. Your healing will not be had by any mental motion you choose to put in play but instead through the activity of your spirit. Forgiveness will challenge your very sense of justice and common sense. This is where the mystical alchemy enters into the picture releasing your spirit to soar to places your mind can't imagine.

Forgive Us Our Debts as We Forgive Our Debtors

In spite of everything, I still believe that people are really good at heart.
~ Anne Frank

Everyone's been hurt at one time or another and whether through omission or commission you've probably caused hurt to another. Pain is so prevalent that there are more people walking around this world in pain than you'd ever expect.

You must be careful with your actions and words because once they're out there they can't be neutralized. Years ago, while I was travelling, a neighbor had a tree company cut my towering shade-giving trees back to look like cotton swabs so he could have a better ocean view through my property. His forthcoming heartless apology meant nothing in the context of returning my trees to nature's original splendor. What I'm saying is, you can't put the branch back on, nor can you take back the energy you cast into motion once it's been put in motion. When you're living from the mountaintop you tend to see and understand the energetic ramifications of the unfoldment of your actions and words *before* they are taken or spoken. The cycle of past, present and future is laid out before you in an instant. When coming from an elevated, more compassionate perspective there tends to be a deeper understanding of the impress of the energetic patterns you set in motion.

It's abusive when you judge others for their perspective and misdeeds. Adding this kind of energy to the collective consciousness is unnecessary and damaging. Let your vision be to see the truth and not to change someone else's perception or make them come over to your side. Those who've committed the gravest of offensives are the ones who need to remember the spiritual truth about themselves. I've often been reminded while sitting with the dying, how unresolved issues can come into their minds before their physical transition. For some, these issues can escalate to the point of personal psychological torment, and this is on their deathbeds. By being a compassionate, nonjudgmental place of unconditional love a safe environment is created and they're fully able to confess their felt transgressions. This is a tremendous release often producing a peaceful healing for the soul. Being a vortex for the mystical alchemy of grace and forgiveness to enter into the experience is a blessing which enriches you and the one admitting their apparent mistakes in their journey through this lifetime. You come to know, not only is forgiveness possible but also essential. It's never too late for forgiveness to enter into someone's life to make a difference. Your transcended, Higher Self is always ready to resolve its human issues.

Go outdoors for this meditation

The power of imagination makes us infinite.
~ John Muir

This meditation is best done outside because the air and sun will stimulate your pineal gland, creating a deeper connection with the silence.

When leaving the body behind, it's always a good idea to know how blessed you are in this field of grace in which you play. Before meditation, take a moment to state:

I know all is well and wherever I go in my expanding awareness, all is good and I am safe. I'm surrounded by and live in an Omni Dimensional Life Force that can never be violated, because there is nothing opposed to it. I move on the very currents of Life Itself and I'm free to notice all things without attachment to anything. Free to move beyond any image at any time and courageous enough to remain in it. I open to a graceful guidance on my soul's adventure, surrender my demands to logical understandings, and welcome new and unknown states of consciousness for my soul's evolution.

Take a few breaths to bring your attention back to the center of your body. Find a natural rhythm for your breath to fall into. See if you can follow your in-breath into your body . . . Exhale. Take with it any tension, worries, or concerns while creating more internal room. Find a natural rhythm to your breathing and following your next breath, let it take you deeper into the space beyond your body temple, where past and future dissolve into the present. Your inner awareness becomes the threshold you move across, where now your exhale *propels* you further into the openness of the void. Allow yourself to become available and receptive to a deep hearing and heightened awareness to move you to greater good.

Notice you are in a vast expanse with infinite points of light as if you are in a galaxy of stars . . . Allow your awareness to be drawn to a beautiful blue orb that is calling you home . . . feel an attraction and relational remembrance to the vibrancy of this world. You move in closer and when you do, you see the pristine snowcapped mountains, the wooded forests, the lush green jungles, the expansive deserts, deep canyons, still lakes, running rivers, and the all-embracing blue ocean . . . Your soul is deeply moved by the physical beauty. As your awareness of the magnificence of this place is heightened, you feel the call of this earth for the gift you have to bring. You return to your perfect mountaintop . . .

As you look out to the west, the land of the setting sun, you sense the autumn as it whispers to you with a hint of moisture in the air from the change of the seasons. Feel peaceful and comfortable from your bountiful harvest and a life well lived. Lean back in quiet repose and gaze out through the imagined portal right in front of your brow or forehead, observing the billowy, white clouds floating through the unchanging blue sky.

Cloud gazing will help you slip out of your three-dimensional awareness, supporting you with the expansion of consciousness as you gain insight and illumination. This home portal of spiritual vision has the ability to see with a clarity that far surpasses your earth bound sight. It not only sees but understands cause and its effect and knows the motivation behind actions. You'll also find your empathetic connection to the whole has awakened, affecting a greater understanding of the higher senses.

Direct your awareness to the endless expanse of blue sky the clouds inhabit, feel your soul expand to reach beyond any seeming limitations of mortal seeing. Let loose your imagination as you freely follow the clouds...

A large fresh white cloud settles in your sacred circle and you feel your ethereal body lift out of your slumbering form and settle on this soft air cushion of support as you feel it drift away, leaving your body behind . . . There is a great relief as you sense the comforting embrace of these clouds. It's as if you're journeying home with your expanding perceptions lifting you higher from the ground but paradoxically leaving you feeling more connected to all things. You have a clear vision with this eye of wisdom and knowing. This kind of seeing activates the brain to self-mastery of the body and an enlightened understanding of your world of affairs . . .

You feel the winds of change gently blowing you beyond any earthly distractions which are causing a lack of ease in your life. With a greater depth of vision and clarity, you'll know the symbolic messages these distractions are attempting to convey. See your ascension dissolving the small illusions that entomb you to the issues in your life . . . What comes up each time you are offered something to heal and transform? . . .

Breathe in, filling your lungs with the jasmine -filled celestial air . . . Sense a lightness that lifts you to a level that isn't about your projections rather about your observations. You develop the fortitude to maintain a cosmic perception in the midst of the pull of smallness. Your intimacies with the universal qualities of Life merge into your awareness losing all outlines of form leaving you with a deep understanding of how it's all connected.

Paradoxically, these prolonged revelations last only moments, but leave you knowing the little self has been replaced by an indescribable cosmic love. You had nothing to do with making this happen. You surrender the desire for description because there's a conviction in the depth of your spirit of oneness with life that no words can depict. This knowing will last a lifetime. You have shifted into a new perception of humanity . . .

See the sun's rays reflecting on the clouds creating

rainbow circles in the sky. These vibrant hues lure your desire to float through them. As you penetrate these orbs of color you are absorbed in their brilliant frequency and tones which realign your body and spirit . . . Any imbalances, eye strains, headaches, learning disabilities, confusion, bouts with panic, nightmares, difficulty in focusing, or memory challenge come to your awareness for healing as you gain greater clarity in these vaporous swirls of color . . .

Your intuition is amplified, deeper understandings in your discerning faculties are enhanced, your imaginative abilities to bring the ethereal into form are heightened . . . The blending of the physical senses with the wisdom of the all seeing eye of knowing is trustingly incorporated into your new way of being.

People talk about having your head in the clouds as if drifting in thought is not a good thing, but you've realized this is a gift to see beyond the control of the mental... Coming through these colors you enter a dream realm of towering white puffy clouds floating in the unchanging powder blue backdrop of a sky. These clouds take on amazing, whimsical, implausible, shapes telepathically reminding you of another time and different realm with their messages of insights into your struggles and triumphs depicted in their imagery. What images do you see passing before your sight? . . . This deeper understanding doesn't mean all hassles will disappear now and you won't have future issues, rather, they become initiations and invitations to expand your consciousness. Your spiritual vision welcomes the inner exploration and the metaphoric significance of the images that come before your eyes. You learn to live in harmony with your multidimensional integration of seeing beyond the physical.

Engulfed in a blaze of sun setting colors you realize you are the essence of its brilliance. The vision of the fuchsia sky bathes you in its intensity while the piercing rays of the setting sun shoot up as it sinks into the west. This intense light filters through the clouds, with oranges, pinks and purples blazing off their bottom edges. This dazzling array of color vibrantly awakens your awareness reminding you of the realm of illusion to know truth beyond the common understanding. What images are calling for you to see aspects of your life from the light of another dimension?

As you watch the sun set into the ocean, a green flash catches you by surprise and in that instant you are reminded and understand that all your life's interactions play into supporting your destiny . . . take a moment and reflect upon some charged experience that has lingered in your memory unresolved, and invite a new understanding as to how it has aided you to develop what's needed in your life now . . .

You surrender to the emerging dusk, leaving you to bath in the indigo sky of the early evening. You have walked the world below in an almost unconscious state, but now in this catalystic moment your perceptions become conscious in knowing you are moving to the threshold of the Oneness Realization . . . There is a remembering of some of your inner travels, whether in sleep or meditations, and the illumined understanding they've brought. What are some of these revelations?

When you come back from the mystical experience you no longer desire to leave this world but feel empowered to walk in a new way through this dimensional realm, so you let go to the darkness and find yourself carried back into your body awakening to the light of your mountaintop. Allow this experience to resonate without description in the vibrational level of your body as you rest on your sacred mountaintop . . .

You return to your world of activity refreshed and renewed. Know once you've been somewhere you can easily return to that somewhere by simply calling it back to your awareness. There is always more work to be done, but for now, pull yourself back into your body permitting gratitude for your discoveries to fill your field of awareness . . . Feel a joy knowing you'll be consistently returning to your sacred space, but for now, choose a path down the mountain . . . Familiarize yourself with this trail back into the world of form. Know there is always this passage back to the elevated perspective of your world. Touch some of the trees as you pass by them and feel the earth move beneath your feet.

As what you saw in a distance comes more into focus returning your attention to your breath. Breathe . . . When you are ready, slowly move your fingers and toes, stretch, gently open your eyes and sit for a moment to reacclimatize to your physical world. Take your pen and take some time to write out your experience. It doesn't matter if it was memorable and you are certain you'll never forget it, you should still capture it on paper – later, you'll be glad you did.

Soulful Adventures

- How do you attempt to numb or ignore painful experiences? What dire difficulties have you faced and what gifts did you find at their center?
- What kind of miraculous healings have you experienced or heard about in regards to the body or relationship?
- What answers are knocking at the door of your awareness that are not yet in your present conversation? What can you do to introduce them into your space?
- Hold a court of consciousness; take a seat in a fairly empty room. Open the windows and doors and invite a guest to join you in consciousness. You will watch all sorts of scenes, individuals; temptations and shames fill your awareness. See and listen to what stories they have to tell.
- Where do you need to take back your power?
- Where are you choosing rotted fruit over the sweetness of a ripe life and why?
- Awakening to your wholeness can release a whole mindset taking with it a full list of issues rather than dealing with each individually. This is what happens when you enter the mystical realm, transcending the reason and acting within the power of divine mystery. What linchpin, if pulled, would bring down a whole structure with all of its issues for you? Why don't you

pull it?

- Is there someone you can't connect or heal with? Intuitively you can connect to do some quality healing work. One way to shift your perception of a perpetrator against your peace is the old tried and true process of visualizing them as a young innocent child or a frail, penniless old fogey. In doing so, you can connect with the humanity that lies below the surface of the personality.

- Write out your transgression. Whatever difficulties you have, it's time to let go. Read them out loud to a confidant if possible, reenact the ritual of confession. Write it out, read it out loud and then burn it.

Body and Soul Practice for Connecting

Body Connection

Satori breathing is usually done lying on your back and involves breathing with full awareness in a circular pattern. Breathe in with a pause between in-breath and out-breath. Twenty minutes of open mouth breathing oxygenates the body to such an extent that the body releases from its cells suppressed emotions that have crystallized in them. Emotions and memories may come up for you. If emotions arise, breath through them allowing yourself to feel through them. Too often we stop breathing to hold our emotions in check.

Soul Connection

Find a comfortable place to sit outside or lie on the ground and watch the puffy clouds take shape, bringing to your mind . . . what? Have some fun and sit with a friend and call out what you see to one another.

Mystical Writing

The Learn'd Astronomer
When I heard the learn'd astronomer;
When the proofs, the figures, were ranged in columns before me;
When I was shown the charts and the diagrams, to add, divide, and measure them;
When I, sitting, heard the astronomer, where he lectured with much applause in the lecture-room,
How soon, unaccountable, I became tired and sick;
Till rising and gliding out, I wander'd off by myself,
In the mystical moist night-air and from time to time,
Look'd up in perfect silence at the stars.

~ Walt Whitman
1819-1892

Chapter 8: Mystical Grace

*I tell my kids and protégés, always have humility
when you create and grace when you succeed,
because it's not about you. You are a terminal for a
higher power. As soon as you accept that, you can do
it forever.*
~ Quincy Jones

The bridge of grace, which connects through the crown chakra, has proven itself to be the first challenge I have had finding words. Here's why. This is the expanding vortex through which Life enters into human form and beyond that, this is where human form connects to Source. So, what happens when one has reached a sense of oneness is a lack of opposites- thereby presenting a dearth of associative examples for me to give you to consider. It's within that scarcity of good and bad, right and wrong, black and white that I've come to rest on a more attuned and perhaps more illuminated description of this leg of the journey to the mountaintop, having gained even more perspective myself through the process of writing this book.

Have you ever had an unexpected encounter with someone who proceeded to change the course of your life? Be it a teacher, soul mate, child, or pet, they might have touched your life in a way that raised your vibration to a level you wouldn't have known to even dream. What about having an idea that impacted your whole world just coming to you effortlessly? How did that happen? Today you woke up thinking about how you'd soon be sitting in traffic on your way to work where you'd make and take calls and write proposals. How was it that in the midst of doing what you'd planned, you got a call from your best childhood friend who you hadn't spoken to in thirty years? Time collapsed and grace entered and you weren't living the daily grind. You were reliving childhood memories you forgot you had and making plans for a whole new future that included someone from the past. Did you even suspect grace would show up in your world when you hit the snooze button on the alarm clock?

How about when that little voice of unparalleled wisdom spoke to you from inside as you faced your last tough decision? Ever had a sickness that miraculously turned around? Have you ever found yourself caught in a moment of jaw-dropping awe by the beauty of an everyday sight?

Sometimes grace comes in the form of not acting. Have you ever chosen not to say something you knew would hurt someone? Better, have you ever been the conduit for an otherworldly love that entered an argument in perfect time and neutralized every ounce of animosity present? What seemed to be a moment in which you were miraculously led to an answer you'd been searching for is the hallmark of grace in all of its glory.

Occasionally grace appears in the form of a knowing, like all of a sudden when you knew the perfect investment or when you were able to locate that lost key to the twelve-year-old scooter sitting in your storage shed. Other times, grace comes as a helper message, like a guardian angel that helps your life be just a little bit smoother or safer. Have you not looked to the heavens and thanked your guides as you were barely missed by an oncoming car or for making you late and missing a train that later collided with another?

Perhaps you've experienced the gentle touch of a person who you knew had the healing powers of an angel. I'm not just talking about a massage therapist or even a Reiki practitioner, though they are often powerful conduits for much grace and healing energy. When I take the hand of my son, and I feel his gentle fingertips in my palm, I shudder knowing I am having a mystical experience in my form just being in his very presence. Touching an angel on earth is a magical feeling punctuated only by the observation and awareness of it in the very second it occurs.

Maybe you know someone who was so lost in life they were on the edge of hopelessness, unable to see their way through when, as if miraculously, they found a positive direction to bring them out of the darkness into the light. Have you ever had a moment of anxiety quelled by a calm that seemed to float into your awareness from out of nowhere? You called, and help answered, and you believed it to be heaven sent. Whether you find yourself getting lost in a dance, a piece of poetry or moved by art, it's grace that is moving through you and pushing aside human form for you to experience a boundless bliss.

Likely at some point you've experienced an animal giving you unconditional love, the presence of a loved one who's no longer alive, or a healing in your body or worldly affairs just when you needed it most. On the heels of grace, wisdom enters and an almost indescribable clarity is known. Peace and harmony expresses itself in and through you, and there's an ineffable feeling of 'all is well with the world'. Surely you know it, as we have all known grace. The question is, when it showed itself, were you aware and did you observe it in its right action? These are just some of the many examples of Grace appearing in everyday situations.

The grace experience is not a mental one, nor an intellectual one, but rather it's an experience of the soul. Your spirit can know grace but only through a direct encounter with it. You can learn about other people's grace-filled mystical moments. You can even closely study the steps to grace, but all you'll know is what the mind makes of it, not the experience of grace itself. My description of knowing grace through holding my son's hand is no doubt beautiful and touching, but does it leave you with a better understanding of grace in your own life by hearing it? Reading a book on grace and finding a formulaic process to finding it is all well and good, but to truly experience grace, you must feel it through your own soul.

I'm reminded of the story of a foolish lover who finally sits beside his beloved after months of rejection and pining.

Having put so much energy into a collection of unsent letters he wrote about his burning desire and the pain he felt in their separation he now sat next to her on the park bench. Instead of basking in the grace of the love that was present, he resorted to reading the ramblings of the unrequited moment. "You fool," she says, "I am sitting with you now and all you can do is read me what you wrote months ago?"

The experience of grace is what remains from a brush with the Divine. Grace comes from the sacred encounter with Life. It's a realization that shifts your world to a softer, kinder trust in knowing all is well in the now and what's unfolding is moving you in a perfect direction. Grace is, Life presenting Itself.

Regardless of the blocks, mistakes and challenges of this world, there's a part of you that's never been violated. This area of consciousness is always alive and alert in its receptivity to whatever brush of grace may come from any place at any time. Grace will rework and re-pattern every aspect of you for a greater walk as light. And no, you don't need to become a monk, minister, nun or rabbi to know or live in grace. The invitations to know and experience it are plentiful in your life. Look around to find the spaces where you can take the higher road. When someone says something offensive to you, grace responds with kindness spontaneously rather than the natural human reaction of defending and attacking. Living by your mighty egotistical-power and battling through is not the way of harmony and balance. When you tire of the fight, grace invites you in.

There is a delicate nuance you must be aware of, however. Setting an intention for grace and then attempting to grasp at it will result in only pushing it further away. Do what you love with an abandoned passion and without a shadow of a doubt you'll feel grace as it gives you the full experience of Life moving through you. Grace lies in going full out for what your spirit must express. Being true to this is where the ultimate fulfillment lies. This is the truth irrespective of what critics may be telling you. Pay heed because grace is not about going for the gold without consideration of how you'll get there. Going full steam ahead without full observation will only create anxiety. Grace is detached from results; rather it serves as a conduit for your passion to express.

You must remember, the gift of who you are is already stored within you and has been complete since the moment you came into self-awareness. Your only mission is to bring it forth from within and of course to recognize it when you do. The motion of Life operates through your consciousness. You are the Activity of Life and your success and experience of grace will come when you allow yourself to be an instrument of Truth by simply being authentic.

Reason is Powerless in the Realm of Grace

The more you commune with the Life Force without need for result, the more results you get. When you come into a harmonic resonance, listening with a receptive heart and quiet mind you'll be led into a peaceful feeling that shifts all things. Reason is powerless in making this happen. The graceful expression only happens when you're present for it but not when you force it. As in love, love alone reveals love. The formless reality can only take form as you leave behind all the limited dogmatic concepts of what it's supposed to look like. That's when dormant gifts like grace and love are activated. Within the state of grace you're seized by a glorious Power and thrust into a radiant bewilderment. The expanded knowing of the unknowable brings torment and elation, like knowing the joy and beauty of youth and not being able to return to it. You know you are eternal yet able to experience the immanence. When you awaken to grace, there is a heightened perspective of the eternal verities revealing a masterpiece unfamiliar to you. In becoming aware of the potential of this holographic image, you sense the lure to merge with it. As it fans out its charmed dimensionality, you'll skip straight through the existence of the second and third dimensional worlds on a direct course to the fourth.

Court the beloved and see grace everywhere. What you admire you become. In this awakened state you know the divine secrets. If your reference is for the world of form is all its flash and gossip, you'll find that neurotic impression cutting off your connection from the sacred. This path of dominating images, sickens your psyche and misleads you away from your conscious communion with Life. Get back to your mountaintop and listen to your observer who is not influenced by physical phenomenon.

You can always get back to a state of awareness by upholding regular rituals that continue to invoke grace. Daily meditation and a commitment to sitting in silence will bring you back to connection with Source. Are you guilty of not being able to find the time in the busy-ness of your day? *Do you tell yourself you don't have time because your so-called priorities are more important than a connection with the Infinite?* Your spirit craves intimacy with the Life that breathed movement into it. You were born as a living, animated avenue for grace to express for humanity. It's really a mindset. When you show up as if you're being called to bring the unseen influence of grace to heal and transform through all you do, it happens. It's not done as a result of your cleverness but through your ability to empty yourself of self so grace can flow unhindered through you.

Self-dissolution is no easy or small task. The little sense of self wants to hold onto the struggle and pain which gives it familiarity and meaning. Clearly, this impairs the flow of grace. Though, because grace is omnipresent, it's the state of disbelief that becomes your arch rival. Grace neutralizes disbelief - it can be that simple. Now is the time to let grace in. When you do, you will be living unaffected by the trappings of disbelief. The more grace, the more miracles. The more you focus on grace the more grace is focused on you. Stop listening to your observer, and you won't hear its insightful guidance. Stop visiting your mountaintop and you'll be stuck in a myopic view of the insignificant. Whatever you take your attention away from goes away, whether it's a blessing or a curse.

You must be available to grace to enter into it. By disregarding your true nature, you may slip into the fear of the temporal power, whether in the form of physical intimidation or the malpractice of consciousness.

The great secret of the mystical life is to trust grace in all situations. Keep your awareness attuned to it. Create an affirmation to support the truth that you don't control Life, you are one with Life. Create the inner dialogue to support your knowingness of this truth of grace. The Divine Presence within you arouses the Divine Presence in everything around you. It has become the purpose of the awakened ones to trigger the memories of those whose paths they cross. By being a true expression of your higher self, the one who has the elevated view of all things, you will quicken the opening to grace for all of humanity. This is why it's important to become familiar with your mountaintop so you can always access and know Truth from a higher place.

Your intuition is a wonderful skill, but don't be fooled into thinking it's a mystical one. Intuition is an ability that you can acquire, expand upon, and use to help tune into the vibrational field of choice. It becomes your link to the subjective realm and, with that; it guides you as you move through your perceptual filters of interpretation. Grace is a breath that bypasses the logical lobes of your brain and is not of the self. It's not a hunch that expands, but a knowing that is complete and indisputable. Unlike intuition, it's mystical in its nature because it comes from the realm of Oneness and directly impresses, without interpretation through revelation. Good luck figuring out what it means half the time, other than the overwhelming sense of wellbeing you're left with as you realize it has come and gone.

You can't box grace into any neat package like a word and there are no gestures for it. It's just not conceptually understandable. Like the magic of a heart in love can't be put into words, though the greatest of poets have tried, grace is something that must be enjoyed personally to know. When you enter into the mystical where the walls between the head and the heart dissolve, you'll find yourself in the barrier between where silence and words vanish. Esoteric elimination of the essence of this space will thrust you into another dimension of knowing beyond thoughts and conceptualization. Here, All-Knowing images and interconnectedness of all things are revealed and there's an unalienable trust that dissipates all fear. When you are passionately energized to follow your dharma while embracing life, rather than attempting to escape it, you'll know for certain that you're in the stream of life with no end.

The Insatiable Urge from the Exalted States

What comes from awakening and listening to the peaks of your being must be a sacred expression. What else could move through you from the rapture of the exalted states but an insatiable urge to share with those around you whether it's through art, music, poetry, or dance among others. They're all glorious expressions of your jubilation of the ineffable, but in truth, they pale in comparison to the brightness and clarity of the experience itself.

Bliss is a natural state of oneness with the flow of the Universe. Having cosmic Life flow through you in a unique and perfect way isn't only a blessing to you but one for all of humanity. Bliss is the full movement of Life appearing through you. It's all pervasive with its known radiance, coursing through every aspect of your physical and energetic being. Your awareness of this from your witnessing self is grace making Itself known.

Grace frees you from any karmic debt. When it is present, you are no longer bound by the law of cause and its effect but instead, released by forgiveness. No longer will you be punished by your mistakes. Grace liberates you. You don't operate under the vibrational law of energy but of the breath of grace which unshackles you to express Life.

When you give up attempting to get the Universe to respond to your demands, you submit yourself to the service of the Divine and lo and behold, that is where you'll find ease and grace flourishing throughout your life. You'll come to recognize there are no real obstacles to overcome in the field of grace because Life is the only power and there's nothing outside of that with any real or true meaning. So stop endeavoring to bring the Infinite down to your level of the finite and surrender to the grace that seeks you as an avenue of its glorious expression.

Graced by Grace

There will always be a desire to share with others the grace that graced your life. Bliss is hard to keep under wraps and you'll want to share what feels so good to you with anyone who will give you the time of day. It's natural to want to save others, yet it's easy to get dragged down to their level rather than pulling them up into the light. Have you ever seen a rescue operation in a drowning? A drowning person will take their rescuer down, not purposely but with super-human strength in the chaos of the fear. It's nothing personal. It's survival. In the case of saving someone through the insights of grace, it's dangerous because they're holding onto heavy burdens and aren't really ready to let go. Be careful not to get so full of yourself that you begin to believe you can save the world. Find comfort in the possibility that in the radiance of your presence, people may catch a glimpse of grace in action and have a realization of what's possible for them.

Mystics are those in conscious communion with the All Animating Essence of Life. The veil is thin for the bringers of the invisible to the visible helping others to see the evidence of things not seen. Wait until someone reaches out to you before you share what you've experienced as grace. It's not your job to convert the world. You wouldn't want someone to impose their will and perform some medical intervention you didn't agree with even if they felt it was right for you. Nor would someone want you to meddle in their consciousness with what you think is the answer to their issues. Your job, if you choose to accept it, is to continue working on yourself so when someone does ask to partake of what you have, you'll be able to relate from a revelation-filled experience rather than from a heady, intellectual understanding. Though you stand at the door and knock they must open their consciousness to the power of their own experience of grace.

Once you are a conduit for grace to flow it won't be long before people begin calling on you for guidance. If you commit to your mountaintop practice, when they reach out, you'll be ready for the healing power of grace to move through you. The grace that brought you the request in the first place will fulfill the work that's before you. Relax in the deep knowing you aren't the one who provides the transformation, but grace itself delivers the answer. If your only desire is to know grace, be in a grace realization, and have a conscious communion with it with no attachment to outcome, then the miracles will come. Living as an avenue of grace supports you as your needs are met naturally. Abundance is yours, and your dependence on earthly vices like medicine will be reduced if not eliminated. Your meditations deepen as you absorb with your heart and soul as opposed to your intellect and you'll find that you'll no longer live by the letter of the law, but by the spirit of truth that sets you free. There's a big difference between knowing the truth and living it.

Grace Can Only Be Found In the Now

When grace is upon you, the motion of its transcendental experience shifts your world. Blessings will be yours and others will experience it. The world is filled with the bright light of grace waiting to be felt by everyone, transforming fear in its wake. As a conduit of love, you will embark on a journey of service so others can sense the grace through your actions. As you keep your awareness on grace, it's reflected in everything you feel, speak and otherwise express. The grace you knew yesterday was yesterday's. Last week's food filled your stomach and sated your hunger then, but you have a need for nourishment this week, and will next week, too. Your present experience of grace is just that. Today's grace, not yesterday's, is the only thing you can bring to serving others. Grace can't flow in your field of awareness if you have concern, anxiety, worry, or fear. There's just too much future blocking out the present. The same goes when grace can't flow in your field of awareness because you have regret, guilt, resentment, and anger. In that case, there's just too much past blocking out the present. If you're going to be serving as a vortex of grace, a healing channel or transparency for it, you must be present in the now. An unprecedented stamina in your vibrational expression of grace comes from the recurrent infusion of the Life Force through your visits to the mountaintop.

Service activates the flow of grace. When you choose to live in the field of grace you'll find it constantly renewing itself and any hesitancy to share yourself and your mystical gifts will give way to the affluent flow of Life. Your radiance will bring a peaceful sense of calm along with inter-connectedness to all of Life.

Sacred Service

I slept and dreamt that life was joy. I awoke and saw that life was service. I acted and behold, service was joy.
~ Rabindranath Tagore

Service is a love that comes from the heart. When the

Essence of Life moves through you, It brings something which can't be purchased or quantified. It's a sincerity that's palpable. This kind of Love cannot be contained; it *must* express itself through service. When you lose yourself in service, each day becomes magical with unexpected gifts.

My days seem increasingly filled with stories that reflect the miraculous healing of those in service. Just recently I ran into an acquaintance who, in response to an early bout of cancer, devoted her life to advocating awareness and fundraising for a large national cancer organization. As is known to happen, her cancer reappeared with a vengeance not too long ago and manifested in many organs of her body. To the detriment of her limited ability to treat it, she opted to go with a holistic approach choosing health rather than a battle with cancer. Her body leaned into the support approach rather than away from the figurative war on cancer and she achieved a balance through naturopathic healthcare using live foods, vitamin supplements, visualization, prayer, service and meditation. Within four months the medical professionals who had previously recommended radical treatment scratched their heads after diagnostic tests showed her cancer was in full remission. Not for one minute of her illness did she push aside her dedication to her life's work with the organization that provides service and support to so many.

When you put another's needs before your own without a desire for return, your intention is coming from a high place. More important than the action of giving is the attitude you had in the process. You are Life's delivery system for love and caring in everything you undertake. It's easy to get so caught up in the delivery of the deed that you forget it's about the spirit you bring. The Danish mystic, Soren Kierkegaard said, "As soon as love becomes self-centered, it's out of its natural element." Gifts are given to those who choose to be in service to others. Those who've been blessed have the responsibility to share those gifts.

Seva is a Sanskrit term for selfless service which means it

is shared without consideration for anything in return. There's an essence of feeling honored by giving. In serving, it's not as if you do your duty and then say, I'm done, and I did it. It's a lifelong practice that keeps you in the Infinite Flow. Knowing you, yourself, are a blessing is a compelling reason to share how blessed you are by recognizing others without concern for what is or isn't coming back to you.

Seva can take on many different faces or practices. While one person's seva might be helping a community be stronger, another person's selfless giving might look like reading to a child, cooking a meal with love, or assisting someone on their computer. Some aid the infirm, support the confused, or lend a hand to the impoverished whether they are on the other side of the world or in their own backyard. For you, perhaps, the greatest seva would be the opportunity to be present and talk with someone who needs you. It's all about showing up for someone or something outside of yourself because it feels good to be used by Life. Your energy is a boost to others which is why your clean attitude of service is so important. If you can't feel good about giving, then don't. Go work on yourself until you have the revelation that you're not the source but the channel through which the Infinite passes. Then you can bring blessings to those whose lives you reach out to touch. More bliss is found in service to others than in only caring for your own needs. Service quickens the oneness experience much faster than just reading about it. The Buddha taught the triple truth that a generous heart, kind speech and a life of service and compassion are the things which renew humanity.

True happiness comes of serving others. It's so easy to get caught up in the human consciousness of ego-based concern, forgetting your journey is about being a conduit for Life to flow. You aren't here to withdraw from the world but make a deposit to it. As you serve the one before you, you serve all of humanity. Serving strengthens your spirit to be a clearer channel for grace to flow. *Why do you have the gifts and talents you have if not to share them with others?*

You are always serving something, whether it's intentional or not. It's good to get to your mountaintop and see what you are giving your energy to. As Joshua asked, "Are you serving Spirit or mammon?" Pause and become aware of what you're serving. Do you kowtow to your fears, anxieties, prejudices, race mind, and family patterns or is your energy directed towards a divine vision, a greater possibility, and your dharma? Pains and abuses like racism, environmental issues and wars stem from the illusion of separation. The best way to heal a schism is to enter the field of grace by serving where you see a need calling out to you. *Where have you been too busy to support a cause that touches your heart?*

There's a beautiful coherence in the field of grace. Yet too many live a life of disconnectedness because of the noisy distractions surrounding the human experience. The more you pursue the distractions the less you know of grace. There is no way to know the Infinite with a finite mind. Attempting to bring the Infinite down to finiteness cannot possibly work. Life won't just respond to your will, instead, you must become responsive to the expression of Life. You can shift your expression by submitting yourself in service and being an instrument through which Life flows. The more consciously connected you remain the more blessed choices will be yours to live. *Would you be willing to be in sacred service if you were never to be recognized and someone else got the credit?*

The best way to find you is to lose yourself in the service of others.
~ Mahatma Gandhi

Hey ... You Over There

The masterful art of being a conduit for the illumination you find on the mountaintop is manifested in your life. While it might sometimes feel like the cacophony of the three dimensional life drowns out the waft of knowingness when you return from the mountaintop bearing insights, it is always available to recover, in full awareness. But in that truth is another law, and it's that observation is such a double edged sword. Those in the sciences studying Quantum Physics say form changes through observation. DNA is rearranged through the minute factor of attention that is paid towards it.

When I find myself aware of the truth that I am of Source, the mystical sweeps me to a center of joy and full enlightenment that becomes so all encompassing, my mind becomes interested. "Hey, you...hey, over there, what are you looking at" my mind asks curiously. I hear its voice, its dialogue tinged with an antagonistic tone. "Ahem, yes...you, witness, where are you in this moment you are not in your mind?" My head turns in a figurative way to observe the voice of the mind, and when I shift my awareness, the moment of mystical empowerment becomes a distant memory, and sometimes like it never happened at all. Sigh. Akin to waking from a dream during which the secrets of the universe were downloaded upon me to find I remember nothing, I'm left wondering how to incorporate the mountaintop mindfulness into my living form when my mind's voice distracts me so fully.

Grace is the ability to know in that moment, when you are not sure what it is you experienced, that the truth is the experience of the observation. And that observation includes the mystical as well as the mindful. In fact, mindful awareness becomes a key to opening the door to the mystical. Employing the knowingness from your adventures of the mountaintop in a practical way becomes the ebb and flow of your new being. Your behavior will change just knowing that you can observe what is happening around you from a higher perspective any time you wish. You can connect with all that is, every spiritual guide, and the realms beyond your physical existence with the recognition that comes of your witness watching. Grace comes of not what is wanted, but of what is needed for you to continue moving on in your journey towards your higher empowerment. Sometimes that means a revelation, and sometimes it means feeling like that revelation is like a word or an old joke, just on the tip of your tongue having slipped your memory banks in a surprising way.

You can experience grace from any level of mountaintop expansion; be it the lower vibrational levels or the higher, esoteric completely out-of-form energies. Each level carries a different personality of that grace, but all support your journey to knowing your life's purpose in a way your mind will always question.

Relating to the mind feeds it more energy while watching the mind's conversations withdrawing energy from it. Wherever you may be in your journey you must acknowledge the Life Force by witnessing it as everywhere. This is a never ending process that keeps you consciously in the field of grace. When you are devoted to being in service to its flow, it's *that* devotion that activates the vibration of grace all around you, not the act of service at all. This all pervasive, Omnipresent, Elegant Blessing that Life is, you know without a doubt exudes as you!

Praise It and Raise It Up

One powerful devotion is the language of praise. A commitment to applauding Life's expressions opens the cosmic doors to a greater sense of Oneness with Life. Praise is a celebration hailing the glorious revealing of the breath of Spirit taking form in your field of awareness. Every day you must appreciate and honor the magnificence of Source to live in grace. Praise is the key to opening the door so you can return home.

In the spirit of honoring the light that flows through someone, praise can shift energy around whatever the situation is. Remember as a child being praised for something you did or said? Didn't it make you want to do more of whatever it was? You should have seen your eyes twinkle with delight as you processed your gift of praise. If I were to praise you today, what amount of false egoic humility would stand in the way of that return to twinkle? What keeps you from taking praise in so you can feel even more of the ecstasy of grace and a desire to shine even brighter? *What would it take for you to feel at home in your skin?*

In the nanosecond of the mystical glimpse of home, you know the evolutionary promise within you has changed you forever. The unlimited potential of the cosmos is instantly available as you from all the dimensions of possibility. Let this grand panoramic backdrop of consciousness be your inspiration to remember the Source is within you and is ever flowing. The great mystic Rumi wrote, "You are not a drop in the ocean. You are the entire ocean in a drop." Try stepping away from considering yourself as merely the drop. You are the ocean, in all its splendor right where you are.

The possibility you see in the world or in others becomes your responsibility because you are the one who's been charged with the vision. Grace will guide you in making it so. No longer is hiding in apathy and denial an option for bowing out of your expression of grace. Your place in the cosmos is being revealed. Your servitude as an expression of unconditional love to those creating atrocities including bankers whose greed is suffocating this world, politicians caught in the game, wounded warriors coming home from war, and blind abusers of mother earth will shift the tides and change the planet.

Your unconditional loving expression of grace is the *only* frequency that can penetrate the hardened facade around the aching souls of those needing your guidance. Your selflessness will help to bless the magnificent soul in its torment, recalibrating its expression to a return to wholeness. As much as one might want to add an 'I told you so' to the lesson, grace doesn't reprimand. It points to the evolutionary emergence in all directions and allows every soul to be stirred with the dream of what's possible. Let your expression come from the wisdom of the mountaintop view. For the blessed emergence of life to always be remembered, you must be a reflection of this beauty. In the midst of darkness you are the bringer of the light. In the midst of struggle you are the reminder of ease and grace. In the face of death, you know life is eternal and this has merely been a pit stop along the evolutionary way.

The breath of grace is the carrier of the sacred secrets, revelations of the whole, and the sacred unity of all things. There's really no other way to explain the ineffability of grace, though I'm trying. It can't be described as a belief because the dispassionate mind is incapable of a transformative soul experience. Rather, the direct experience of grace will bring a certainty of recognition while annihilating all previous personal settings in your brain. This will end up leaving you bewildered, yet transformed and under grace's spell. You are no less than a distributor of the Divine. Allow your every word, thought and action to be in accordance with the infinite pulse of Life. The mystical life is about being a beholder of Spirit, now in action everywhere, including through you. As a mystic, your desires will dissolve and you'll become a transparency for grace to express to Its end not yours. If you seek grace, be still and allow it to move through you. Any thought of grace is self-created and in your mind, so drop the graven image. Remember it's a soul experience that comes to visit by brushing your being; it's not something you can conjure up. Think of it like sitting in your garden and willing a butterfly to land on your hand. It's not just going to happen because you will it. It'll only happen if it's meant to by an act of grace, and of course if you live in a climate where there are butterflies.

When you look out from the elevation of the mountaintop, you're above words and thoughts. Don't get me wrong, they aren't eliminated; you just aren't reliant on them for communication any longer. When you live by grace, and it's what produces your words and thought images, you become the channel through which it creates your expression. No longer are you attempting to overcome the human world with its challenge of forms. You rise above knowing the truth, to *being the Truth*. You become this Truth through the transformative experience of moving beyond your body's outline to the revelation that a living spirit never dies. Rest in this realization rather than frantically attempting to over-intellectualize the concept. As your observer watches the experience expanding as you, all of your communication will now come from the high place of a greater conscious connection. So now that you've stepped through the door and are a glorious expression of grace, you can rest confidently in a quietude of peace.

Meditation

When leaving the body behind, it's always a good idea to know how blessed you are in this field of grace in which you play. Before meditation, take a moment to state:

I know all is well and wherever I go in my expanding awareness, all is good and I am safe. I'm surrounded by and live in an Omni Dimensional Life Force that can never be violated, because there is nothing opposed to it. I move on the very currents of Life Itself and I'm free to notice all things without attachment to anything. Free to move beyond any image at any time and courageous enough to remain in it. I open to a graceful guidance on my soul's adventure, surrender my demands to logical understandings, an welcome new and unknown states of consciousness for my soul's evolution.

Take a few breaths to bring your attention back to the center of your body. Find a natural rhythm for your breath to fall into. See if you can follow your in-breath into your body . . . Exhale. Take with it any tension, worries, or concerns while creating more internal room. Find a natural rhythm to your breathing and following your next breath, let it take you deeper into the space beyond your body temple, where past and future dissolve into the present. Your inner awareness becomes the threshold you move across, where now your exhale *propels* you further into the openness of the void. Allow yourself to become available and receptive to a deep hearing and heightened awareness to move you to greater good.

Notice you are in a vast expanse with infinite points of light as if you are in a galaxy of stars . . . Allow your awareness to be drawn to a beautiful blue orb that is calling you home . . . feel an attraction and relational remembrance to the vibrancy of this world. You move in closer and when you do, you see the pristine snowcapped mountains, the wooded forests, the lush green jungles, the expansive deserts, deep canyons, still lakes, running rivers, and the all-embracing blue ocean . . . Your soul is deeply moved by the physical beauty. As your awareness of the magnificence of this place is heightened, you feel the call of this earth for the gift you have to bring.

You return to your perfect mountaintop to help open the crown of your head. Lift your gaze to father sky, the ancestral realm of untold wisdom. The countless stars in the majestic night sky of unfathomable reaches as well as the bringer of light, says, I am here, living in you, moving in and having my being as you. I am of the One Life Force, the expresser of the One.

With each breath move your attention to the top of your head and sense a deep violet glow filling your mind. Bathing in this violet light, see a closed white lotus flower hovering above your head . . . As you reflect upon this thousand petal lotus flower it starts to slowly spin and one by one the petals of this lotus flower begin to open. As layer after layer opens it reveals the next, then the next, then the next as the speed of the multidimensional white lotus increases its rotation. Each new level of the blossoming layer reveals another opening of a previously closed chamber . . . As all the petals unfurl to their fullest revealing the receptive vortex of calm in the midst of the spinning pinwheel of light, feel a connection to the sky above, sense a white light moving through the crown of your head connecting you to the earth and the entire ethereal realm in-between so there is a total absorption in the light, leaving nothing but light and you are one with all that is . . .

Repeat to yourself, I am one with the light that created me . . . Breathe with the pulse of this light and say to yourself, I am in harmony with the beauty and grace of Life . . . Repeat to yourself, every aspect of my body and life is bathed in this healing expression of light . . . All negative past remembrances I harbor are instantly erased from the file of my memory by grace that now realigns all my thoughts and words to the light vibration . . . Breathe in the light and repeat to yourself, I am perfect, whole and complete now . . . I am all that I shall ever need . . . I am love expressing . . .

Knowing your connection is with all that is; worry dissolves as you face your life knowing you are not alone. Consciously aware of your connectedness with the universe, you know you have the universal power at your disposal instantly neutralizing all fear. Realizing you are an integral part of the grand scheme of it all, you surrender to the magic carpet ride of grace leaving behind all that no longer serves you. All your challenges dissolve in the brightness of the light.

Repeat to yourself, bathing in this light of grace I am healed and whole and move to a greater rapport with the universe. Merging in this Oneness my expanding awareness broadens with an understanding of the interconnectedness of all things. Breathing in wisdom integrated to the very core of my being, I now know all resources I need to fulfill, who I've come here to be and what I've come here to do.

It's time to return to your world of activity refreshed and renewed. Know once you've been somewhere you can easily return to that somewhere by simply calling it back to your awareness. There is always more work to be done, but for now, pull yourself back into your body permitting gratitude for your discoveries to fill your field of awareness. Feel a joy knowing you'll be consistently returning to your sacred space, but for now, choose a path down the mountain. . .

Familiarize yourself with this trail back into the world of form. Know there is always this corridor, this passage back to the elevated perspective of your world. Touch some of the trees as you pass by them and feel the earth move beneath your feet. As what you saw in a distance comes more into focus returning your attention to your breath. Breathe . . . When you are ready, slowly move your fingers and toes, stretch, gently open your eyes and sit for a moment to re-acclimate to your physical world. Take your pen and take some time to write out your experience. It doesn't matter if it was memorable and you are certain you'll never forget it, you should still capture it on paper – later, you'll be glad you did.

Soulful Adventures

- Close your eyes, touch your heart and enter some remembrances of moments of grace.
- Where in life do you find yourself on the battlefield?
- How might the good emerge if you were to surrender to grace?
- What can you do to bring forth dormant gifts that are waiting to be awakened?
- What "flash and gossip" of this world is trapping you?
- What could you do to extricate yourself from their hypnotic trance?
- If you are going to be in service, a vortex of grace, a healing channel, or a transparency for grace you must be present in the now. If in your field of awareness you have concern, anxiety, worry, fear, you've got too much future blocking out the now where grace flows. Where do you harbor anxiety, worry and fear? Are you willing to let it go?
- If in your field of awareness you have regret, guilt, resentment, anger you've got too much past blocking out the now where grace flows. Where do you hold regret, guilt, resentment, anger? Are you willing to let

it go?

- What gifts and talents would you be happy to share with the world?
- Where are you being called to serve? What's enticing you to get involved? What's keeping you from saying yes to this request?
- Always being on the lookout for the good and praising it will keep you seeing good and living in grace. Make a joyful noise and start praising more.

Body and Soul Practice for Connecting

Body Connection

Give yourself a head massage and open up your crown chakra.

Soul Connection

You can do this exercise sitting in a chair, but sitting crossed legged on the ground is better. Interlace your fingers and place your connected hands above your head with your elbows out making a circle with your palms facing down above your crown. Roll your eyes upward towards father sky attempting to see the heavens out of the top of your head. While keeping your gaze upward, close your eyelids, keeping your hands in their position. With a deep long slow breath in, feel and see the energy and light coming in through the top of your head. Allow it to move slowly through and down your spine energizing and healing your whole body. Slowly release a long exhale out the bottom of your spine depositing into the earth any undesirable energetic toxins. Then again breathe in this Life animating energy, allowing it to cleanse and remove what doesn't belong back into the earth. Then, take another energizing breath from the top of your head through your total being awakening your Kundalini. After seven minutes, keeping your eyelids shut, let your gaze to the heavens return, bring your arms down and briskly rub your palms together. Then, lovingly rest them on your eyelids.

Mystical writing

". . . I want first of all - in fact, as an end to these other desires - to be at peace with myself. I want a singleness of eye, a purity of intention, and a central core to my life that will enable me to carry out these obligations and activities as well as I can. I want, in fact - to borrow from the language of the saints - to live 'in grace' as much of the time as possible. I am not using this term in a strictly theological sense. By grace I mean an inner harmony, essentially spiritual, which can be translated into outward harmony . . ."

~Anne Morrow Lindbergh
1906-2001

Chapter 9: Masters of Brightness

I wish I could show you when
you are lonely or in darkness
the astonishing light of
your own being.
~ Hafiz

Nothing can dim the light which shines from within.
~Maya Angelou

The Toughest Step

Legend has it that there once roamed this earth a mythic Kodiak bear so beautiful that a description of it couldn't be put into words. Those who heard stories about the bear knew him as both terrifying and awe inspiring in his sheer size no less his instinctive nature. With claws the size of tree branches and the ability to rip through rock, golden hair that glistened with splendor in the light, and a roar that could be heard across continents, few brave ever lived to tell of their incredible encounters with this magnificent creation. It was written that whoever advanced towards the bear and courageously rubbed its head would walk away unscathed and indeed, be blessed for the rest of their life. But if at the last minute, there was any scent of trepidation, the infuriated giant would take his enormous incisors and tear its visitor apart before they even knew what was happening. Not for fear or even for retaliation, but because of the poor judgment one had of him.

Despite the obvious dangers, after studying all the lore enveloping the iconic marvel, one trepid soul ventured off alone through seasons across the Arctic Circle's backcountry in search of this impressive beast. He knew his defining moment would come only as he stared straight into the bear's eyes. Then, came the day. As he looked up from where he had bent over to wash his face in the icy glacier stream he witnessed the Kodiak eyeballing him from just a few feet away. In an instant, everything he'd done to prepare himself for this instant evaporated and all he had was the moment he was in as he stared in the face of the behemoth. Was he struck by fear? Would you be? What would you do? Nothing up to this point counts if you don't see it through. No matter what hoops you've had to jump through, and no matter what Kodiak bears you come upon, it's all moot unless you take the final step which is often the hardest one of all.

All your study, classes, conversations, meditations and silent retreats have brought you to this place where the next step into the light will take every bit of trust, faith, and courage you can muster. You won't want to take this step and then fall back into your old patterns of being. You want to take it and fall into a new pattern of being. And just because you took that expansive step into the Oneness today doesn't mean you won't face the bear tomorrow or the day after. But, each day you let go of the known you will deepen your ability to let go the next time.

If You Want the Rapture, You Can't Remain

To access the Infinite you must merge with the boundless. You will enter into a state beyond perception. Even your imaginal body, the externalized image for your awareness to know through, must be surrendered.

Absorption occurs when you let go of direct attention and find your equanimity in the radiant brilliance of consciousness. Find yourself letting go of even *that* awareness so you can unite, expand and let go again and again into the rapture of the limitless realms of the exquisite state of pure oneness. Many blessings will come of this immersion. Alignment with a full sense of Oneness will invite healing, deep calm, clarity, psychic awakening, visions of other times, astral travel, and lucid dreaming among only some of the takeaways. But, wait! It's imperative you recognize that delights to your world are the extras from the amplified realms and not the reason why you seek a sense of Oneness. The extras can become forcefully tempting, tantalizing you to succumb to a piece of the power while missing the whole. If you want to experience the rapture you can't remain in it.

No matter what heights or depths you realize, the swag of form do not bring the freedom you seek and if you remain there the bliss will never be realized. All must end for the new cycle to begin. To validate your truth, remember to ask yourself, *who is witnessing this oscillation of being?* The only release from attachment is letting go. No matter how extraordinary the domain of consciousness you activated seems, you must surrender from it as you did to it.

I spent my summers as a kid growing up in a then bohemian community called Malibu. I can still conjure up memories of digging clams at Big Rock, the smell of the salty sea air that wafted through the pier, and the funky sign outside Wiley's Bait Shop. Like clockwork, my friends and I would spend afternoons building elaborative sandcastles and fortresses. This was some serious business, this castle building effort. Each one of us was delegated responsibilities including managing delivery of the wet sand, water, and the silt that held it all together. From the spires to the moats, there wasn't a grain of sand out of place and passerby's praise fueled our expanding excitement. Years before SPF50 had even been considered no less invented, we'd spend hours and hours in the blazing sun constructing our architectural masterpieces, yet to what end? Lo and behold the tide would roll in as it has done every day since the beginning of time and reclaim what it begot through our efforts. Our early life lessons in letting go came of working so hard at building and defending what we alone had created. As the sun set, we were as likely to run home for dinner as we were to run out to the beach the next morning to start all over again. So goes the cycle of creation, attachment and letting go, always leaving room for what's next.

All the dimensions of awareness you carry for the amazing constructs in your life have their place and joy, but you can't go back tomorrow, because you won't find it where you built it. Maybe you took a picture of it and can talk about it after the fact, but you can't control and maintain the impermanent by calling it mine or yours. There's a trust that evolves from seeing emergence and completion demonstrated by the passing moments. Freedom is letting go of all and opening up beyond the observer, in a place which can't be identified.

Oneness

My family has a ranch in Montana called Mystic Mountain. I go there to reconnect, but whenever I return to my full-time home I find the experience turns into a dream. Old patterns surprisingly and quickly reappear and my calm body is easily activated into recalling anxiety, concerns and pressures of doing my dharma. What is real and matters is what I could touch, smell, feel and know in Montana. But it slips away to the call of chaos. Hard as I might try, I can't live in an enlightened memory. What becomes clear is spirituality exists only as what you're doing in the now. As much as I'd love to put down roots in my idyllic otherworldly experience, I must return to where I'm doing life and remember what's before me is my spiritual practice.

Knowing it's not the time in my life to make Mystic Mountain my new permanent residence, I attempt to bring the mental images of towering majestic pines as they sway to and fro to my memory. In my meditation, I see the glassy calm lake reflecting the snowcapped mountain peaks, hear the wings of the eagles soaring in the pristine blue sky, watch with delight as the fish jump through the glassy surface of the sparkling blue lake, and rest in the bodily sensations of the whole of it all. In a moment of sheer mystic memory, I am breathing the crisp, clean fresh air and listening to the thunder of silence while next to me a dragonfly in its metallic blue finery lands on a springy cattail. I am free of the mass of modern radio magnetic frequency waves that wash over me in my other bustling life. When you lean into the silence the stillness allows you to catch only little glimpses or pieces of the image. The longing comes of the truth that as much as you try, there's always something more to capture in the mental picture. Yet, close your eyes and you'll feel and hear nature inviting you back into her embrace. Time and space dissolve as you lucidly enter the picture again and realize you are as much a part of nature as the trees and the animals.

You are the experience the trees are having in the moving world. When you stop attempting to take images with you and allow yourself to enter into that setting you become conscious of the role you play as the Infinite in the now moment. It's because of the power of the now moment that you actually become part of the picture rather than attempting to recall it. Contrary to the possible belief that you are a separate observer, you always have access to every aspect of the beautiful when you choose to be part of it rather than just an on-looker. Whenever you consciously enter the timeless realm, a realignment of your wholeness is an instant option. You don't just have to survive with a goal of trudging through day after day. That kind of mentality is what disconnects you from your sense of Oneness to everything around you.

Harmony

Like most of the mystical, the realization of harmony can't be arrived at through words either. Imaginative thoughts are your steps to the doorway beyond them. You'll know you're there when you cross the threshold of individual consciousness into the atmosphere of Life Itself. In that state of glorious harmony, all conflict subsides and duality no longer exists because there is only One.

Stepping over the threshold doesn't mean you won't still face repeated challenges in your world. I've no doubt you'll be caught in fear, longing, jealousy, anger or whatever melodrama your life will throw at you from time to time. But, now you'll hear your observing self say, "Really? You got snagged by that one again?" In that liberating instant you'll become conscious once more, chuckling at yourself from the mountaintop. Your spiritual path calls for watchfulness. In other words don't get all cocky in your success. Just because you got it right this time doesn't mean you won't be tempted to slip up in the future.

The war in your mind creates a dark corner. When harmony enters that wounded space, it can approach conflict without aggression or resentment. Harmony knows that you are one with the assailant. If billions of stars can live in harmony in the cosmos, you too can live in harmony with the billions of thoughts and stories swirling through the galaxy of your awareness.

Living in Harmony is your true nature. Harmony dissolves the self-centered consciousness where feelings of fear and separation dwell. The cosmic consciousness feels its oneness with the universe where all is. A 40 watt light bulb will illuminate the darkness but a 150 watt bulb will reveal so much more. Rather than fighting off what you don't like, turn on a brighter light. Discovering what brings you fulfillment will eliminate a lot of irritation and is crucial to living in harmony. The strength of electrical power traveling the same wire into a building can be harnessed in different ways. Depending on the demand, that power can light either a 500 watt stage light or a nightlight. It's all a matter of your choice.

Mindfulness and discernment are your tools to assess every moment, keeping you aligned in harmony. Watch as you bring your present awareness into harmony and instantly your whole world will look brighter. Every day you're present here you play the part of bringing more harmony to the world. No expression too small will go unnoticed. Whether it's a smile, a soft touch, or a kind word; it's a wave of loving light that flows from you touching more people than you'll ever know.

Rhythmic consistency produces specific manifestations. The vibration that emanates from you is regulating and producing your harmony. Too often people attempt to force things into happening. This kind of battle keeps you from coming into harmony. Rapport with harmony eliminates blockage and opens the energy flow to reestablish the motion of your chi or life force. When you are at peace with yourself, you know your place in the universe.

When you're in harmony, you have no idea what inner guidance might emerge. You have to leave your ego at the curb to make room for a Greater Presence to present Itself. No matter what your academic accomplishments are, you can't figure out inspiration, it's just something that shines through you. When you don't follow your dreams it'll feel like something is dying in you. And no, you're not the only one who's ever felt that way. It's supposed to feel just that awful, because you're out of harmony with what you're meant to be doing. The closer you are to your true nature the more balanced and harmonic your life is, even in its extremes.

The mystical marriage is the only fitting conclusion of saying yes to love. The union of discordant perspectives and the fusion of clarity with a different view for a greater intention is pure ecstasy. With this marriage comes a new call to action and below the surface is all that's necessary to midwife this urge into being. You'll find a new creative expression awakening within. When you say yes to the new harmonic vibrations, a brighter light shines on a higher path that can only lead you into a pure, unadulterated state of bliss.

Blazing in the Glory of Light

There is a peace that surpasses understanding. It's a power that can stop wars, transform economic systems, and bring forth a desire to live in harmony with the earth. It also brings order out of chaos. Come closer to the center of the light, where there are no variables, no shadows and see this peace for what it is. Turn and face the light and make a commitment to take the tough step, face your discomfort and come to know the vital breath of light that fills your awareness. Be free from your ignorant emotional habits. The mastery of living is yours for the taking now. Too many turn away from the responsibility of the light and the joy of being consciously in the beam it casts. Your awakening is needed now. As the mass of humanity there are more contributing to tipping the scale of living unconsciously and out-of-balance than there are living in perfect harmony. Your role of living from a higher view of the mountaintop and as an expression of conscious living is needed now more than ever before.

You've been prepared for a time such as this. You must remain vigilant in your insistence to listening to your observing self. Remember, you are the light of the world. It can only uniquely exist with you as its conduit. Blaze with this glory of Life and let others hold on to their melancholy; you are a light worker and have much to do here. Through your work, much of the discouraging human condition will be purified and transmuted. When enough individuals come into this light you'll witness planetary issues reversing their course. You will be able to tell your children's children you *did* do something to make a difference. Keep your light bright and you'll never be held hostage to the strains of the mass mentality, for you'll always be a deliverer of the light.

And just to clarify, darkness can never snuff out the light. You are always free to choose between the darkness or the light and it's in this freedom that the stones upon your path turn to dust and the concerns of the past dissolve into nothingness. But, you must be patient with yourself on the path of light. Don't be tempted to seek another road to travel and still expect to reap the rewards of the sweetness in life. Follow the light and you'll be freed from the calcification of your ethereal and energetic astral shell. Remember, sensitive psychic individuals see the subjective fields and not the realm of the All Animating Creating Life Force. They aren't coming from the mountaintop because they're still operating from the vibrational realm of cause and effect. You can and will go vibrationally higher than your average oracle reader.

You, who temporarily inhabits your body, won't become any more spirit when you leave the flesh. The very one who listens to the mountaintop voice of the observer is actually the observer whose voice you hear. It's just the doubting and non-accepting, that tempts and torments you into believing a separation from the light is even possible.

When your consciousness operates from the mountaintop of light, you are no longer susceptible to the thought process of those in the flesh causing discomfort. Everyone makes mistakes but if your greater desire is for a greater expression of Life all of those mistakes will be absolved in the light. The human impulses that compel your attention like errors, personalities, and diversions are all passing elements of human expression. Know that no matter what experience you might be caught up in you can always move to the place of quietude beyond silence and be freed from responses that would keep you earthbound.

You'll discover a confidence and strength that comes from knowing harmony within. As dramas noisily work themselves out, don't allow yourself to become dismayed in your quiet bringing of the light. Don't undervalue your unseen contribution to the emergence of the light because indeed, your role is significant. As those around you chose to put their faith in the adversary and live instead through fear, you will have chosen to live from within. You have placed your trust in the Light from within disintegrating the evidence of the senses. Infinite Love meets every endeavor.

As you're only generally conscious of the eternality of

now, when you're coming from your high resolve it's so beyond your ordinary comprehension, you may not even notice anything taking place within you. Don't forget, your mind can't come along for the ride when you enter the higher realms of consciousness. But your gentleness is able to merge and observe. You are about as far away from Oneness as you can be when your mind keeps you distracted journeying down every side road. It won't go down without a fight if you entice it to surrender its dominance. When your mind surrenders, pressures and tensions ease, but the shift may be as subtle as when the captain of a cruise ship changes course and the passengers are completely unaware that a new horizon is in view.

You will soon see the inner-connectedness of all things when you bathe in the Light. Surrender to the guidance from this mountaintop perspective and the holographic fullness of history and potential will make itself known instantly in the present moment. The reality of you is invisible and intangible which is why being an observer of your life is essential to keeping you in touch with the imperceptible and un-manifested parts of your soul's expression.

Remaining in touch with the indiscernible aspects of who you are will make it easier to reestablish your authority in the visible world. By virtue of an acknowledgement of knowing your union in the Absolute you are empowered. Even when you get pressed by the heaviness of events in your life and you seem to disappear under their cloak you will know your strength in Oneness. If your desire is to be the conduit of the Infinite, then no littleness can deny Its expression. The two just can't coexist. The more open you are to what is beyond your understanding, the more available you become to a greater realization of what lies within you. You become clearer and more present to what is being revealed to you. Nothing has scale to the limitless, Infinite and Transcendent. Nothing. In context, your daily tasks and challenges in and of themselves can seem almost insignificant.

Do not run with the wailers and complainers of your mind

allowing yourself to tarnish under your beggar thoughts. Instead, be persistent in allowing your radiance to shine. You serve as a collaborator of Life's unfoldment by bringing the light to wherever you are in thought or form. Your charge is to enlighten mortal confusion and restlessness in the mundane sphere of the earth plane.

Be lifted by the wave of light. It will incinerate the heaviest of impurities; liberating you to stand on higher ground enabling you to see the expanded vistas. The light will awaken you from your slumber revealing you have been cleared from the hard law of consequences. You've been set free from needing to spiritually scrutinize all your trials and tribulations in an attempt to find something of significance to please your mind. You are called into action now.

There's no effort in the light, though something in you feels as if you must do something that exhausts you to validate your efforts. Stop with all the spiritual busybody stuff and get to your mountain peak touching the stars, right away. Don't face choice in the dark. Follow purposeful action with an enlightened view of all that's yours to do - and do it with no ifs, ands, or buts!

Beings of Brightness

When you master the light the darkness will disappear. In the most esoteric of ways, you've been created for the light but kept in the dark. Rebels. We all know them and often even try to suppress that aspect in ourselves. The rebels are the ones who shine the new light where the controlling elements prefer no one to look.

The euphemisms, or the standard clichés of the day, put the spin on truth so you don't see it in the light for what it really is. Some examples of this Orwellian doublespeak include referring to the Department of War as the Department of Peace. How about the use of sanitized, ethnic cleansing to describe genocide, or the even more politically gentle correctional facility instead of the term jail? Lest we forget the more politically correct way of referring to someone getting fired as having been let go. Let go from what?

Visionaries who are excited and revitalized about new possibilities are framed as fanatical and extremist by those who prefer a robotic, non-questioning conformist. *Are whistleblowers the heroes of our times or are they the criminals some would want you to believe?* So, darkness is cast and people move into fear forgetting at any time they can flip the switch turning on the ever-available light. If you don't flip the switch, it'll never matter that it was available to you all along. The first hint of light can reveal new insights beyond what's been seen and known by many and defended by few.

The first domino is strongly defended to prohibit it from starting an unstoppable chain reaction of occurrences bringing down those who call the shots. When the walls do start their downfall, eye-opening surprises are exposed that have been tightly guarded. Protect that first domino, even if most don't know where it is, as it needs shielding from exposure to any kind of question that could topple it. An excellent example of this is the ongoing denial of planetary weather change despite reams of validating and credible proof. The violent defensiveness of those that denied and continue to deny its existence is in the face of the growing numbers who know its damage. At this point, it seems only those that are literally shielded with blinders could not acknowledge the damage greenhouse gasses have inflicted on our planet, yet the debate seems to continue. Follow the money and you'll find those who benefit by not changing present patterns of destructive behavior.

The blanket that has been cast on this world has put most people in a state of forgetfulness, a sort of collective amnesia. False impressions promote separation and combativeness. People are walking around like zombies in a functional black-out, and the result is a prolific number of them don't wake up until the time of their impending death. It's no wonder they spend their final hours in agony, their hearts filled with unexpressed appreciation and love put on hold for decades.

The bringers of this new bright light reorganize priorities from their inter-dimensional viewpoint. Master the light, now, while you're healthy and able to travel through the inter-dimensional portals beyond the battle of opposites. Don't wait to find resolution in a pained heart later when you're exhausted and your body no longer functions as it once did. It's better to store up on the light while things are going swimmingly in your world than when the rip tides roll in. You're far better prepared to deal with the chaos with a good amount of spiritual insurance in the bank of your consciousness.

On your journey, you'll come across beings of brightness so light they can't take on the density of human form. But the wisdom they have to share with you is ever available for transference because it's not bound by form. You have been and will always be welcome into the light and you've never been more prepared than you are in this moment.

Close your eyes and imagine you're a golden chalice whose bejeweled bowl awaits the fruits of the vine. No longer apprehensive, you reconnect to the cellular knowledge of the unknown precious cargo you've carried with you on your journey throughout this book. With this knowledge you can very carefully bring forth this exquisite treasure from within your being welcoming the outpouring of this extraordinary light. Engage and open your earthly body's arms, palms facing up, as you watch and feel the transference of the light wisdom being poured into you as the receptive chalice. Breathe in deeply, filling your lungs with this brightness of Life. Exhale and breathe in even deeper, filling your earthly body with revitalized, replenishing wisdom. Continue this practice until you are full. Be there, bathing in the fullness of the light, filled with the undifferentiated potential of the Infinite just waiting for you to give it form. When you're done, and you will know without a shadow of a doubt, quickly open your eyes without moving your body and feel the stark difference. Without moving your head, shift your glance around the room and notice the sudden contrast from where you were to where you are now. Feel the lingering memory of both moments anchored within.

There can sometimes be a feeling of dissonance when coming back from the lightness to this density of form. When you are first developing your mystical practice, it can feel as if you walked out of a movie theater after a double feature in the dark. When you entered the theater, the daylight wasn't jarring, but after a few hours entrained to watch the projection of light on a screen in the dark, your vision adjusted. Now you are pushing the door of the theater open again and the sunlight and your system is shocked by the general commotion of life after losing yourself in the theater. You'll find it can take a few moments for your eyes to adjust and your mind and system to re-acclimate again; the same can be said for returning from your mountaintop.

When the light reveals the realm of Truth, the desire to conceal through control becomes a non-issue. You speak the truth because you're in the light and there's nothing to hide. Light makes everything clearer. You know as well as you are known. You see as well as you can see. George Orwell wrote, "The further a society drifts from truth, the more it will hate those who speak it." When the suppressed truth is released it explodes like a volcano disrupting present form. *How can the truth set you free if you're not paying attention?*

You don't need to reject experiences and facts; instead, you must allow them to teach you another lesson. If you allow the light of your heart to shine into your open mind when you're stuck, you'll be able to see what's going on around you. Mindfully notice and care to understand what's true rather than imposing a need to impress your will. Don't so quickly refute the natural experiences of anxiety, heartache and death. In this high tech low touch era, it's easy to drift away from our inner screens of truth. Sadly, the technological age gives so much information online that many lose touch with the innate intelligence with which they were born.

The technological revolution has even changed the traditional method of checking the weather. Instead of walking outside your front door or looking out your kitchen window, you can sit at your computer and surf radar maps and meteorological websites. It's just too easy not to. Instead of opening windows some choose to walk across the room to adjust the thermostat. Rather than seeing death as a natural part of evolution, the elderly get sent to homes inoffensively referred to as Eldercare facilities when all they really want to do is go home. The media deluges everyone with smiling ads of photo-shopped body types parading around and pretending that this typical made-up reality is true while aging isn't. My grandmother, mom and dad all died in our home, and that seems pretty natural to me. Sending loved ones elsewhere to die in a sterile facility, on the other hand, seems like someone else's version of what they think is good for the masses because it's pleasant and innocuous.

Your Fractal Self

The intention of living in the light is to become beholders of it everywhere. You'll no longer have needs because they're long met before you're even aware of them. When your motives no longer matter and, in fact, cease to exist and you serve as a conduit for Life to flow unrestricted as you, you are living in the light. You'll find your desire to be nowhere except where you are. Now is the only time that exists. There's no worrying about tomorrow because now is the only time that exists. When someone reaches out to you for help, there is no room for contemplation. There is no hesitation while you craft a response. Give that approach up and just listen to find the wisdom speaking through you. If you try thinking of a truth to say to make something better, you're attempting to give that statement power. Remember, no statement has power. If you want to give it power in that moment, or you are waiting for your profound statement to change that person or their circumstance, then it's just a graven image. It doesn't matter if it's a golden calf or perfect sentence structure with some flowery words, it is not the power. Your egoic mind must be distanced from the formulation of thought so the true power of Life can move through you. There's much to be said for the power of positive thinking, and while it's better than negative thinking, it's not the power either. Be the place where the power of Life Itself flows through you. When someone asks you for help, confidently quit your thinking and instead, allow the Power of compassionate wisdom to do Its thing as you.

You must become the Truth, because you are the Truth. No matter how briefly in earth time it is, when you enter the realization of the Truth of your being, you'll be forever changed to match your new vibration. You'll become a finer, more acutely attuned version of who you knew as yourself. It's almost as if you've been endlessly wandering in a nightmare of separation. In the moment of your awakening you will realize you have returned to your familiar home of awareness and all the separateness that's haunted you is gone. You're freed from your association to prerecorded self-images, prior experiences and the concern about what's on your life's horizon. This brief encounter activates a cellular recall of wholeness leaving a graceful wake of recollection.

The veil will part long enough for you to catch a glimpse of your fractal dimension of familiar reality to realign with the part of you that's without dimensional limitation. Your iteration into form is the boundary you put on the Infinite. Actually, it's not so much a border as it is a set of margins between which you live your reality. But, your True Nature of Life is not there. This marginal dimensionality seems real to you but it's important to recognize it's only a fraction of the whole containing all possibility. Your agreement to participate in this time and space means you've allowed amnesia to cover the Absolute Awareness and consented to move around within the agreements of this dimension. Your small story only applies to your small self. But, no matter what constraints you encounter, who you are will always be a fractional part of the Whole. That is Truth and who you are can never be lost in the small story. It's always available, easily recalled and never goes away. All form and astonishing visions will at some point pass, but don't weep in sadness. Life is always changing, as it reflects an expression that is forever reaching, emerging and birthing Itself into greater form.

When you know the Absolute as yourself, it's as if Life Itself will be looking at Life with Life's own eyes. The power in understanding this is in sensing the Divine with the Divine's own spirit-loving-life. The mind is left behind in the direct mystical gnosis; the theophany of the soul as your spirit opens to love and light.

Distinctions and Dimensions Vanish

The One Mind, the One which knows all, is the timeless witness to two distinct dimensions within your life. The first dimension is the ever-changing flow of experience and the second, is the participation you take in living that experience. You can be one with the unfoldments or you can live in the pain of endurance. Your choice lies in the decision whether to resist or surrender to the flow of those unfoldments. Dissolving into the flow of life is an effortless experience that can't be figured out. It's something which usurps any power you think you have. The love and joy of life, which is ever available 24/7, can't come to visit if you're busy trying to control the way everything happens not to mention the outcomes. You must be open and available to experience the effulgence. It just can't be mandated.

Your life is full of road signs; the aim is to follow the flicker of light back to the source and become one with it. That merging of you and the light-source is the consummation of your journey through this realm. In the light there is no darkness. In the light there is only eternal wisdom, total knowingness, and illumined sight. Through the integration with the richness of Life, the Eternal projects its intricacies and multi-faceted expressions in the field of form.

When you're the transparency for the unseen to be seen you have only unparalleled elation to look forward to. When the manifest world, with its intrigue and mysteries, gives way to the Light of the Ultimate Truth, you will be absorbed in its love and grace. It's as effortless as moving from one room of your house to another; you simply pass from one state of awareness to another one with a fuller understanding and a greater wattage brightening the higher perspective. Secure your gaze on the emanating light and don't look back. In this light there is no creation or demise, yet all creation and transcendence takes place within light. As the light splits apart, if you choose to ride the beam from what appears further from the source, you'll be identifying more with your false self, forgetting the all-embracing, graceful glow of eternal oneness.

As the sun's beams shine through the many different windows of your house, they eventually unite as one light once again. Multiplicity disappears as what starts out as different streams become one. It's just that simple and when it all streams into one, it becomes brighter and all that was hidden is known. As your perception becomes more acute you perceive beauty and joy with an ecstatic knowing that what you're looking at is not separate from you. You are no longer looking out at it, but are being and knowing as it. All distinctions and dimensions vanish as you shimmer and glimmer as the all-knowing Light.

Now that you carry the light, in you as you, it's time to come back to doing your dharma while remaining as consciously connected to Source as possible.

There's a wonderful story that depicts the nature of life after enlightenment with perfection. A disciple who spent a number of years in a monastery experienced many moments of deep knowing and felt he was finally ready for the ultimate and ecstatic transcendent experience of light. With that intent, he went to the monastery's Master Teacher and announced his readiness and excitement to go to the mountaintop to become enlightened. He explained that he'd either stay up there until he received it or died. The teacher recognized his student was indeed ready, and granted his request. After embarking on his trek, the student climbed higher up the mountain and the trail became narrower and narrower, the air thinner and the edges steeper when he came upon an old man heading down the same mountain path he was trekking. With his weather-worn skin and torn outer clothes, the scraggly old gent looked tired but satisfied as he hauled a big bundle of something over his shoulder. When they came upon one another the student saw a glint of wisdom in the old man's eyes and approached him kindly. "Do you know what enlightenment is?" he asked him. The old man looked at him squarely and set his bundle down and in that instant, the disciple received enlightenment. Still amazed in both the realization and the simplicity of it, he sat down for a moment as he digested the knowledge that enlightenment was just a matter of putting one's burden down. As he assimilated the information, he became so excited he naturally stood up and began hiking back up the path when something occurred to him. *Wait, he thought, now that I'm enlightened, what do I do next?* In that instant, he turned back towards the wise old man. "Old man," he hollered and the echo caught the wise one's attention as he turned his glance back up the path toward the student. "Old man, now what?" To which the old man responded with a shrug as he picked up his bundle, slung it over his shoulder and continued back down the path. The student realized the simple yet profound answer in the old man's response overwrote his own expectation of what enlightenment would look like. Indeed, after the burden-free mountaintop experience, you will still have to come back and walk this world.

When you're really ready, I mean *really* ready, your answers will come in revelatory interactions with others or ephemeral visions. You might catch a glimpse in poetry, or art may remind you of a realm without rulers. Perhaps it will be music for you as it might activate your natural rhythm of an illumined heart. The activation of enlightenment is only the beginning of your next step on the cosmic path down from the mountaintop and back into life. Only then can you integrate what you've come to know. You have been entrusted and shown a lot and much is needed from you. So pick up your bundle and bring on the light.

Light Meditation

When leaving the body behind, it's always a good idea to know how blessed you are in this field of grace in which you play. Before meditation, take a moment to state:

I know all is well and wherever I go in my expanding awareness, all is good and I am safe. I'm surrounded by and live in an Omni Dimensional Life Force that can never be violated, because there is nothing opposed to it. I move on the very currents of Life Itself and I'm free to notice all things without attachment to anything. Free to move beyond any image at any time and courageous enough to remain in it. I open to a graceful guidance on my soul's adventure, surrender my demands to logical understandings, and welcome new and unknown states of consciousness for my soul's evolution.

Take a few breaths to bring your attention back to the center of your body. Find a natural rhythm for your breath to fall into. See if you can follow your in-breath into your body . . . Exhale. Take with it any tension, worries, or concerns while creating more internal room. Find a natural rhythm to your breathing and following your next breath, let it take you deeper into the space beyond your body temple, where past and future dissolve into the present. Your inner awareness becomes the threshold you move across, where now your exhale *propels* you further into the openness of the void. Allow yourself to become available and receptive to a deep hearing and heightened awareness to move you to greater good.

Notice you are in a vast expanse with infinite points of light as if you are in a galaxy of stars . . . Allow your awareness to be drawn to a beautiful blue orb that is calling you home . . . feel an attraction and relational remembrance to the vibrancy of this world. You move in closer and when you do, you see the pristine snowcapped mountains, the wooded forests, the lush green jungles, the expansive deserts, deep canyons, still lakes, running rivers, and the all-embracing blue ocean . . . Your soul is deeply moved by the physical beauty. As your awareness of the magnificence of this place is heightened, you feel the call of this earth for the gift you have to bring. You return to your perfect mountaintop . . .

Sitting on your mountaintop, you see brilliant rays of light streaming through the silver-lined clouds . . . You notice that there is one cloud that seems to open up and as it does a bright white ray of light shoots down right through its thinnest layers towards the top of your head refracting a prism of colors. Within the frequency of each color is an energizing power, a life sustaining vibrancy flowing toward you and entering the different layers of your auric shell with its rainbow of colors right above your head . . . splitting through nature's natural prism you are bathed in this kaleidoscopic spectrum . . . you feel these colors enter your auric shell penetrating deeply into your body, mind, and soul.

Feel the base of your spine tingling . . . feel as it comes alive from the red light waves awakening your physical energy. The sacral awakens to harmony in your emotional layer from the orange wave of light . . . The solar plexus rouses to the yellow beam of light stirring your mental field . . . The green beam finds residence in your heart space bringing balance to your astral layer . . . The blue ray brings strength to your throat center finding a power in your etheric layer . . .

The indigo wave imbues your brow bringing balance to the celestial layer activating the third eye's ability to see the celestial realm . . . The violet ray permeates your crown illuminating your ketheric layer bringing a golden radiance to your countenance, for there can be no luster without the light. Feel this light pouring in you, over you, and through you, fine tuning your light frequencies. Feel the merging of the rainbow within you. You are the pot of gold pouring forth the luminosity as brightly as it is pouring into you. You are a transparency of the shimmering, iridescent light fountain sparkling beautifully. Feel the power of the multifaceted luminescence coursing through your body as a perfectly blended laser of white light.

This surge of energy passing through your spinal cord is as if the flood gates have been opened, the breakers have been flipped, and the high beams turned on. The array of light activates your dormant potential. Through this, innovation flows, your awareness becomes inspired, and you simply become a higher voltage of power. In this state of heightened awareness, you will witness the pulse and vibrational frequency of all things. There's an abundance of the vital force moving through you. These waves of joy and bliss that move up and down your body intensify, purify, cleanse and heal all that you are. Feel lighter and more energetic as this attunement expands your clarity of awareness. This sweeping light can no longer be contained by your body or your auric shell . . . Feel the expansion of your light filling the room . . . but notice that the room cannot contain the light of your being as it expands beyond the walls blessing your neighborhood . . . Your exponential expansion moves beyond even your city to grace the nation . . . Watch as your light expands far beyond the earth to fill the sky and blanket the earth . . . Your cosmic light expands beyond even that until you shine like a star in the sky realizing you are a portal of the Infinite. Be with this for a while . . .

Are you a star looking at you, looking out at the star-painted sky from where you just came, or are you looking at the star-painted sky dreaming you are a star looking back at you . . .

You return to your mountaintop refreshed and renewed . .

. Know once you've been somewhere you can easily return to that somewhere by simply calling it back to your awareness. There is always more work to be done, but for now, pull yourself back into your body permitting gratitude for your discoveries to fill your field of awareness . . . Feel a joy knowing you'll be consistently returning to your sacred space, but for now, choose a path down the mountain. Familiarize yourself with this trail back into the world of form. Know there is always this corridor, this passage back to the elevated perspective of your world. Touch some of the trees as you pass by them and feel the earth move beneath your feet. As what you saw in a distance comes more into focus, return your attention to your breath. Breathe . . . When you are ready, slowly move your fingers and toes, stretch, gently open your eyes and sit for a moment to re-acclimate to your physical world. Take your pen and take some time to write out your experience. It doesn't matter if it was memorable and you are certain you'll never forget it, you should still capture it on paper – later, you'll be glad you did.

Out beyond wrong doing and right doing there is a field of luminous consciousness. I'll meet you there.
~ Rumi

Soulful Adventures

- When in your life have you put in a great effort and at the last minute balked? What kept you from rubbing the head of the Kodiak? What were the mental images that came to mind keeping you from taking the toughest step? Are those images still residing in you now? When you took a big step, how did your world change as a result of your courage?
- Looking back, what sandcastles of form did you defend so vehemently despite them not meaning much to you

now? What if you had this present kind of detachment in the moment you exuded a fierce defensiveness. How would your behavior have been different?

- A 40 watt light bulb will illuminate the darkness but a 150 watt bulb will reveal so much more from the same darkness, bringing greater clarity and depth. Where can you replace low wattage bulbs with higher wattage bulbs in your life?

- What inspiration is stirring in you that you haven't given life to? If you say yes to that stirring, can you imagine the level of bliss that will arrive in your world?

- What contributions of harmony are you making to keep the scales from tipping in the other direction? How else can you bring harmony to your world?

- How does your doubting mind create separation and problems for you? Where would trusting bring more ease and joy to your life?

- By remaining in touch with the indiscernible aspects of who you are it's easier to reestablish your authority in the visible world - where would you like this brighter light to shine? How are you being called to action?

- Be the light and go express some love and appreciation today.

- Is there somewhere that being more truthful would create a volcanic eruption in your world? What do you fear from this truth that is keeping you a prisoner of the dark?

- Your iteration into form is the boundary you put on the Infinite. They are not borders so much as they are the margins between which you are living your reality. What margin of your reality can you stretch into a fuller experience of your greater expression?

Body and Soul Practice for Connecting

Body Connection

Want to become lighter, give something up. Try some abstinence from something that is weighing you down for 30 days and observe the difference and conversations going on in your head. Keep a journal and notice the shifts in your world from just removing that one Achilles heel. Look at those shifts with curiosity and play in the new energy created where there was once heaviness. Assess if what you gave up is something that is better left behind.

Soul Connection

Find a comfortable spot to sit, close your eyelids and focus internally on the black void behind the brow. Alternatively, sit or lay down in a dark room. As images come along, dissolve them and stay focused on the nothingness you see in front of you until you see a light appear, eventually popping you through a portal to the other side where you can lucidly look back upon your physical body in the room. There's no need for concern, you're safe when you are in this light and space. Allow yourself to be where you want to see knowing in the fourth dimension you can instantly be anywhere. After a time your awareness will want to be back in the body, just say yes and you'll find yourself gliding back into form.

Mystical writing

Enlightenment is like the moon

Enlightenment is like the moon reflected on the water.
The moon does not get wet, nor is the water broken.
Although its light is wide and great.
The moon is reflected even in a puddle an inch wide.
The whole moon and the entire sky
Are reflected in one dewdrop on the grass.

~ Dogen
1200-1253

Chapter 10: Freedom

I have learned silence from the talkative, tolerance from the intolerant and kindness from the unkind.
~ Kahil Gibran

You Choose the Ride

Are you an adventure hound? Do you look up longingly at wild rides coursing through the center of theme parks like unwieldy veins? Are you transfixed with an inexhaustible childlike excitement at the thought of taming a beast that rattles and clangs while spinning and tipping and flying through the air? It's so true that a roller coaster always returns you to where you started a bit more excited than when you hopped on. The definition of a good adventure is one that returns you home safely but changed. A good roller coaster is an exhilarating thrill ride whose primary intention is to take you on an adventure to the outer limits of, and in some cases beyond, your comfort zone. Most start off slow with a gradual chain-clanking pull up to the monster's apex giving you a quick glimpse of where you're about to go (not that what you see is what you are actually about to experience). But wait, did you have an unbridled moment of fear as the 15-year old park employee reached over your lap and buckled you in? Not that far-fetched, since the fear removes freedom from whatever circumstance you are facing down. There's not too much freedom within the experience once the seatbelt is tugged tightly across your chest. You are about to have the ride of your life. Your pounding heart and pumping adrenaline feels as if it's about to pop through your skin as the carriage drops, leaving you floating in the air above your seat, with only your seat belt keeping you attached. Yes, you'll survive the steep drops, accelerated twists and turns, soul-searching inversions, and bone-rattling spiraling banks. With outrageously messy hair and maybe a little color left in your face, you'll pull back into the station where it all began with a grin from ear to ear. As wild a ride as it was, though it may not have felt it, you were always safe. No doubt you were caught up in the adventure; but, you were always connected to a track that was going to return you to where you started filled with joy and a greater sense of freedom for having faced the unknown.

Can you see where I'm going with this? Your adventure begins the moment your mind catches a glimpse of what's possible. Something comes more alive in you when you are standing in line, or signing up for a class, or hearing about new states of consciousness. Not until you address what has captured your awareness will you be freed. Your soul adventures are demonstrations that you're always on your perfect track because your spirit is not bound to your physical experience. You'll come back to this world with a newfound freedom from what had gripped your mind before you left on your mountaintop excursion.

There are no gray areas when it comes to being free. There isn't an "I'm kind of free" space, you either *are* or you *aren't.* Freedom isn't a gift of the governments, it's an inalienable right you can choose to exercise or give away. The challenge comes when you've ceased to own your own personal power of freedom. When your awareness gets sucked into identifying with the distractions and activities in your environment, it's no longer empowered by your freedom. It will only be known as the aspect of you it attached itself to.

After a thrill ride, surviving a wipe out, coming through a dark night of the soul, or a tumultuous spin through this life, you have the potential to awaken the inner freedom of your spirit which, in hindsight, you'll realize was the purpose of all of this when you stepped onto the adventure ride to begin with. You, who is observing, gets to decide if what's calling for your attention warrants further investigation. *What rides are you choosing to take in life?* Do you find the climactic drops and intoxicating speed exhilarating or terrifying? Are your relationships with others a ride on the Tilt-a-whirl? Does your career feel like a House of Terrors or an adventure cruise? Are the addictions in your life like the Spinout?

Will you or won't you allow a ride's gravitational magnetism to pull you onto its track? Like those clouds, the ones that move through the sky but don't change it, you can let the low vibration temptations pass on through your awareness without changing you or your perspective. After time, nothing will be able to remove you from the driver's seat of consciousness. As soon as you notice an imbalance of heavy awareness, stop talking about it. When things go wrong you don't have to go wrong with them. Let them move on through and out without you. Remain unchanged, but allow the heaviness to move through you.

There will always be an unsolicited yet constant invitation to jump into the old memories, future plans, doubts, guilt and judgments that clash with your sense of freedom; but, there's no need to engage your energy. Just don't get on that ride. Instead, remove your attention. The beauty of consciously focusing your attention on staying grounded is when the loud distractions that are begging to be noticed just pass through your field of awareness. You've come to know there isn't any truth about a problem, there is only truth about the Truth. Through your mystical goggles, you'll begin to see the perfection in the imperfections.

Is It Beneficial?

Too often, only one option is seen. It's usually not the richest or most life enhancing of choices, either. The mystic has an espy kind of vision seeing beyond the limited to the waiting Infinite. The mystical mind understands there is a knowing of much, rather than being stuck in a particular. Not that there's a right or wrong choice, it's just that some directions are beneficial while others are not. Freedom brings with it the opportunity to see multiple tracks with a diversity of choices instead of being caught, albeit comfortably, in the mundane routine of normalcy. Gone is the abandonment of developing your ability to hear what the witnessing self has to say.

You returned to the station from where you started, and yes there is full validation that you were on a wild ride but now you know through having had the experience that it didn't kill you. You didn't die. There are cycles of adventure that come to an end only to be the foundation for a new beginning. Each frame of the movie is complete in itself but yet part of a fuller picture. Fear of death is gone and the longing to be anywhere but where you are now, is over. You are lifted to see perfection and wholeness in this very moment rather than thinking you're missing it elsewhere. You come to know your essence, your true nature, as a component or fractal of pure reality of Life Itself, perfect, whole and complete as you. You know you were all that before you were born and you will continue to be after your departure from this dimension. Remember, you are the one observing your choices, your body and activity in this time in space. The experience itself is not you.

There is brightness in your countenance around your newfound freedom. You've been liberated from your self-imposed prison of fear. Does it feel like you've been released from a straightjacket? It should, because you have taken the power back by journeying through the dark night of your soul questioning everything you held to be true, including what your five senses told you was the truth since you first experienced the three-dimensional world as a human being.

You transcended time to join the initiates of the great mystery schools of antiquity to discover you are not bound by your body in this dimension. You are far more than the frequencies and shapes of what your eyes tell you is the truth here. You are a diverse and abundant expression of Life loving Itself as you. In this kind of realization all separation dissolves and healing occurs gracefully because you've become a master of the light, returning to the station of your form and bringing the relevance of an expanded awareness with you.

After you begin to adjust to a greater clarity and depth of light in the level of human form it becomes as effortless to employ your new filters to every area of your life as walking into the next room. What used to feel like chaos as your children bickered over who got to use the laptop next now feels like an invitation for growth and understanding. In their inability to agree you're able to see their distinct points of view and even better, the lesson each will learn from the consequence of the intended outcome. The babysitter's tardiness and overall inconsideration for leaving all those dishes in the sink and your living room looking like a tornado hit it, welcomes your loving kindness rather than an empty form of confrontation leaving everyone concerned shrouded in dense negative energies. Within every wound, within all crisis, within every experience that used to confound you as emotion took the driver's seat and you found yourself pushed to the waaay waaay back now exists the power to heal itself, prioritizing the lesson and the greater spiritual insight with virtually no effort. And isn't that the key? Isn't that the ultimate irony, that the less effort you spend trying to figure it all out and 'cope' with the difficulties that they themselves do the heavy lifting and work themselves out without much more than your observation?

Have you ever tried to untangle a necklace? While your efficient approach to conquer multiple knots and snags may seem easily scientific, the truth is, the needle and tweezers are best left in the drawer. Better, breathe deeply, know that the truth of the jewelry is in its finding its right place, and gently lift it off the table knowing it will direct you how to move it to recover its uncompromised length. Watch and wonder how a half hour of acute untangling is met with alchemy as it gently untangles itself with a few directional sways of the hand. Like in the divine plan of nature, how the grass knows how to grow, how the trees regenerate every

Spring, how the birds know how to fly south, how the necklace knows how to untangle itself . . . in the divine plan of human form we're all an integral part of a unified and diverse picture that is best met without resistance.

So you ask yourself, is it me that has changed? Well, in a way, yes and a way no. Your observer's perception is far different from the egoic charged filters you used to see through before the mountaintop filter came to be. So, it depends how you define the me that is you. Remember when I had you look in the mirror to unpeel the sense of you under the you seen in your mirror's reflection. What *has* changed is how you, the witness, sees and perceives everything outside of your human form. It's almost like being reborn. A question to ponder is whether it was the witness or your ability to understand the witness that has changed.

What I'm trying to say is, once you've put on your mountaintop lenses, you are still 100% at choice. You can choose to go with the perspective you've come to know as grace or you can choose to respond in your old, pre-mystic patterns and simply endure the painful experiences in the way that served you until you found unparalleled bliss. Seems a relatively simple choice to make if you surrender to the ease rather than fighting the battle, but sometimes the response comes from a place of disappointment (egoic will). Wanting dinner and finding yourself stuck in a meeting are two mutually exclusive situations. Again, coming back to the choice of what you observe and what vibration you wish to view it from is always a freedom you can exercise.

Libraries of Consciousness

Entering the mystical is like walking up the uneven stone steps of an enormous old city library. Ever wonder how many footsteps gently tapped each stair to cause the pavement to be so worn? If each visitor brings an unconscious curiosity alongside their task to complete at the library, imagine the vibrational amalgamate of spirit in that house of words. That is, after all, what a library is. It could easily be defined as a mansion of word-smithing, communication, ideas, truths and stories - some as old as time itself. Each carrying with it the energy of those who wrote it, lived it, not to mention every single person in history who'd ever read or heard it. What a metaphor of collective consciousness!

Stepping through the doors to the magical home of all this wisdom, you find your physical and subjective senses inundated with an intense and vivid overload of impressions. The rich history and knowledge stored there is calling to be heard, felt and assimilated. The scent of aged parchment wafts through the halls carrying with it alchemized images of possibility aching to be known again and again. Don't you just know that feeling in your gut? That, "so many books, so much knowledge, so little time" overwhelm in the moment you realize you want it all. You crave to sit on the floor and inhale the contents of every single word in the building. There is excitement stirring in the anticipating soul for secrets to be revealed. Your freedom lies in this omniscient realm of the unformed fifth dimension eager to birth itself again through you and your choice to embrace it within your awareness.

This expanding numinous awareness of your being releases you from a defensiveness to know there is more for you to know. Mystics are conscious of their connection to the Infinite. *What's going on in your world that is keeping you from grabbing a new book off the endless shelf of wisdom?* What is making it difficult to live from your observer's mountaintop view? Freedom is born out of our ability to work with any dynamic or difficulty that arises.

When circumstances of the body, heart or mind keep recurring, it's an indication, whether a subtle nudge or a loud message, this caller of consciousness is asking for your fuller awareness here. Take the time to be quiet with this persistent caller, invite them in and have a deeper exchange with what is being brought to you. Whatever of significance that comes into your sight, just be present with it. Freedom is your ability to enter wisely into all the frequencies of this world, awesome or awful. You'll find freedom in the everyday events of your life if you choose to see them as points of your spiritual practice. Those situations where you struggle and are most vulnerable, are the access points to unlock the arcane mystery of your life. These points always require relinquishing your fortified perspective, and you can only do that if you are free enough to trust.

There is a peace and wisdom that comes with being alright with not having to hold the knowing for everything. Insight comes alive in the presence of mystery when the awareness is open to what's possible beyond the known. The mountaintop view comes into clearer focus as you mature into trusting more in love than knowledge. Follow what you love and you will find a passage into a supported joyous way of being. You are not labeled by your past, you are prepared by it. Your history is not keeping you from your success and fulfillment but propelling you into it. You must learn to trust your brilliance more than your disappointments. Because you said yes to that brilliance, it makes life more beautiful. Engage with what you said yes to and you will find a freedom in the commitment as everything unlike it becomes clearer for you to release.

Dawn of Your New Epoch

After your revelation of the emergence of the Whole as you, you realize your conscious connection is about your contribution to Life. This involvement is a key to your energy living on long after you pass through. As you follow your joy you'll find yourself in service to humanity and participating at the dawn of a new epoch. Old axioms like 'what's in it for me' and 'I'm in this alone' give way to 'We are all in this together' *Is it odd that 'not bad' is somehow considered 'good' in the context of two choices?* An example of this might resemble a conversation over tea with a friend about the destruction in the rainforest being minimal or a celebration of losing only three or four animals to extinction this month. The dialogue of this mentality is decimating our environment and it's time to contribute to the collective again.

There's an inter-dependence within all domains of life. You are part of an emerging civilization with heart. This awareness of your inner connectedness will guide the planet's unfoldment of a new and better approach to education, economics, media, the arts and governance. It's imperative that, as a civilization, there is a commitment to setting aside the negative and dominating effects of patriotism that are exploiting and destroying our planet and its life forms. Integral to the discovery of global harmony is the inescapable emergence of our interconnected future. Cultural isolation is no longer an option with interdependent monetary systems, scientific collaboration, digital tracking, and global commerce unifying the planet. Your heart's voice is more important than ever in directing a new global ethic to the fresh and emerging memetic planetary story. There's just no going back to how it was. Evolution doesn't go backwards without total annihilation. By following your joy, you become a contributing voice to the global heart that must continue to guide the unprecedented abilities our species has been developing. One's fear of artificial intelligence (AI) overtaking humanity does not take into consideration the fields of thought outside of what science can define. Matters of the heart and soul along with beauty are ineffable and transcend data, leaving the consideration of AI as a competitor or human replacement, ridiculous. Without those esoteric elements to Living, there is no evolution of the human soul.As evolution relates to commerce, the number one international business on this planet right now, above petrol or medical, is the trade to support war. If it were to stop right now, there would be an economic crash beyond anything we've ever seen. Your spirit must be added to the new story which is the new meme of our current collective connectedness. Our evolutionary advancement has taken us to a place where we can now make conscious choices to be co-creative agents as opposed to insignificant parts of the whole. Our destiny lies in coming together, and we are, but how successful that coming together is, is in your hands.

Our planet is in crisis. The evidence of destruction is compelling as wars kill the innocent, children are abandoned, ten's of thousands of people die daily from starvation and dozens of species are disappearing from our planet every day. The polar caps are melting at unprecedented rates, old growth forests are being decimated, nuclear annihilation is both prevalent and palpable, a majority of our ocean fisheries are gone, an unparalleled level of pollution fogs our planet and access to fresh water is increasingly in jeopardy. Too many who are not 'directly' impacted are living in comfort while choosing to believe there are no planetary issues.

Though we know this to be an ignorance rather than a truth, the days of living in isolation are gone. The commons include our air, water, environment and collective consciousness. It seems rather extraneous to think that one person's negative behavior as it relates to something we all have in common affects everyone, but it's the truth. What goes on in one part of the world affects all of us. Some might try to live in denial that what took place in Fukushima, Japan doesn't affect the waters of the west coast of the Americas, or the winds that blow through the hemisphere. What we must all work towards is waking up those that are complacent to the realization that we are all connected! The caller of consciousness is at the door and the intensity of its knocking is getting louder. The tools of change are here in this new epoch, but it will take all of us to shift global behavior to a sustainable, interconnectedness.

An Emerging Moment

The good news in all of this is there have always been those emerging moments in the evolutionary process where a leap takes place to a new collective level of being. Historically, it was demonstrated biologically when one cell split or fish migrated onto land. Culturally, when trains changed the speed of transportation, airplanes made the world smaller and wireless communications connected us all, instantly, we were witness to this new collective. We've always made the leap; the question is whether or not we'll be able to do it all together before we totally deplete our Earth's banked resources. Wisdom will rise to meet whatever challenge is before it since the Infinite contains all answers, it's just a matter of whether we're a part of the solution or not. Answers already sit on the shelves lining the halls of consciousness. They're just waiting to be plucked from the libraries of the All Knowing and implemented with the many answers waiting to be utilized for the next leap of evolution. It's already taking place.

Freedom transpires when you step beyond the limits of your inadequate perception and are willing to open your mind and understand more than you had known before. This mountaintop view promotes the unity of the human family and our shared planet, not separation and segregation from one another. It's not about same-ness where everything gets thrown into a soup pot creating one blended flavor, either. Rather, humanity is likened to a salad with its distinctive contributions maintaining their unique flavor while simultaneously creating the one experience called salad. It would be ridiculous to think that the lettuce would stand with a superior attitude because it makes up the majority of the contents or worse, attempt to make a tomato be like it. It's what each is and brings in its distinction that is its most valuable contribution to the whole. When you live with an inclusive heart, you'll find freedom by honoring differences while knowing we are all One. Our flavors and textures all add to the sum of the whole being greater than its parts.

Absolute freedom is your true nature and you are the only one who has accepted your constraints. It is right to be free from your limitation, pains, and fears, returning to soaring through your native heights. I can't think of a better anecdote to cite than the old, often told story of the student who asks the teacher, "How can I ever be free?" To which the master replies with a question right back, "Who said you were imprisoned?"

Many along the path hope they will find liberation someday when they die. You can be freely moving about this world while completely aware and conscious because it's as spiritual here as any other dimension you might travel. The Life you are is Omnipresent. Your freedom isn't located off in space somewhere, so looking for it somewhere else is unnecessary. Those approaches are meaningless. This now moment is the only thing assured. Take the time to do good now. Show your love now. Give those who could use your forgiveness the understanding the situation calls for now. By returning to your innate and instinctive innocence, you align with the harmony of the cosmos moving in the rhythm of Life Itself now.

Spiritual Illiteracy

You become spiritually illiterate when you forget the twists, turns and disruptions on the soul's path bringing valuable insights and lessons on the lifelong journey to a greater conscious connection. This illiteracy occurs when looking outside of yourself for answers and embrace conformity to religious ways that will entrap you to the institutional forms. No one is going to be in their total joy until they find an inner intimacy with their true nature. In realizing this union a deep peace prevails through every action that is undertaken. Mystics know Life is well and carry this awareness into everything they do in the now.

To be free you have to pass where you last stopped. Just beyond the last red light is the expansive Infinite waiting for you to dance in any direction of your choosing. It will only become more magical as you bring the mystical calm into the exploration of your soul's newest adventure ride. It helps to keep your eyes open to the objective mountaintop view in order to see so much more of Life's beauty that is waiting to be experienced.

Contemplation and deep reflective thoughts like meditation activate an inner realization that moves the question of concern to an integration of what your soul experiences as direct encounters of a perfect unfolding order.

Let's say you are in the grocery store on Wednesday afternoon. You, like everyone else in town, are gripping the weekly circular in search of the freshest organic fruit and vegetables on special. You push your cart towards the well-stocked shelves daydreaming of fresh guacamole but as you get closer you see one large bin with nothing but a few badly bruised avocados. As you realize this might mean the store has sold fresh out (pardon the pun) of the avocados you built up an expectation for, you might be tempted to put on the victim role. Perhaps before you experienced life in a state of bliss, you might have had some self-directed deprecation, internalizing and regretting whatever errand you ran before the grocery store. This left you personalizing the lack of avocados as a potential consequence of your own poor planning. Screeeeech. That was the version of needle scratching across a vinyl record. In the observer's practice of mindfully noticing and caring to understand what's true rather than impressing will, all the dense, low-emotion vibrational energy associated with the disappointment was not the truth of the situation. The truth is, you were in the perfect place in the perfect moment and the Fruit and Vegetable manager was merely unaware that the bin needed a refill. Your will screamed scarcity, but the truth is always abundance. Your response was not the truth. Your will made you feel like it was, but the truth is perfect and right in every moment. The thing is, though you now know the perspective that can and will change your entire expression in human form, it's still work to stay aware of the opportunities for mind-blowing clarity and freedom.

You'll be moved beyond just knowing about mysticism to being a mystic. The non-dual, non-conceptual transcendence is a direct experience. This realization of the Infinite in the midst of the temporal will free you from the prison of limitations. Once touched, the certitude changes you forever. The intensity of the mystical is undeniably clear. What once seemed solid and true is now a flow of thousands of discernments emerging and dissolving in each moment as you, the observer, melt into the perception. With this sapiential sight, you are always at choice, no longer fooled by form, with a realization that you are in relationship to activities of your world and you can align with another perception of the Infinite. But when your grip won't let go of your fixed position you are no longer free to frolic among the ever-available options. You're not doing yourself any favors by holding onto what isn't serving you just because you are afraid of what you haven't yet realized. Whether it's a relationship you are holding onto because being without a partner is too scary, or a job you can't leave despite the fact that your gifts are not appreciated because the possibility of being without an income overwhelms you, you are literally cutting off the flow of freedom that Spirit is offering you. Pema Chodron said, "The truth you believe and cling to makes you unavailable to hear anything new." Just dump your limiting beliefs for a bit and the imperishable secret of secrets will appear before your availability.

But The Vision Remains

As great an idea as it might sound in theory, you can't remain on the mountaintop forever. Because you must return to report through the known, the conscious awareness beyond your brain can not be proven in any tangible way. To walk this world you must fully return to it. But once you've seen and come back from the mountaintop, the memory moves through you. You ascend, you see, you return and while it is true that you are no longer actively seeing, what you had seen, the vision from the mountaintop, remains an integral part of you. When I leave Montana, I'm still a part of it and it's a part of me. Your unification with that integral observation changes everything. How you move through your world can be motivated by what you saw rather than by the controlling programing of a fear-based reality. The mystic sees and feels Life's self-awareness declaring, I *am* this.

The freedom comes as the thoughts drift away and awareness moves to the heart. The stillness moves beyond the energy of words not to be uttered and begging description to those of waves and vibrations moving through the vastness of the heart's compassion. Notice how, in the mystical state of being, the totality of your identity drops away and you find yourself breathing in the blissful void of equanimity. This blissful unconditional emptiness is at the core of your I am-ness. You are a still point in a peaceful place beyond comparison; a definitive edge of consciousness. Any awareness angling for your attention is not only unpleasant in comparison to the stillness, but also wholly unwelcome.

Clinging to a false sense of separation from Life, keeps you from opening your awareness beyond your sense of self. The separation will fall away to this noumenon awareness. There is a deep knowing of wholeness as your true nature. Resting in this grace and grateful for the ease in the return home from your journey your soul-filled heart will beat with a greater sensitivity. Its reward is its liberation from the mountaintop's vibrational remembrance in its expression in your present form. This harmonious, balanced expression of compassion and joy will align you with all Life. You'll journey through your life with an interconnected realization alongside many who still won't give a hoot about your experience or what they might be missing.

Freedom is your very nature and you are always at choice to step away from the unfolding causes of pain. Try leaning into the bright flow of Life, instead. Each individual is an integral part of the multifaceted diamond sparkling in the brightness. Some facets will sparkle with joy and love, while others will express pain and suffering. Some will have great clarity while others present as dull and lifeless. When you do meet with a true heartbreak you'll be able to experience the sadness without being lost in it forever. You know the ups and downs, perfections and imperfections of the journey and that holds true for all facets of life. Birth and death, pleasure and pain, creation and destruction are all a natural part.

Walking With the Spirit of the Mystic

Each experience calls for you to awaken that deeper knowing inside. You can fall into a pit of gloom and despair never to emerge again, or you can choose to be free and embrace the sorrow and find Life there. When you realize you are expressing as consciousness knowing Itself, you'll transform the world around you because you'll have every resource in the universe in your repertoire. Do you have room for a greater expression or are you holding the despair so tightly you've forgotten you were just passing through? If you were walking down the street with hands full of groceries, mail, your phone and a cup of coffee and you saw a beautiful multi-faceted gem sitting on the ground but your carrying capacity was full, what would you do? Would you put something down to pick up the gem? *Life is always offering gems but are you creating space for the new possibilities presenting themselves to you?*

Crisis calls for healing; healing is an invitation to participate in your own evolution to freedom. This mystical awakening is the change agent to surrender what's unnecessary for what is emerging. And, what was held together by shreds of false truths just may crumble leaving a shock wave in its wake. Your mystical expression isn't about keeping you one step ahead of the next catastrophe, but learning to be present for Life's Grace to land. You'll be free to know you'll never avoid all the pain of this world but rather be lifted by the mountaintop view so you'll be enlivened by it. Rest assured you'll enjoy being liberated from worldly thoughts beyond the valleys of logic and reason which have successfully created a bunch of cranky people. There's already enough belligerence in the masses. Choose to walk with the spirit of a mystic and, as Ghandi said, "be the change you want to see in the world". If you don't listen to that great perceiver of your being, the one who is observing all of who you are, the one you betray the most is yourself, the one who knows.

You'll come to know the knower, when you are free enough to go into the not-knowing to listen to what is beyond the foreseeable. An excellent example of this is embracing imminent death. You have to be willing to let go of what you think may happen so you'll experience what can happen. You can only truly know freedom by moving forward into the greater yet to be. Released from a reliance on support, you will no longer have a concern of loss. Don't allow fear to keep you from your celebration. When you become fully present allowing your past to remain in its historic locale, its influence ceases to have authority in your now moment.

This moment will never come again. You will never be with the one you are with now in the same way. The next time you'll be different, they will be different and it will be a new now. You'll never repeat that moment in time with your child again. The sound they made for the first time coming down the slide will never be heard again. Every experience, every relationship including the one with self is transient and impermanent.

Everything is relative to the moment defined as now. Yes, there will be new moments but not this one ever again. Choose happiness to be your link of interconnectedness to the moment with others; because there's no going back to change the exchange. With no regrets, let your spirit lovingly express passionately as if you have the ability to transform the world - because you do.

Life's blessings are pouring forth but are you in perfect alignment with them or are you still earth-bound? Your world is immersed in grace, it's just a matter of being in the right frame to witness it. When the body aches and is in pain, it's hard to say I am not my body. When the finances are tight and the debts add up to more than what's in the bank, it's difficult to say, I live in an abundant universe. When your relationship feels dead, it's hard to say, it's vibrant and alive. Sometimes when it's difficult to rally the strength to live your vision, it's perfectly OK to find a spiritual practitioner to remind you of the truth of who you are. Never give your power to them but instead, allow their deep knowingness and faith to re-launch you to the mountaintop so again you can see the truth above the struggle.

The ultimate freedom from the weight of the world is knowing there is a divine purpose for the dense, stuck, lower vibrations that attempt to pull you down into their muck. Returning from the mountaintop with an electrified understanding of the truth added to the simultaneous perspective of the non-truths leaves you prepared to embrace a fuller awareness. It gives those sticky, negative, unhealthy vibrations the boot. When you can see the negativity for what it is from your mountaintop, isolated only by the reflection and meaning you once gave it when you were looking at it from a three-dimensional perspective, you'll find a deepening of the gifts that freedom brings. Yes. Deep feeling perspective begets deeper perspective and the deeper you go, the more liberated you'll feel. First from the traffic and the maddening crowds, then from the media . . . you see how it works? Even the fear mongering news channels will be outside of your peripheral concern, as spirit uses more and more of your experience in form to raise you and everyone around you to a new thought.

Be free of those peripheral concerns in order to follow what your soul loves and you'll evolve in mystifying ways discovering amazing new capacities you never knew were in you. You'll stop listening to your controlling earthbound littleness and begin hearing, evermore clearly, your intrinsic urge to be a frequency for a greater expression of Life. Turn away from the wall of trepidation thinking you can't do what you want to do and watch as you're lifted into a grander version of you stepping into your freedom. Use what is before you to shift your world into a finer vibration of a higher channel.

This grander version of you doesn't necessarily mean big, bigger or super-sized. It means deeper. It's the authentic, genuine, fractal expression of Life knowing Itself unimpeded by the concerns of this dimension as you. And however that takes form is perfect, even with its imperfections. Listen to your inner stirrings; the ones calling you to rise to know more in all situations.

Yes, there will be time to hang back and recharge. While at other times, you'll pick up the pack and re-enter life to do what you love and be rewarded with some of the most energizing, in-the-flow, moments of self-expression. You'll discover expanding opportunities to reveal the magnificence from the depths of your spiritual reservoir. You'll move from struggling to cope to feeding your spirit. Life hasn't been holding you back. You've been holding It back. You're here not to get but to be an avenue through which good is given. Withholding your light isn't serving anyone and truthfully, it doesn't work anymore, anyhow. You don't own that light or energy. You dwell in it. You're a transparency and light travels through the window of your soul and filter of your choice. Your individualized perspective is part of a greater whole that is the interconnection of the Omnipresent All. Within the Totality are multiple domains of awareness. Being moved by illumination is exciting and might leave you wanting more, not unlike addiction, which is all about you. Greater awareness about what's possible is good but your spirit, mind and body will not be an enlivened awareness of compassionate knowing until you drop the demands of the desirous-self. Looking beyond your local perception has far greater rewards than any human desire could manifest.

You come into expression out of the One. So when caught in your residential perspective, a walk in the woods may lift you to a higher knowing. Or maybe, you might find yourself caught in the gravitational pull of a loss when a call from a friend, inspirational quote, or piece of mystical art activates a higher remembrance returning you to the Loving, Abundant One. This unity is liberating, serving to remind you of instantly available higher states. To be unified in the One is synonymous with the dissolution of a sense of self taking with it all the struggles of the local awareness.

Watching your child intensely playing in a basketball championship game, maneuvering, shooting, blocking and running up and down the court may have you on the edge of your seat guessing, wondering and hoping with heart-pounding, nail-biting excitement. Next to you, a neighbor waits to give you a ride home but has very little interest in the same game you are so deeply engrossed in. All three of you, the child, you the parent and the neighbor serving as the driver are in the same place with three entirely different realities of that place in time. It's all perspective. We've all chosen different rides in this adventure park. For some it's Eden and others a trail of tears, and still, for others a magic mountain.

There's a wonderful book series whereby making certain choices for the protagonist at integral points in the story allows its reader to craft a different adventure and, of course, ending to the same book. Depending on the multitude of decisions you make each and every read-through is unique. Trevor loves these books and every night as I read them over and over with him, I too am mesmerized, but perhaps for a different reason. For me, the possibility of breaking the code to get to the same ending twice teases me. Innate to the writer's concept was a realistic sense of unpredictability and with its tricks and endless page loops I have not yet been able to see through the complicated formula. I realize that I have become fascinated by both the adventures and the control Trevor and I have over the story line. I can't help but use it as a metaphor for the freedom of choice you have relating directly to the cause and effect you see in your life. You are the protagonist in your own life story; ultimately one that is led and supported by the decisions you make. How liberating it is to know you have the choice to lose yourself in the story as it plays out as static and immovable or fluid and flowing? Of course, a collective decision can sometimes be different than your individual decision and keeping alert to how that changes your behavior is important. If you are not stuck in a story, you can always choose a new perspective from your higher observing mountaintop without the heaviness of the collective norm. I would ask you to consider what you might have recently agreed to that is not really the direction you would like to be going?

Zen Story

Zen Master asks his student, "Where did you come from?" His student takes a moment to ponder the question and responds thoughtfully, "Master, I don't know."

Zen Master asks yet another question of his student, "So, where is Mind?" His student, now gazing towards the horizon, responds, "I don't know."

Zen Master thinks for a moment and asks a final question of his student seeking only the student's truth in his answer. "What is consciousness," he asks?

The student, now somewhat ill at ease that he is somehow letting his Master down with his answers sighs and answers, "Master, I do not know."

His master nods and with a keen sparkle in his eye responds, "Good answers. Now keep this 'don't know mind' for your meditation."

I trust you are finding your way to your mountaintop more quickly and with greater ease than when you began. Perhaps you are able to get there by simply closing your eyes and observing from a higher place without attachment? So in this last meditation, without guidance from me, simply close your eyes and allow your higher wisdom to guide you to see what it is that wants to be known through you.

I know all is well and wherever I go in my expanding awareness, all is good and I am safe. I'm surrounded by and live in an Omni-Dimensional Life Force that can never be violated, because there is nothing opposed to it. I move on the very currents of Life Itself and I'm free to notice all things without attachment to anything. Free to move beyond any image at any time and courageous enough to remain, I open to a graceful guidance on my Spirit's adventure and surrender my demands to logical understandings. I welcome new and unknown states of consciousness for my soul's evolution . . . and when it's time to return, do so with gratitude and appreciation for the journey . . .

Soulful Adventures

- How have you been changed by your chosen roller coaster ride through life?
- Where do you feel the gravitational truth pulling you to a track in life you don't want to get on? Are you abandoning the heed of your witnessing consciousness?
- Where you don't see multiple paths or directional options, set the search down and rest from the struggle and come back to it later. Put a pen and paper next to your bed and sleep on it. Ask the question of yourself before you go to sleep and let your all-seeing-self deliver some answers through your dream state. Before you get out of bed write them down for consideration in your waking hours.
- Where are some places that you'd like to bring the relevancy of an expanded view into play in your life?
- What's going on in your world that's keeping you from grabbing a new book off the endless shelf of wisdom?

What's making it difficult to live from your mountaintop view?

- How can you be more conscious? Where do you act unconsciously?
- What callers of consciousness have come knocking for your attention? Are you giving your attention or will the callers need to get louder?
- Those situations where you struggle and are most vulnerable are the access points to unlock the arcane mystery of your life. These points always require relinquishing your fortified perspective, and you can only do that if you are free enough to trust. What are the fortified perspectives that are keeping you jailed?
- Do you feel you'll find freedom while walking this world or only after you die?
- What are you clinging to that's making you unavailable for greater good?
- Crisis calls for healing; healing is an invitation to participate in your own evolution to freedom. Do you have any crises in your life that could actually launch you to greater freedom rather than just irritate you?
- What are some of the strongest insights your observer delivered while you were reading and practicing, Living from the Mountaintop?

Mystical writing

I know why the Caged Bird sings
The free bird leaps
on the back of the wind
and floats downstream
till the current ends
and dips his wings
in the orange sun rays
and dares to claim the sky.
But a bird that stalks
down his narrow cage
can seldom see through
his bars of rage
his wings are clipped and
his feet are tied
so he opens his throat to sing.
The caged bird sings
with fearful trill
of the things unknown
but longed for still
and his tune is heard
on the distant hill
for the caged bird
sings of freedom
The free bird thinks of another breeze
and the trade winds soft through the sighing trees
and the fat worms waiting on a dawn-bright lawn
and he names the sky his own.
But a caged bird stands on the grave of dreams
his shadow shouts on a nightmare scream
his wings are clipped and his feet are tied
so he opens his throat to sing
The caged bird sings
with a fearful trill
of things unknown
but longed for still

and his tune is heard
on the distant hill
for the caged bird
sings of freedom.
~Maya Angelou
1928-2014

Epilogue

Don't cry because it's over, smile because it happened.
Dr. Seuss

Joy

All of the mystical ideas we've covered are fun to explore in the realm of thought, but the greatest joy lies in putting them into practice. Like the old man coming down the mountain who put his burden down, eventually he picked the pack back up and returned to his world of activity. Through your practice of regular visits to your mountaintop you will be able to observe your activities of life and not lose power or perspective to the world of form. The more mystically you see the world the more inspired you are to be here and contribute your spiritual perspective to it.

The process of writing this book has been an extraordinary journey for me. For close to ten years I have been formulating theories and jotting notes on everything from notebook pages to cocktail napkins. I taught classes on Mysticism using curriculum I developed from many respected authors and spiritual teachers and throughout I held very close to my chest my inner knowing that I had a significantly different and unique perspective on the mystical experience. It wasn't so much that I was procrastinating the effort it took to put words to the concepts, it was in the perfect timing that I was able to find the freedom to choose opening myself to the flow. As soon as I did, Spirit delivered the support system I needed and the spigot was turned to full on. And flow it did, when I allowed it. The key to allowing was always making myself available by declaring the wee, pre-dawn hours of nearly every morning for over a year to the creative process.

Daily, long before Kalli and Trevor even entered their

mid-sleep dream states, I was affirming my gratitude as my eyes opened spontaneously to look at the ceiling of my darkened bedroom. I pushed the matted hair back from my pillow-creased cheek, wiped the sleep from my eyes and shuffled to the sink to splash water on my face before staring down my keyboard. There alone the discomfort reigned, having only handwritten my previous eight books, the learning curve of technology itself was enough to overwhelm me some days. I must admit to losing several chapters to my own inability to knowing how to save them to something called the cloud that I was just beginning to understand.

There were times I would sit for hours and nary more than a paragraph would come, which I found both frustrating and humbling. Other times, the words tumbled out of me onto page after page as though I was merely the typist; like water from a fountain, pennies from heaven, insights from the one and only Spirit with the man I see in my reflection serving as scribe. There is nothing quite like the moment you realize you are at one with the One Mind. The zone of total and undeniable connection with Spirit confirmed over and over as I reread full pages that I don't remember writing. What a glorious and surreal experience. Was I actually shape-shifting into a writer?

Mid-weekly, I met with my editor who'd pull out her virtual scalpel after we dined and laughed about writers block, documentaries we enjoyed, and what local farmer's markets we each favored and I'd notice the slight muscle tension between my shoulder blades radiating down to my lower back with each and every sentence she clipped. I learned early on that feeding her before we sat in front of the computer tamed her incisions in my weekly work as if it were an anesthetic for both of us.

There was, of course, the time I wrote for fourteen straight hours only to finish and realize it wasn't in keeping with my vision and I faced the delete key with a sort of rancor. Fourteen hours, my aching back and worse, my soul so spent from forcing words that didn't communicate what I knew I wanted to say. Yes, scrapping that day's work was a true test to my ability to stay in the now moment. Saying YES to writing *Living from the Mountaintop* meant for me a number of new experiences and a level of joy around creation I perhaps had not experienced prior - as if writing about it paralleled the employment of it in the process in a special, more acute way. I share this journey from a place in the hopes you will all have the same opportunity within this blissful learning process. I share this to illustrate that my perception, at times, was all that remained between it being truly excruciating and joyfully existential.

All the struggle and energy you've been expending to unlock the gates to higher consciousness is over now. Up to this point, you've been attempting to unlock a door that was never locked. Now you have the realization which opens the door and welcomes in the objective witness of your life. The more conscious you are the more concurrent your life is between your higher beliefs and actions. The more conscious you are the more liberated you are and with more freedom comes the joy you'll live in as you experience the divinely ineffable in all you do.

Are you filled with joy the moment your consciousness awakens to the new day? Start your day by going to your mountaintop and seeing life from a higher place. Because woofing down breakfast before throwing your clothes on and running out of the house to do your day leaves too much empty space to be bombarded by whatever wants to drop on your path. The situations you meet in your day will be reflective of the vision you entered into in the morning.

The mystical connection to the greater aspect of being and Life Itself is a far greater quandary than most people realize. Having a purpose for Life to move through you is an activity of the heart and spirit, not just of the mind. The mental approach alone is missing an integral player. The heart is a large part of the activity to be led by your spirit. Yet it's the alignment of your spirit, mind and body that leads to mystical success. There's so much talk about the out-of-body experience from the ego-centered perspective because of its mysterious intrigue and novelty that the search for it can become lopsided. Your true path of oneness calls for the greater challenge of the in-the-body experience. Being present where you are with a greater realization of the Oneness of Life sounds so simple, doesn't it? I'm smiling right now because as simple as it is, it's been my life's most joyous work, being present where I am. Leonardo da Vinci wrote, "Simplicity is the ultimate sophistication."

Welcoming simplicity will help you become more conscious of your deeper connection to Life. When the mind is stilled, your true nature has a better chance of being revealed. Most simply, all you have to do is awaken from a belief in two opposing powers, whether they be sickness and health, fear and faith, good and evil, or lack and abundance. You can fear no evil if you know there is no opposing power to the Infinite One. The vision of One Power is not accessible to only one esoteric sect, but is available to all people who are open regardless of spiritual or scientific persuasion, religious or non-religious views. This direct realization beyond the intellectual deciphering of wisdom is now available to any who are willing to see from the mountaintop.

Dr. Martin Luther King shared an intuitive message on the eve of his assassination, as though he knew exactly what prophesy he was to fulfill. He spoke with great passion as he proclaimed, "Well, I don't know what will happen now. We've got some difficult days ahead. But it doesn't matter with me now. Because I've been to the mountaintop. And I don't mind. Like anybody, I would like to live a long life. Longevity has its place. But I'm not concerned about that now. I just want to do God's will. And He's allowed me to go up to the mountain. And I've looked over. And I've seen the promised land. I may not get there with you. But I want you to know tonight, that we, as a people will get to the promised land. And I'm happy, tonight. I'm not worried about anything. I'm not fearing any man . . ."

The expanded vision is tantalizing and it's easy to get swept away thinking it will last forever, but you must come back and enter this world. There is a certain fragility to your understanding of what you can carry and what must flow through you. If only it were as easy as tying a ribbon around your finger to remind you of your joyful perspective. You can return with a sense of joy knowing It is all Life and all connected. Or, you can mope about wishing you were in the blissful place rather than making where you are the blissful place. Joy is the dance of the divine living in harmony in the human experience as it presents itself.

A greater bliss comes when you stop dividing your life up into neat little compartments. One part spiritual, another part work, yet another compartment saved for family and vacation behavior. You've got your love life and your spiritual practices and the two just don't seem to meet. Why the division? Do you think some things are sacred and others are something else? It's a lot simpler to allow your wholeness to dissolve the fragmented behavior. Your mystical expression will move you away from your anxious petitioning off of different aspects of yourself, by allowing the concurrent stream of life with all of its flaws, faults and failings to be unapologetically part of your whole expression. The thing about the ego-centered mind is it leads you in the direction of separation from the All Knowing You. The commitment to this spiritual practice will reveal to you that you can trust yourself absolutely. There is no second guessing when you're empowered with a sense of Wholeness that results from a personal commitment to embracing all of Life.

Whatever your perspective is of a mystical life, being authentic is imperative. Are you effortlessly walking in joy and comfort through your world? Or is that natural state of being shrouded by your struggle with the need for perceived appropriateness? It doesn't mean you have to change what's going on, just your approach to it. It's liberating to realize you can listen to your observer and make a self-adjustment so your joy of life can return based on your choices, not other's. Your life will always need adjustments. Be grateful for that because it means you are alive. The moments when I feel most alive are those when I'm awakened to a new aspect of myself that I must shift to embrace. You're in tune to see the signals, so work with, not against them. They will help lead you to an even happier and healthier life.

As the Tibetans like to say, when you come from a good heart it makes your choices easier. Your internal and eternal wisdom will joyously free you from the constrictions of the human conditions of question with the revelation of an elevated mountaintop awareness. Your compassion deepens and your love expands when the conditional constraints are dropped. The loyalty to a particular group or nation that served evolution so well must now include all of humanity or we just may not survive as a species on this planet. Does your patriotic pride get in the way of loving others? There will always be a devotion and affinity to your "clan" but the deepest devotion must be to express Life if humanity is going to continue to inhabit this planet.

There is no shortage of blessings because they come from the Infinite. The things you work so hard to accumulate necessitating a defensive line to protect what's mine and not yours are eradicated in a state of conscious Oneness. So there's nothing for you to defend. You can battle the world all you want with no guarantee that the achievements of your victories will ensure a legacy of any sort. But, if you walk this world in joy and harmony, the path you take and footprints you leave will be a blessed contribution to the collective consciousness of humanity.

Being in the presence of someone who lives in joy feels truly magical as it touches your soul uplifting your very countenance. You are this someone! Through your mountaintop perspective, a greater sense of connectedness wraps around you like a soft warm blanket from your childhood bringing with it a sense of security in remembering that the world is a good and safe place for you. Take the time to go home, and in that, I don't mean a physical home. I mean a moment in time rather than a physical space; an internal place where you can feel your true wholeness. Find your home in a sunset, on the wings of a bird as you watch it sailing through the air, or in your car as you sit watching planes fly overhead. And through that connection with your place of refuge and the sound of your inner remembrances of your own nature, you become receptive again to the synchronicities of the web of life. You live in harmony with the flow that there is enough because separation evaporates into the nothingness from which it came. With a greater, more conscious connection to life, loneliness gives way to the inner-connected revelation of the mountaintop.

Get out of your own way and live in trust of the perfect rhythm with the unfoldment of time in your space, knowing all that needs to happen, does. Exactly in its perfect timing. We all find ourselves here at this time for a reason. Within this convergence of elevated souls who embrace a mountaintop vision as individuals stepping out of the old rigid paradigms, each plays an integral part in the evolution of this mystical renaissance. The planet couldn't be saved a moment before now without your participation because you are part of the whole. You've been called here now for a time such as this. If not for divine timing, why you? Why now?

In a state of mystical awareness you come to know the sacred secret that the whole universe is in harmony. The beauty and significance of this is incomprehensible to the un-awakened mind, but for the mystic immersed in gnostic ecstasy there will be laughter at the human folly and joy in knowing all is well.

There are bon-voyage parties as one heads out on their enchanted journey, whether it's off to college, a new career or arrival at birth upon this planet. We celebrate the completion of the degree, retirement, and death. What appears to be forgotten is where we spend most of the time, in the middle; forgetting to applaud, praise, rejoice and honor every footstep on the path of our way to the completions. Remember to celebrate Life expressing as you, as this moment will never come again. Love yourself enough to take the time to appreciate a Life well lived. It's your Life! And, it's now! Through this mystical journey you have taken a wild ride expanding the monumental spectrum of what you know as sacred. Listen to your witness and live in joy and freedom. When you're done you'll see the bundle you've been carrying is weightless and easily slung over your shoulder as you embrace your newfound peace on the path of Life.

"Patriots have sometimes been asked to "think imperially." Mystics are asked to think celestially and this, not when considering the things usually called spiritual, but when dealing with the concrete accidents, the evil and sadness, the cruelty, failure and degeneration of life. So what is being offered to you is not merely a choice among new states of consciousness, new emotional experiences - though these are indeed involved in it, but above all else, a larger and intenser life, a career, a total consecration to the interests of the Real. This life shall not be abstract and dreamy, made up, as some imagine, of negations. It shall be violently practical and affirmative, giving scope for a limitless activity of will, heart, and mind working within the rhythms of the Divine Idea. It shall cost much, making perpetual demands on your loyalty, trust and self-sacrifice: proving now, the need and the worth of that training in renunciation which was forced on you at the beginning of your interior life. It shall be both deep and wide, embracing in its span all those aspects of Reality which the gradual extension of your contemplative powers has disclosed to you: making the inner and outer worlds to be indivisibly One."

~Evelyn Underhill
Practical Mysticism: A Little book for Normal People
###

Glossary

Terminology I've used to describe aspects of the mystical in this book

To support you in reading this book, below you'll find a legend with some of my interchangeable terms in the glossary. What's more important to me, is your experience of where the word is pointing rather than the word itself. Feel empowered to replace words that make sense to your personal journey through this book.

Absolute - anywhere in this book a capital begins a word other than at the beginning of a sentence, it indicates the Life Force, The Intelligence of All, The Alpha-First Cause, Infinite, It, Spirit.

Akashic Records - the interactive influential energetic imprint, encoded in a non-physical plane with every thought, intention and experience that has occurred and is the central storehouse of all information for individuals and the world.

Archetype - a typical example or original model from which all things of the same kind are copied or based, the first form of a certain person or thing.

Aura - A field of subtle, luminous energy surrounding a person or object.

Base Jumping - the most extreme of extreme sports. Jumpers leap from very tall fixed objects, some may wear a wing suit where they can guide their fall before opening a specially designed parachute for rapid deployment.

Bliss - a state of perfect happiness as to be oblivious of everything else.

Causative - what makes something happen or responsible for something to happen.

Celestial - pertaining to the universe beyond the earth's atmosphere.

Chakra - Sanskrit term for wheel or disk. According Tantric tradition, everyone has seven spinning vortex or energy centers that serve as a junction points between the body and consciousness.

Clairvoyance - clear seeing without the known human senses.

Coherence - the quality of forming a unified whole.

Collective or Cultural Think - group of thoughts or entities creating a common whole.

Consciousness - awareness.

Conscious Consumer - living consciously, spending wiser in a more sustainable way. Purchasing from companies whose values one trust.

Cosmos - the universe seen as a well-ordered whole.

Craniosacral Therapy - a form of bodywork focused on regulating the flow of cerebrospinal fluid by using therapeutic touch to the patient's skull, face, spine and pelvis.

Crown Chakra - the seventh and highest chakra represents the ability to be fully connected spiritually.

Dharma - a Sanskrit word with a varied of meanings having its origin in the myths of Vedic Hinduism where the gods created the universe from chaos. Its behavior and action necessary to all life in nature, society, family as well as at the individual level. Most simply, it's used in this book to describe your life work, your calling your passion. It is what is yours to do in this life.

Dimension - serves to define the location of an element within a given space or plane.

Discernment - a perception in absence of judgment with the view to obtain higher understanding.

Diversity - the quality of having differences. Encompasses acceptance, respect and understanding of each individual as unique expressions of Life.

Doublespeak - is a language that deliberately disguises, distorts, or reverses the meaning of words.

Ego- the small mind, controlling mind, character, persona, psyche, subjective, are all names used in this book to describe the personal thinking, feeling, and willful self-distinguishing itself from the selves of others.

Epigenetics - recently developed science proving the genetic code, the DNA, can change with our environment as well as with beliefs, emotions, and thoughts.

Esoteric - opinions or ideas preserved or understood and taught by a small group of the specially initiated.

Eternal Verities - truth that is forever

Euphemism - an indirect word or expression substituted for one considered to be too harsh or blunt when referring to something unpleasant.

Fractal - each part displays self-similarity having the same statistical character as the whole across different scales.

Field - a region or space in which a given effect exists.

Frame - the edge around a space that holds something.

Frequency - the energy of vibration is transferred by waves which in turn can produce new vibrations. A single vibration is called a cycle. The number of cycles made in seconds is the frequency of the vibration.

Gaia - Mother Earth.

Higher Self -observer, witness, watcher, original self, true self, souls connection to Infinite.

Holistic - diverse field of alternative approaches in which the "whole person" is focused on, not just the malady itself in its quest for optimal health and wellness.

Holographic - each piece of a hologram contains the full image of the original picture, no matter how small of apiece.

Hypnotic Trance - an altered state of awareness characterized by a heightened suggestibility and receptivity.

Idiomatic Beliefs - common phrases used in place of direct speech.

Imaginal body - the separate externalized image of the self that carries your awareness through the different dimensions.

Ineffable - indescribable, beyond words.

Intuition - the ability to acquire knowledge without reason. Natural power or feeling to know something without any proof or evidence. Direct perception of truth.

Karmic Debt - putting one in debt with the give and take / action and reaction of the universe. Karma of any action is a force that continues to have an effect until it is used up or exhausted. The Tibetan Buddhists have a term, lenchak which translated would be "occurrence attraction."

Ketheric layer - the seventh layer of the aura is associated with the Divine or Universal Consciousness and is related to the crown chakra.

Koan - an introspective question or thoughtful puzzle that cannot be solved with the logical mind.

Lucid dream - the dreamer has conscious control over their participation within the dream or is able to manipulate their imaginary experiences in the dream environment.

Meditation - focuses and quiets the mind helping to reach a higher state of awareness and inner calm.

Meme - an idea, behavior, or style that spreads from person to person within a culture. A unit for carrying cultural ideas, symbols, or practices that can be transmitted from one mind to another through writing, speech, gestures, rituals, or other. A field of study called memetic rose to explore the concepts and transmission of memes in terms of an evolutionary model.

Mindful - focuses the awareness on what is being sensed moment-by-moment by being conscious of thoughts, feelings, bodily sensations without right or wrong judgment.

Mitochondrial Eve - in the field of human genetics, the name refers to the kinship with the mother of most recent common ancestor of all currently living humans.

Morphogenetic Field - the more with a common habit, whether of knowledge, perception or behavior, the stronger it is in the vibrational field; thus, making it easier to replicates in a new, non-local host. - The Hundredth Monkey Phenomenon.

Mountaintop View - to observe from an elevated or higher perspective. The ability to clearly look out over a whole scene and see where and why it started and how it unfolds without judgment.

Myopic View - lack of discernment of long range perspective, short sighted.

Mysticism - is the passionate conscious union with the Pure Essence of Life Itself.

Noumenon – an object or event that is known without the use of senses. Phenomenon.

Numinous – appeals to one's higher senses, felt sense of a spiritual presence, surpassing comprehension or understanding, mysterious.

Occult - beyond the natural or typical powers displayed by the five senses.

Omnipresent - present everywhere at the same time.

Paradox - when two apparently exclusive views are held at the same time.

Quantum Leap - an abrupt and non-linear transition of an electron, atom, or molecule from one quantum state to another. Metaphorically used to describe dramatic sudden changes in life that appear to come out of nowhere.

Realization - becoming fully aware of something. The act of making real or achieving something that was first imagined.

Resonance - two objects that vibrate with the same frequency.

Re-pattern - to change the regular and repeated way something happens or is done.

Reptilian Brain - part of the brain responsible for species-typical instinctual behaviors involved in aggression, dominance, territoriality, and ritual displays.

Revelation - surprising and previously unknown truth made dramatically known.

Sacred Space - a distinctive space differentiating it from its surroundings where meaningful and significant occurrence transpire that amplifies the world beyond the five senses and brings it to earth.

Sapiential - having, sharing, showing, expounding and providing wisdom.

Satori Breathing - is a type of consciously connected breathing that facilitates a significant escalation or an elevated spiritual awareness of greater understanding.

Seva - Sanskrit term for selfless service.

Shape-shifting - the ability to change into another form.

Societal Norm - expected patterns or behavior and beliefs held within a society, a standard of average performance of people.

Soul - your essence, your spirit. I have used Soul and Spirit interchangeably in this text.

Standard Operating Beliefs - established recurring operational procedures guiding one with the internal information and methods as to how handle a task.

Subjective - belonging to personal or collective realm of thought as to how a moment is experienced; beneath the threshold of consciousness. The sum total of all of one's thinking both conscious and unconscious.

Sympathetic Vibration - harmonic phenomenon wherein a formerly passive vibratory body responds to external vibrations of the same frequency.

Synchronicity - the simultaneous occurrence of events that appear significantly related but have no discernible causal connection.

Talisman - an object representing and reminding one of their ancestry or mythic past and having the power to cause good to happen.

Tao - the way of nature.

Telepathy - thought transference or transmission of information from one to another without using the known sensory channels.

Theophany - The personal experience of the visible manifesting Presence and glory of the Divine.

Therianthropy - the ability of humans to metamorphose into animals and deities through shape-shifting.

Third Eye - the inner eye, an esoteric concept referring to a speculative invisible eye which provides perception beyond the ordinary senses located in the middle of the forehead and is associated to the pineal gland - referred to as the master gland.

Transpersonal - the spiritual dimensions of human experience beyond the person.

Transformation - a dramatic change.

Transcendence - experience beyond the ordinary and physical senses.

Vibration - slight shaking movement, quivering, pulsing, oscillating, reciprocation or other motion about an unchanging point.

Vibrational Healing - process whereby vibrations are introduced or transferred into the physical and energetic bodies so the resonance which has become unbalanced is readjusted. All systems of the human body have an ideal vibration. When there are imbalances there is dis-ease.

Vipassana - insightful or noticing approach to mediation through concentration on the body.

Acknowledgements

Heart felt appreciation to Lori Gertz for Wednesdays with Lori. I'm grateful to you for making sure every word was in its proper place, adding the ones that were missing, and for cracking the whip to keep me producing. My gratitude deepens for lots of laughter and snacks to keeping it fun. Your inspiration and know how came from the Mountaintop filling the project with infinite possibilities. The journey has been a joy.

Lots of love to my beloved spiritual community, the Seaside Center for Spiritual Living. You created the space to unfold, work and rework all these ideas through my weekly talks and classes. Your support continues to encourage me to stretch so I have so much more to bring home to you from the Mountaintop.

Deep thanks also go out to Linda Amorsen and JoAnne Millison for putting up with me in the creative mode behind closed office doors on Wednesday afternoons for almost two years